RAND | PROJECT AIR FORCE

T0290817

A Survey System to Assess Abuse and Misconduct Toward Air Force Students in Occupational Specialty Training

Laura L. Miller, Coreen Farris, Marek N. Posard, Miriam Matthews,
Kirsten M. Keller, Sean Robson, Stephanie Brooks Holliday, Mauri Matsuda,
Rachel M. Burns, Lisa Wagner, Barbara Bicksler

Prepared for the United States Air Force
Approved for public release; distribution unlimited

For more information on this publication, visit www.rand.org/t/RR2692

Library of Congress Cataloging-in-Publication Data is available for this publication.
ISBN: 978-1-9774-0203-5

Published by the RAND Corporation, Santa Monica, Calif.
© Copyright 2019 RAND Corporation
RAND® is a registered trademark.

Support RAND
Make a tax-deductible charitable contribution at
www.rand.org/giving/contribute

www.rand.org

Preface

This report documents a RAND Corporation study designed to adapt a survey system for monitoring abuse and misconduct in the Air Force Basic Military Training (BMT) environment to extend it to the next stages of the Air Force technical training and flying training environments. The report provides background on the structure of the Air Force technical training and flying training environments, survey revisions to tailor the BMT survey content to apply to students in these additional training environments, results of a pretest of the survey, strategies to promote open and honest participation, and recommendations for future survey administration and reporting of results.

This research was sponsored by the commander of the Air Force's Air Education and Training Command (AETC) and was conducted within the Manpower, Personnel, and Training Program of RAND Project AIR FORCE.

RAND Project AIR FORCE

RAND Project AIR FORCE (PAF), a division of the RAND Corporation, is the U.S. Air Force's federally funded research and development center for studies and analyses. PAF provides the Air Force with independent analyses of policy alternatives affecting the development, employment, combat readiness, and support of current and future air, space, and cyber forces. Research is conducted in four programs: Force Modernization and Employment; Manpower, Personnel, and Training; Resource Management; and Strategy and Doctrine. The research reported here was prepared under contract FA7014-16-D-1000.

Additional information about PAF is available on our website: www.rand.org/paf

This report documents work originally shared with the U.S. Air Force on March 23, 2017. The draft report, issued in June 2017, was reviewed by formal peer reviewers and U.S. Air Force subject-matter experts.

Contents

Figures

Tables

Summary

For incoming officers and enlisted airmen, initial skills training (IST) provides basic knowledge and skills specific to their designated occupational specialty in the U.S. Air Force and prepares them for transition to their first duty assignment. It is a developmental period, particularly for those first transitioning into the responsibilities of adulthood, and these students enter as the newest Air Force members at the lowest levels of the officer and enlisted hierarchies. They are seeking admission into career fields for which they must prove their capability, and, in some cases, they must compete for limited positions in their subspecialties. For these reasons, these technical training and flying training students may be particularly vulnerable to abuse and misconduct from one another and from those who have greater experience than they do or hold authority over them that could shape their entire careers.

In fiscal year 2013, RAND Project AIR FORCE researchers developed a survey system to monitor abuse and misconduct targeting enlisted trainees in Basic Military Training (BMT). To extend that survey system to trainees in the next stage of training (technical training or, for enlisted aircrew, flying training), the commander of the Air Force's Air Education and Training Command (AETC) asked RAND researchers to adapt the survey content and administration modes to these more diverse settings. AETC also asked us to begin adapting the survey system to the officer training environments by focusing on the Specialized Undergraduate Pilot Training (SUPT) pipelines, where power imbalances and career consequences for students may increase the risk for abuse and misconduct.

Our research centered on the following questions:

1. What are the characteristics of the technical training and flying training environments?
2. What content should be included in the technical training and flying training survey, and how should it be tailored?
3. How should the survey be pretested?
4. When should the survey be administered?
5. Who should participate in the survey?
6. How should the survey be administered?
7. How should the survey responses be analyzed and reported?

To answer these questions, we solicited input from AETC personnel, consulted the scientific literature, pretested modified survey instruments with technical training and flying training students preparing for different types of Air Force specialties across multiple locations, refined the survey items based on the pretest, and developed recommendations for survey administration, analysis, and reporting.

Characteristics of the Training Environments

The technical training and flying training environments are varied, which led us to recommend tailored approaches to administering the survey. Technical training and flying training take place at many locations across the country, including some run by organizations other than the Air Force, and the length of the training pipelines vary considerably.

Each year, 20,000 to 30,000 enlisted trainees graduate from BMT and, through AETC's Second Air Force organization, are enrolled in technical training for a wide array of career fields. The duration of the pipelines and the number, sequence, size, and location of courses within each pipeline vary considerably—although the majority of the pipelines necessary for obtaining an occupational specialty and associated Air Force Specialty Code (AFSC) take less than six months to complete. This environment differs markedly from BMT, which is a standard eight-and-a-half-week course for all new enlisted airmen. The instructional and residential environments during technical training offer students greater autonomy than in BMT, which may present different types of protections from and vulnerabilities to problematic behavior.

Both enlisted aircrew and officers participate in what the Air Force refers to as "flying training," which falls under the authority of AETC's Nineteenth Air Force. The system is expansive and carries out 44 percent of the Air Force's total flying hours. Enlisted aircrew training is a relatively small program that prepares enlisted aircrew for a diverse set of occupational specialties. The greater proportion of flying training is SUPT, which prepares officers to receive their aeronautical ratings, or "pilot wings," on a variety of aircraft. SUPT is lengthy, taking more than a year to complete. SUPT students may face increased vulnerabilities to potential abuse and misconduct stemming from the concentration of career-decision authority placed in the hands of the instructors and flight commanders.

Adapting the BMT Survey for Technical Training and Flying Training Environments

The technical training and flying training survey was developed to solicit several types of information about the training environment: experience and awareness of abuse and misconduct; at what installation the incidents occurred; reporting decisions, rationales, and consequences; the leader climate in the training environments regarding abuse and misconduct domains; and perceptions of leadership and support staff. The overall purpose is to track incidents and target systemic problems. The survey is not intended to identify specific incidents for investigation, as this would be redundant with other reporting channels and could jeopardize students' willingness to reveal unreported incidents through the survey, and thus obscure leaders' window into behaviors that are otherwise not visible.

The adapted survey covers six domains of abuse and misconduct, which are not necessarily mutually exclusive:

1. bullying of students by other students, including cyberbullying

2. maltreatment or maltraining of students by military training leaders or civilian or military instructors

3. unprofessional relationships between students and military training leaders, civilian or military instructors, or prior-service students

4. sexual harassment, gender discrimination, and sexual orientation discrimination against students by anyone

5. sexual assault of students by anyone

6. hazing of students by anyone.

The first three of these domains also appeared in the BMT survey and were generally adapted to the technical training and flying training environments by updating relevant terminology, modifying response options to better connect to the varying lengths of the training courses, modifying or adding items to reflect differences between the BMT and the technical training and flying training environments, and deleting items that did not pertain beyond the BMT environment. These revisions are discussed in detail in this report (Chapter 4). As an example of adaptation, a new cyberbullying subsection was developed in response to AETC student input and AETC leadership concerns, as enlisted students gain access to technologies during their IST that were off limits during BMT. Some bullying elements of the BMT survey were modified to reference both in-person experiences and those in the cyber environment, and new items were also developed based on research related to the measurement of cyberbullying—in particular, addressing public humiliation and malice.

The sexual harassment, gender discrimination, and sexual assault sections were substantially modified to adopt the new measures developed by the 2014 RAND Military Workplace Study, which included RAND researchers' redesign of the U.S. Department of Defense's (DoD's) Workplace and Gender Relations Survey (known as the "WGRA" for the active-duty population version and "WGRR" for the reserve). Because DoD subsequently adopted these new measures of military sexual assault and sexual harassment for future use, the Air Force elected to incorporate the measures into the technical training and flying training survey to permit closer comparisons to Air Force or DoD-wide responses from that survey. The new measures differ most substantially from the BMT survey in the inclusion of follow-up questions that gather the necessary information to make a more definitive statement about whether the behavior rose to the level of a military equal opportunity violation or Uniform Code of Military Justice–defined sexual assault. In addition to DoD's newly adopted measures, we retained a BMT survey item on noncontact events, such as exposure or exhibitionism, and added an item on sexual orientation discrimination.

Hazing is a new category that was added at the request of AETC because of new DoD policy and emphasis on identifying and preventing hazing. We developed a series of survey items to encompass hazing behaviors, drawing from previous studies on hazing. In developing these questions, particular attention was paid to ensure that the items clearly differentiated between abuse or misconduct and authorized training exercises or techniques. This distinction was important because of the unique nature of some training pipelines, such as battlefield airmen pipelines, where students undergo particularly rigorous and intense physical training necessary to prepare them for real-world mission environments.

A Pretest of the Survey Content and Administration

We pretested the survey content and potential administration modes with both technical training and flying training students. We administered the survey in classrooms and computer labs at five U.S.-based Air Force bases that train large numbers of students in a wide range of occupational specialties. Students took the voluntary survey using Air Force computers to connect to the Air Force survey website. The data from the pretest helped fine-tune the survey (e.g., determine whether the questions were understandable, whether response options were complete, how long the survey takes to complete), develop survey administration methods, and collect additional feedback from students.

Survey System Recommendations

Our recommendations for AETC's future survey system were informed by input from AETC leaders, key staff, instructors, and students, as well as the survey pretest responses.

When to Administer the Survey

There are two primary options for the timing of the survey. The first option is to administer the survey at a single point in time, capturing a snapshot of all technical training or flying training students at that same point. This method focuses on the training environment as a whole at a point in time, but it captures students at a variety of points in their training pipelines. This approach could be used to estimate how many students at a given point in time had experienced any abuse or misconduct during their training or during a set period of time (e.g., the past six months). The second option is to connect the administration of the survey to the training pipeline itself—for instance, by surveying students at the end of the awarding course or at the end of the first course.

Given AETC priorities, we recommend building the survey into the training pipeline, which allows the survey to serve as alternate feedback system for all students, especially those not willing to report incidents through other channels. This strategy allows the survey to be incorporated into standard course schedules. Also, provided there are sufficient response rates, the pipeline-connected approach enables leadership to compare average annual responses from students in the larger pipelines (e.g., security forces, munitions systems, aerospace medical service) who were surveyed at the same six-month or graduation point in their training—thereby providing a mechanism to determine whether interventions and policy changes to mitigate abuse or misconduct appear to be having an impact. Given unique characteristics of the technical training and flying training environments, we recommend slightly different timing for each training environment.

For non-prior service students in enlisted technical training who do not go on to participate in flying training, we recommend surveying students at the end of their training pipelines or at approximately six months, whichever comes first. Research suggests the accuracy of recall for life events declines substantially seven months after the event (Raphael, Cloitre, and Dohrenwend, 1991). Because most technical training pipelines are shorter than six months, accuracy of recall is not a significant concern, and the survey will capture their entire experience during technical training. However, surveying students in longer pipelines at six months will circumvent concerns about recall and will capture students' early training experiences—a period during which students may be at their most vulnerable to misconduct. Additionally, this time frame will allow for a more timely leadership response to emerging problematic trends than waiting until a lengthy training pipeline has been completed. If AETC leadership is concerned about misconduct occurring six months or more into any of the lengthy technical pipelines, they have the option of deploying the survey again to follow up.

Students training for enlisted aircrew AFSCs could be surveyed at the end of flying training and permitted to indicate experiences in both the technical training and flying training phases of their pipelines. The results for the technical training phase of enlisted aircrew training could be analyzed and reported separately from their subsequent flying training experiences, given that different chains of command oversee each.

For officer SUPT students, we recommend a modified survey administration schedule. Because the undergraduate pilot training pipeline is much longer than other pipelines, and because it occurs in distinct phases, **we recommend surveying officer SUPT students at least twice**: at the end of their primary training (with the survey asking them to include the time awaiting pilot training and pre-flight academics, as well as their T-6 primary training) and again at the end of advanced training (approximately seven months later). In each case, the survey should be administered before decisions about advanced training or aircraft assignments are made so that survey responses, particularly those pertaining to the flying training leadership, are not colored by satisfaction (or dissatisfaction) with those decisions.

In addition, we recommend that students who leave technical or flying training without graduating be invited to take the survey prior to their exits. Those surveys should include an indicator that they were taken by nongraduates so they can be aggregated and analyzed separately from graduates.

Who Should Participate in the Survey

When administering the survey, the Air Force will need to decide how many students will be invited to participate. Two sampling strategies were considered. The first is random sampling, where a select random subset of the population is invited to participate. In the second, referred to as a *census*, everyone in the population is invited to take the survey. **Recognizing that both sample and census techniques have strengths and limitations, and taking into account AETC priorities, this study recommends a census for the survey system.** Arguably, two of the most important concerns in administering the survey are whether students feel comfortable taking the survey and the capacity to capture rare events, such as sexual assault. With a sample, students may conclude that they were purposefully selected to answer the survey, leading them to opt out of participation or give socially desirable answers to the questions. A census allows the survey to serve as an alternate, anonymous reporting channel for abuse and misconduct. Additionally, the survey could serve as a training tool, as the act of reading the survey items could reinforce students' understanding of proper conduct and values in the Air Force.

How the Survey Should Be Administered

Our survey pretest results suggest that certain survey administration methods may improve student participation and comfort in being open and honest on the survey. **We recommend that flight commanders announce the survey and encourage participation,** although, of course, participation should not be coerced. Leaders could communicate how survey results have been used in the past to improve student experiences during technical training or flying training, to highlight to students that leaders will be taking their input seriously, and thus that their participation matters. **However, to promote open and honest participation, only students and a civilian survey administrator should be present in the room during the survey.** No military or civilian authority figures should be present.

Building survey time into student schedules will also ensure that students have an opportunity to participate, particularly in pipelines with full schedules or limited access to computers. This would also avoid assumptions that students who participate are those who experienced abuse or misconduct or wish to complain. **Ensuring that students stay in the room for the full survey session will help protect against pressures to rush through the questions. This practice would also avoid calling attention to students who are taking longer to complete the survey because they experienced several incidents and thus are receiving more follow-up questions than average.** Setting aside time in the training schedule may be particularly challenging or impossible, however, in courses that do not fall under Air Force leadership (e.g., medical courses at the time of this study). **Where feasible, AETC should coordinate administration of this survey with administration of other surveys to reduce survey fatigue.**

Additional considerations could assist with survey access. If Air Force network computers are required to access the survey, **AETC will need to ensure sufficient availability of computer rooms with active connections,** as not all locations will have large labs or classrooms equipped this way. **However, we also recommend AETC explore options for students to take the survey on personal or other military-owned computers or devices**, as a requirement for Air Force network computers may be a hurdle particularly for airmen training on non–Air Force bases.

AETC should also explore the feasibility of not requiring a common access card (CAC) for survey participation. Although our pretest suggested that students who are willing and able to take the survey using their CACs would respond similarly to students who are not required to use their CACs, CAC and local information technology (IT) requirements may present survey access barriers. If a CAC is necessary, survey administrators should ensure that students are registered to use their CACs at the installation where the survey will be administered, that there are a sufficient number of machines available for students, and that students who have forgotten their personal identification numbers have them reset shortly before the survey is scheduled.

Where feasible, installation of privacy screens on computers may promote greater openness in reporting sensitive information by providing students greater confidence that others sitting or passing beside or behind them will be unable to view their screen.

How the Survey Results Should Be Analyzed and Reported

One of the most critical elements of the survey system design is confidentiality for the individual responses. **Without confidentiality, the survey loses its value in promoting visibility of behaviors that students are not willing to reveal through official reporting channels.** The surveys do remind students of their official reporting channel options, should they be willing to come forward. To avoid undermining the survey's added value to leadership, **individual survey findings of misconduct should not be forwarded to squadron commanders or Office of Special Investigations representatives for follow-up investigation.** The survey can prompt other forms of action, as noted above, such as further exploration of cultural or other institutional factors that may contribute to abuse and misconduct, or discourage official reporting or help-seeking behaviors.

Differences in pipeline length need to be considered in data analyses plans to avoid misleading comparisons of incident rates across widely differing periods. In addition, the survey results should be triangulated with other technical training and flying training data. Incidents indicated through the survey could be compared with rates of incidents reported to leadership or service providers to examine how much underreporting may be occurring and to help provide insights on areas of concern, such as reasons for not reporting. In addition to reported incidents, potentially relevant data that could complement the survey data include injury and illness rates, counseling referrals, rates of attrition and recycling, and other student surveys. Survey results could also be used to spark further explorations into problems areas: for example, leaders could hold focus groups or town halls with military training leaders, instructors, or students to present or discuss results of concern, or chaplains or first sergeants could more discreetly raise certain topics when making general inquiries about the well-being of students.

The survey results should be presented in context. Relevant information that may explain changes in survey results include policy changes, changes to training pipelines and programs, staffing changes (e.g., rank, gender, instructor-to-student ratio), and changes in student admissions (e.g., class sizes, screening mechanisms). This information, combined with survey information, may also be relevant for interpreting other training trends, such as rates of attrition.

Conclusion

We have proposed a confidential survey system intended to solicit open feedback from Air Force technical and flying training enlisted students and officer SUPT students about incidents of abuse and misconduct in the training environment, attitudes toward and experiences with reporting incidents, and attitudes toward AETC leadership and feedback and support systems. The system is intended to provide greater visibility of events that may not be reported through official channels and can help identify barriers to official reporting. The survey also solicits information to identify key characteristics associated with incidents (e.g., location, type of people involved) to better understand how to target prevention efforts.

The survey is not intended as an investigative tool. To avoid undermining the intent of the survey, law enforcement should never try to deduce who filled out any particular survey. Meaningful spikes in misconduct should prompt an assessment of changes in the climate, leadership, or student body to learn about possible causes. For example, a civilian behavioral or social scientist hired to lead the survey effort could conduct focus groups, or leaders could hold town halls with students and flight leaders to learn more about the current climate.

For respondents reading through the survey, it can also serve to reinforce the types of behaviors that are not acceptable within the Air Force and as a reminder of the diverse options within the Air Force available to them for reporting incidents or seeking help.

If implemented, the survey would benefit from additional testing to confirm that it is functioning as intended, including as it is extended to enlisted training pipelines not in the survey pretest. Moreover, the instrument will likely need additional adaptation if extended to other officer flying training pipelines (e.g., combat systems officer) or officer technical training pipelines, as these environments may differ from those considered in this study. However, most of the content on abuse and misconduct, reporting channels, reporting attitudes and experiences, and leadership climate is also relevant to these other environments.

Acknowledgments

We wish to thank the many contributors who have offered their expertise and insight to improve this report. Air Force Education and Training Command (AETC) Commander Lt Gen Darryl Roberson was the research project sponsor who established the priorities for the study and provided important feedback throughout. AETC Vice Commander Maj Gen Mark Brown also offered key insights and made critical decisions that enabled us to proceed with the pretests. Members of AETC's Research, Education and Training Oversight Council more broadly, including Christine Burnett and Lt Gen Steven Kwast, contributed to the development of the survey system through their responses to briefings, questions, and survey drafts.

Project action officers Col Timothy Owens, Col Michael Grunwald, Roger Corbin, and Arturo Gomez helped shape the direction of this project, as they provided research oversight and guidance. In particular, the active dedication of Mr. Corbin and Mr. Gomez proved essential to the success of this project. We also benefited from the insights and experiences of Laura Munro, Robert Wilson, Robert Berger, and Jeffrey Nelson, who have been analyzing data from the RAND Basic Military Training survey since it was adopted. We are also grateful for the contributions of Aaron Condel, Milton Turner, and Gina Johnson surrounding AETC's technical capabilities as they pertain to the feasibility of the survey system. The vice commander of Second Air Force during the survey development, Col Malcolm Johnson, provided a careful review of a draft of the survey instrument and offered advice to further tailor it to the technical training environment. Additionally, Second Air Force liaison Stephen Ellis and Nineteenth Air Force liaisons Maj Chris Bennett, Maj Stacie Billington, and Lt Col Oliver Johnson provided valuable project coordination assistance and insights into the technical training and flying training environments. During our initial site visits to Keesler, Lackland, and Laughlin Air Force Bases (AFBs), dozens of leaders, students, instructors, and other key staff took time from their busy schedules to meet with us, review early survey drafts, and offer suggestions for improvement. Their input was critical to the quality of the proposed study design and survey instrument. Similarly, dozens of site leaders and staff at Fairchild, Keesler, Lackland, and Laughlin AFBs helped establish the conditions for a successful pretest administration, and hundreds of technical training and flying training students volunteered to participate in the survey. Their willingness to assist the team was necessary to developing a high-quality survey system for AETC. For their efforts coordinating the pretests, we especially thank Kurt Higgins, Lynn List, Beverly Fisher, Lt Col Art Alcantara, Capt Eric Wells, Lt Col Linwood Wells, Maj Dana Bochte, Lt Col Blake George, Senior Master Sgt Alexander Guerrero, Master Sgt J. Cullen Elliot, Master Sgt Kevin Wulf, Timothy Ori, Kevin McGaughey, and Jim Steele. Not only did their assistance make the pretests possible, it helped us understand the unique constraints and capabilities of each installation where the pretest was conducted.

We are also grateful to Arturo Gomez and Patrick Weatherington, who overcame many technical hurdles to programming the pretest survey instrument; Joseph Bentley, who helped survey ensure network connectivity with each pretest site; and Gina Johnson, who helped manage the numerous technical challenges more broadly.

We would like to thank our RAND colleagues for their contributions. Michael Robbins assisted with the calculations for the power analyses in Appendix D. Chandra Garber helped improve some of the figures and communication of findings and recommendations. We are also grateful for Ray Conley's valuable input at various stages during the study's planning and execution.

Peer reviewers Meredith Klekamp and Laura Werber provided thoughtful, constructive feedback that helped us improve the content and clarity of this report.

Abbreviations

AETC	Air Education and Training Command
AFB	Air Force Base
AFSC	Air Force Specialty Code
AWACS	Airborne Warning and Control System
BMT	Basic Military Training
C2ISR	Command and Control, Intelligence, Surveillance and Reconnaissance
CAC	common access card
CSO	Combat Systems Officer
DEOCS	DEOMI Organizational Climate Survey
DEOMI	Defense Equal Opportunity Management Institute
DoD	U.S. Department of Defense
ENJJPT	Euro-NATO Joint Jet Pilot Training Program
EEO	equal employment opportunity
EO	equal opportunity
FAIP	first assignment instructor pilot
FY	fiscal year
ISR	intelligence, surveillance, and reconnaissance
IST	initial skills training
IT	information technology
JSTARS	Joint Surveillance Target Attack Radar System
MAJCOM	major command
MEO	military equal opportunity
MTI	military training instructor
MTL	military training leader
NCO	noncommissioned officer

OSI	Office of Special Investigations
PIN	personal identification number
PR	personnel recovery
ROTC	Reserve Officer Training Corps
RPA	remotely piloted aircraft
SARC	sexual assault response coordinator
SERE	Survival, Evasion, Resistance, and Escape
SOF	special operations forces
SUPT	Specialized Undergraduate Pilot Training
UCMJ	Uniform Code of Military Justice
WGRA	Workplace and Gender Relations Survey of Active Duty Members
WGRR	Workplace and Gender Relations Survey of Reserve Component Members

1. Introduction

Airmen begin their U.S. Air Force careers with entry-level training. All enlisted recruits first complete Basic Military Training (BMT) at Lackland Air Force Base in Texas, during which they receive foundational training and are introduced to Air Force culture. Following BMT is technical training, where new enlistees disperse to career-specific initial skills training (IST) pipelines to learn the basic knowledge and skills necessary to be awarded their designated Air Force occupational specialty. Enlisted personnel in aircrew specialties will serve onboard aircraft, and flying training for their particular specialties follows their technical training. Enlisted technical training and flying training are conducted at locations across the country, and training pipelines can last from a few weeks to more than two years, depending on the job requirements. After completing their initial skills training for their careers and any additional occupational subspecialty training, enlisted airmen proceed to their first duty stations.

The training program for officers differs. Officers receive their initial socialization and training through their source of commission: the Air Force Reserve Officer Training Corps (ROTC), Officer Training School, the U.S. Air Force Academy, or, less commonly, Commissioned Officer Training. Following their commission, officers enter technical training or flying training for IST for their career fields. Officer IST also occurs at multiple bases across the country and can last more than a year.

Technical and flying training students may be particularly vulnerable to abuse and misconduct from one another and from others in the training environment. For both incoming officers and enlisted airmen, IST provides an introduction to their career fields and prepares them for transition to their first duty assignments. It is also a developmental moment that might test their autonomy, particularly for enlisted airmen, as many young adults are transitioning from their parents' homes to living more independently. Although this period is also one in which they are socialized to adopt Air Force culture and values, the process may still be ongoing and at odds with their norms and values prior to entry. Moreover, these students are the newest Air Force members at the lowest levels of the hierarchy, and thus may not be fully aware of all of the rules, regulations, and boundaries within which their superiors should be operating. Additionally, in some cases, they are competing with fellow airmen for limited slots. For example, the type of aircraft that officers will fly when they become pilots (e.g., tanker, fighter, bomber, helicopter) is determined only after students have completed the first stages of their Specialized Undergraduate Pilot Training (SUPT).

To help prevent potential abuse and misconduct during this vulnerable period, the commander of the Air Force's Air Education and Training Command (AETC) asked RAND Project AIR FORCE to develop a survey system to monitor abuse and misconduct within the technical training and flying training environments. In addition to the monitoring function, data from the survey system will also provide insights into potential cultural or systemic changes that could help reduce the occurrence of abuse and misconduct and increase reporting when it does occur.

In fiscal year (FY) 2013, we responded to a similar request to develop a survey instrument to monitor several types of abuse and misconduct within BMT. The domains of abuse and misconduct on the BMT survey, which we will describe more fully in Chapter 4, included

- trainee-on-trainee bullying
- maltreatment and maltraining of trainees by military training instructors (MTIs)
- unprofessional relationships between MTIs and trainees
- sexual harassment of trainees from anyone in the BMT environment
- unwanted sexual experiences committed against trainees by anyone in the BMT environment.

In addition to identifying abuse and misconduct in each of these areas, the BMT survey also identified factors related to type, frequency, and the severity of these behaviors, such as reporting attitudes and experiences, the organizational climate, and leadership.[1] Although the survey instrument was designed specifically for BMT, these domains of abuse and misconduct and the assessment of barriers to reporting these incidents are also relevant to the technical and flying training environments.

Study Objective and Approach

The objective of this study was to modify the survey system designed for BMT and extend it to the technical training and flying training environments for enlisted airmen and to the flying training environment for officers in SUPT. In addition to the domains of abuse and misconduct already included on the BMT survey, AETC identified hazing as a necessary addition. Because technical training and flying training are transition periods in which airmen are joining a career field, it represents a potentially vulnerable period during which initiation rituals or hazing could take place. Additionally, cyberbullying was identified as another problem behavior that could be present in technical or flying training; enlisted students leaving BMT gain access to personal electronic devices that they would not have had during BMT. Given this change in access, it becomes important to monitor any student-to-student cyberbullying that may occur via these devices.

To adapt and extend the BMT survey system for monitoring abuse and misconduct to the technical and flying training environments, we completed the following tasks:

- based on a review of the scientific literature and feedback from meetings with Air Force students, military training leaders (MTLs), academic instructors, AETC leaders, and other stakeholders, adapted the BMT abuse and misconduct survey items to be relevant in the technical and flying training environments
- administered the revised surveys to samples of technical training and flying training students from several Air Force specialties

---

[1] For details on the development of this BMT instrument and items in each domain, see Keller, Miller et al., 2015.

- based on results from the pretest survey, refined the survey items
- developed recommendations for the design of the technical and flying training survey system, including survey administration, analysis, and reporting
- documented analyses, observations, findings, and recommendations in this report.

Organization of This Report

The remainder of the report is structured around answering the following research questions:

1. **What are the characteristics of the technical and flying training environments?** Understanding who attends training, course lengths, and the instructional environment informed adaptation of the survey and administration recommendations (Chapters 2 and 3).
2. **How will we adapt the BMT survey for the technical and flying training survey?** We developed a misconduct survey tailored to technical and flying training environments, accounting for differences from BMT, such as a broader range of training locations, types of personnel, and reporting channels. We also addressed AETC requests for new content (e.g., related to hazing) (Chapter 4).
3. **How should the survey content and administration be pretested?** We considered how best to efficiently pretest the survey and reach a range of types of students, facilities, and training pipelines (Chapter 5).
4. **When should the survey be administered?** We considered the advantages and disadvantages of delivering the survey at one or more points within each training pipeline relative to surveying all students in the training environment at certain points on the calendar (Chapter 6).
5. **Who should participate in the survey?** We weighed the advantages and disadvantages of asking every student to participate in the survey compared with inviting only a select sample (Chapter 7).
6. **How should the test survey be administered?** We explored options for the survey administration mode and how these options may affect participation, survey responses, confidentiality, and data security (Chapter 8).
7. **What technical or human resources challenges might need to be addressed?** We documented challenges encountered or raised during the pretest survey that could interfere with systematic survey administration across the diverse and numerous training installations (Chapter 9).
8. **How should the survey data be analyzed and reported?** An effective survey system depends on analyses that can be supported by the data, interpreted in context, and reported in ways that are meaningful to leadership and help them meet AETC's goals (Chapter 10).

The report concludes, in Chapter 11, with a succinct outline of the key recommendations for administering the survey system.

For reference, Appendix A conveys additional information about other Air Force and U.S. Department of Defense (DoD) surveys in the training environment. Appendix B provides details about enlisted occupational specialties available to non-prior service students, and Appendix C is the recommended survey from this study that has been revised following the survey pretest.

Appendix D provides more specific guidelines on the types of comparisons that might be possible given the sample sizes and prevalence of abuse and misconduct.

Part I: Understanding Technical Training and Flying Training

2. Characteristics of the Technical Training Environment

In this chapter, we describe the characteristics of the enlisted technical training environment that informed the survey content, administration, analysis, and reporting recommendations, contrasting it with the BMT environment where illustrative.[1] We provide an overview of the range of career fields available to enlisted airmen, as well as the process of training for these careers. In addition, we describe how training pipelines vary by number, sequence, size, and location of courses. We also describe the residential and instructional environment, the increase in student autonomy, the chain of command, and other characteristics of enlisted technical training that differ from BMT and are relevant for the design of the survey system.

Structure of Enlisted Technical Training

Enlisted technical training is overseen by Second Air Force, headquartered at Keesler Air Force Base (AFB) in Biloxi, Mississippi. Each year, 20,000 to 30,000 U.S. Air Force enlisted trainees graduate to airmen status upon completion of BMT at Lackland AFB in San Antonio, Texas (AETC, 2014). After BMT, these airmen enter IST to acquire the knowledge and skills necessary to perform their specific job duties. IST is a "formal school course that results in an AFSC [Air Force Specialty Code] 3-skill level award for enlisted" airmen (Air Force Instruction 36-2201, 2010, p. 111). Airmen can be enrolled in either flying training (for enlisted aircrew specialties) or technical training career paths, which include one or more training courses depending on the career field. Career fields and assignments are organized into seven general *career groups* and two *identifier groups*. The number of new airmen in FY 2016 holding AFSCs in each of those groups is shown in Table 2.1.

---

[1] For this project, AETC requested that we prioritize enlisted technical training over officer technical training, as non-prior service enlisted students are typically younger than officer students, who also often have much more exposure to the Air Force through the Air Force Academy or ROTC.

Table 2.1. AFSC Career and Identifier Groups and Number of New Enlisted Airmen in Each Group in FY 2016

Number and Name of Career or Identifier Group	Number of Airmen with Less Than One Year of Service
1. Operations	3,654
2. Logistics and maintenance	9,475
3. Support	7,153
4. Medical	1,776
5. Professional (i.e., paralegal, chaplain assistant)	49
6. Acquisition	210
7. Special investigations	0
8. Special duty identifiers (e.g., military training instructor, honor guard, recruiter, first sergeant)	69
9. Reporting identifiers (e.g., basic trainee, patient, prisoner, awaiting discharge)	7,231

SOURCE: RAND-generated based on raw FY 2016 data provided by the Air Force.

Upon completion of technical training, airmen are assigned their first duty station, where they continue to receive on-the-job training. The Air Force enlisted technical training encompasses a diverse array of career fields, such as air traffic control, vehicle maintenance, security forces, and mental health service. These career fields change periodically as the Air Force incorporates new technology or reorganizes its operations. No career field is closed to women, and all are gender-integrated. However, the gender ratio varies across career groups and more specific career fields.

There are three types of enlisted students in the technical training environment:

- *Non-prior service* students are "individuals who enter the military with no previous military service or have not been awarded an AFSC" (AETC Instruction 36-2216, 2010, p. 30). The majority of technical training students are non-prior service students.
- *Prior-service* students are individuals who have previous military service (e.g., in other branches) and have separated from the military, but reenter (AETC Instruction 36-2216, 2010, p. 30). The prior-service program is small and highly selective, based on the current needs of the Air Force. For example, for FY 2014, the number of applicants being accepted for the prior-service program was cut from 250 to 50 (Stonemetz, 2014). In addition to non-prior service and prior-service students, the technical training environment also includes retrainees.
- *Retrainees* are airmen who have returned to technical training to earn a new AFSC after serving the Air Force in a different career. These airmen may be permanently changing

careers, or they may be training for a special tour as a recruiter, military training instructor, or military training leader, after which they will return to a position in their original career field.

In this study, we focus on enlisted non-prior service students. The distinction between prior service, non-prior service, and retrainees is important because they are subject to different military training standards, discipline, procedures, and responsibilities. For example, prior-service students (who have completed BMT in another service branch or the first time they entered the Air Force) are required to take an orientation course rather than complete BMT with non-prior service trainees. Retrainees are not required to return to BMT, and, because they already have military experience, they are not assigned an MTL to assist with the transition from civilian to military life during their technical training. Although students from each of these groups may complete their coursework together, the older and more-experienced prior-service students and retrainees are housed separately from non-prior service students. Moreover, retrainees and prior-service airmen are not permitted to socialize with non-prior service students.

Within a pipeline, the required courses may be different for retrainees and prior-service students relative to the standard sequence for non-prior service students. For this study, AETC leadership requested that we focus on those career fields that are open to non-prior service students with the understanding that these pipelines may also include students who are retrainees or prior-service students.

Enlisted Student Population Sizes and Pipeline Lengths

The number of students in each specialty pipeline determines the appropriateness of certain types of data analyses and comparisons across groups and informs the risk of identifying a unique student's responses by inference. In FY 2016, the enlisted AFSCs with the greatest number of new airmen (less than one year of service) were security forces (2,782), aircraft armament systems (674), munitions systems (650), tactical aircraft maintenance (581), aerospace propulsion (550), materiel management (521), and aerospace medical service (521). Examples of career fields with fewer than ten new airmen that year included spectrum operations, special operations weather, and histopathology. Appendix B, Table B.1 lists the range of AFSCs available to non-prior service students and the number of new airmen holding those AFSCs in FY 2016. The student population in these pipelines may include some prior-service students and retrainees who are changing AFSCs, but the majority of students are non-prior service students.

Pipeline length is important to consider, as the risk for abuse and misconduct is greater in longer pipelines relative to shorter pipelines. Wide variability in pipeline length must also be considered when comparing rates of misconduct across groups (e.g., across AFSCs, installations). Pipeline time includes days spent training and days between courses (e.g., time transferring from one installation to another, delays from injuries, time awaiting security clearances, or administrative issues).[2] It also includes holiday leave from the end of December to early January. The longest enlisted technical training pipelines require more than a year to complete (e.g., special operations weather [1W0X2]; pararescue [1T2X1]; and cryptologic language analyst [1N3X1]). The shortest pipelines include logistics plans (2G0X1), aviation resource management (1C0X2), and personnel (3S0X1), which typically last about five to six weeks. Overall, the majority of enlisted technical training pipelines take approximately six weeks to six months to complete.

Technical Training Locations and Pipeline Structure

In technical training, each pipeline consists of one or more courses that a student must complete to be awarded the AFSC for a specific career field. Second Air Force oversees nonflying enlisted technical training pipelines each with a unique sequence of training courses of varying durations hosted at one or more of numerous locations. In contrast, enlisted BMT is a more uniform process, which occurs over a standardized period of eight and a half weeks at a single location (Lackland AFB). Technical training courses vary in length from relatively brief classes that last fewer than 14 days to lengthy language or medical courses that can last more than a year. Some courses support more than one career field. For example, Avionics Fundamentals courses provide foundational skills for students training for the avionics test station and components career field and the various avionics systems career fields. As such, some courses will include students studying for only one career field, whereas other courses will include a mixed group.

Technical training locations are dispersed across the country; however, the majority of enlisted technical training occurs at one of four locations:

- Sheppard AFB near Wichita Falls, Texas: 9,867 students in FY 2015
- Keesler AFB in Biloxi, Mississippi: 6,415 students in FY 2015
- Lackland AFB in San Antonio, Texas: 5,390 students in FY 2015
- Goodfellow AFB in San Angelo, Texas: 3,872 students in FY 2015.

The Defense Language Institute hosts technical training students who are learning a foreign language for their AFSCs. Other training locations include both Air Force and non–Air Force (e.g., Army, Navy) installations nationally and internationally. Therefore, there is wide geographic diversity in locations of technical training both across and within career fields. As a consequence, a plan to monitor activity in technical training requires enumerating all the locations in which technical training courses are offered. Furthermore, any plans for reporting results by installation must also take into account population size.

Next, we describe three sample pipelines that were selected to illustrate the variable nature of the technical training pipeline length and number of courses.

---

[2] For further discussion of such delays and the challenges of managing efficient flows through these technical training pipelines, see Harrington et al., 2017.

Security Forces Pipeline

Security Forces, the Air Force's military police and force protection specialty, is part of the *support* career group. When students in this training pipeline exit BMT, they remain at Lackland AFB for a Security Forces Apprentice course (see Figure 2.1). On completion of this course, they are awarded their AFSC and transition to their first duty stations. The Security Forces Apprentice course lasts about 65 days. In FY 2016, 2,782 new airmen held the Security Forces AFSC.

Figure 2.1. Enlisted Security Forces Technical Training Pipeline, as of May 2014

SOURCE: AETC, "Tech Training Pipelines," slides provided to authors, October 2, 2015b, slide 230.

Cryptologic Language Analyst Pipeline

Crytpologic language analysts are part of the *operations* career group. Upon completing BMT at Lackland AFB, enlisted students in this pipeline begin language training at the Defense Language Institute, which is a DoD school in Monterey, California. Figure 2.2 illustrates the pipeline for a cryptologic language analyst specializing in Persian, but students may specialize in other languages. After language study, students complete their AFSC awarding course at Goodfellow AFB. For this career field, there is great variability in required course time due primarily to language differences, with the longest training for the languages involving new alphabets or characters (e.g., Persian, Korean) and the shortest language training being for Spanish. In FY 2016, 293 new airmen held the cryptologic language analyst AFSC.

Figure 2.2. Technical Training Pipeline for Enlisted Cryptologic Language Analyst—Persian, as of May 2014

SOURCE: AETC, 2015b, slide 57.

Combat Control Pipeline

The combat control career field is a special operations, or battlefield airmen, occupational specialty that was one of the last to open to women when DoD lifted all restrictions on women's service in late 2015. Like the cryptologic language analyst, it is also part of the *operations* career group, but the training pipeline is quite different (see Figure 2.3). After completing BMT, students enroll in a Combat Control Selection course at Lackland AFB (see Figure 2.3). If successful, they complete a Combat Control Operator course at Keesler AFB. Next, they spend time in Airborne Training at the Army's Fort Benning, Georgia. They must then complete an Air Force Combat Survival Training course at Fairchild AFB and Combat Control Apprentice course at Pope AFB in North Carolina. This training pipeline is highly demanding both mentally and physically, and training attrition rates averaged 75 percent from FY 2011 to FY 2015, compared with 10 percent average training attrition across Air Force enlisted specialties as a whole (Lytell et al., 2018, p. 1). In FY 2016, 44 new airmen were combat controllers.

Figure 2.3. Enlisted Combat Control Technical Training Pipeline, as of May 2014

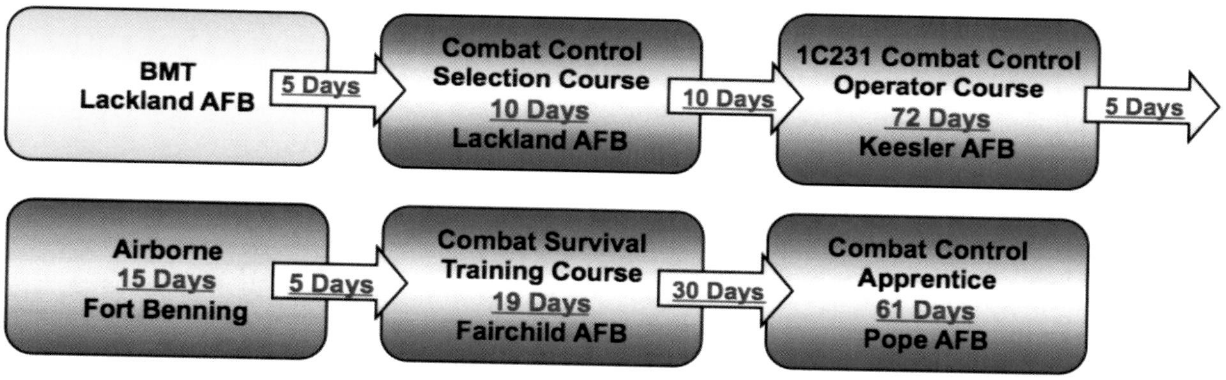

SOURCE: AETC, 2015b, slide 34.

These three examples demonstrate the diversity of Air Force enlisted technical training pipelines. Although some IST pipelines, such as security forces, are completed in a relatively short period of time at a single location, others (such as cryptologic language analysts and combat control operators) require longer durations of training and transfer between training locations. Most enlisted technical training pipelines require travel from BMT at Lackland AFB to at least one other location. Exceptions in 2015 were technical training pipelines at Lackland AFB for

- Safety, Logistics Plans, Materiel Management, and Vehicle Management and Analysis AFSCs (approximately one month of technical training)
- Contracting (about 40 days long)
- Security Forces (approximately two months).

11

This variability holds implications for our survey system design. For example, an end-of-course survey of security forces students would be relatively straightforward, providing timely information to leadership (incidents would have occurred within the past 65 days) at a single training location (Lackland AFB). In contrast, waiting until the end of the pipeline to administer a cryptologic language analyst survey would risk the loss of respondents' recall of events early in their training, as well as reduce the timeliness of feedback to leaders. Pipeline differences also have implications for survey content and result reporting. To help leadership understand whether certain locations or courses are presenting greater risk for abuse or misconduct, it would be valuable for the survey to include follow-up questions about where an incident occurred whenever students train at more than one location.

Residential and Instructional Environment

During their coursework, the majority of airmen in technical training reside on base. These residences are similar to college dorms, with airmen assigned to gender-segregated bays with oversight provided by MTLs and student leaders who are assigned to individual bays, floors, and buildings. Both the residential and instructional environments are more gender-integrated than BMT. Courses are gender-integrated, although gender composition varies across AFSCs. In general, the technical training environment has a more-diverse composition than BMT, as some courses may contain both enlisted and officer students, and non–Air Force personnel may be present either on base or in training courses as instructors or students. Additionally, some courses take place in classrooms whereas others occur outdoors. Courses may emphasize cognitive tasks, physical tasks, or both. We describe other key differences in the populations and instructional environments of courses within different AFSCs below.

Student autonomy. As students transition from BMT to technical training, their degrees of autonomy shift. BMT can be described as a *total institution* (Goffman, 1961); trainees are segregated from society, their time is highly scheduled, and their freedom, privacy, and other privileges are restricted. Daily routines are directed by MTIs. In contrast, technical training provides students with greater autonomy. Although they typically reside on base, students may be permitted to come and go at their discretion after duty hours, may host visitors, and maintain other privileges, such as internet and cell phone use. In addition, MTLs provide less oversight over airmen in technical training compared with the high level of control by MTIs over trainees in the BMT environment.

Chain of command. In BMT, trainees function within a single chain of command of MTIs that is relatively consistent throughout the duration of training, although there are periods where they are trained by MTIs other than those leading their flight (unit). In technical training, non-prior service students have two chains of command: their course instructors and their MTLs. The role of MTLs in technical training is similar to MTIs in BMT; they are enlisted noncommissioned officers (NCOs) who are responsible for enforcing military standards of conduct, accountability, and discipline among airmen completing their training. Course instructors are responsible for specific career field training. Unlike MTLs, instructors may be either civilian or military, members of the Air Force or other branches of the military, or foreign nationals. In addition, airmen required to take multiple courses throughout the pipeline may be subject to serial chains of command. Therefore, there are multiple possible sources of abuse or misconduct from individuals in positions of authority over students.

Attrition and washback. Not all students complete the training pipelines they enter. Some students are required to repeat coursework. Attrition, or failure to complete a course or training pipeline, may be attributable to a variety of issues, such as academic failure, self-initiated elimination, medical holds, or other issues that prevent completion of coursework. Repetition of instructional blocks because of academic failure, referred to as course "washback," is also not uncommon. Instructors, but not MTLs, have the power to fail students in particular courses. Students must then either retake a course or transfer to a different career field. In the past, average rates of attrition and washback have been 8 percent and 21 percent, respectively, with higher rates in certain AFSCs, such as the battlefield airmen specialties (Manacapilli et al., 2012). A full picture of student experiences will include both pipeline graduates and those who do not graduate, as well as those whose pipelines are greatly extended due to injury or course failure. We must also consider the possibility that some students who are the target of abuse or misconduct may consequently struggle with their coursework or choose to leave the Air Force.

These differences between the BMT and technical training environments, and the heterogeneity across training pipelines, were important context for survey development. The survey needs to assess potential abuse or misconduct from both military and civilian leaders in either chain of command (MTLs, instructors) and at each training location. We developed the survey to have the specificity necessary for the technical training environment, while also maintaining enough generality that students in diverse pipelines would find the questions and material relevant.

Conclusion

In this chapter, we described the environment for enlisted technical training pipelines available to non-prior service airmen (with the exception of students who will go on to enlist in flying training, which are discussed in the next chapter). Technical training covers a wide range of diverse career fields. As a result, the duration of the training pipeline and the number, sequence, size, and location of courses within each pipeline also vary considerably. This differs markedly from BMT, which is a set eight-and-a-half-week course for all airmen. Technical training and BMT also differ in the instructional and residential environment and the level of student autonomy, which is significantly greater in the technical training environment. These differences affect the potential for abuse and misconduct in the technical training environment and influenced our decisions regarding an appropriate survey vehicle and strategies for pretesting and implementation, as later chapters will describe.

3. Characteristics of the Flying Training Environment

This chapter describes the training environment for the U.S. Air Force's flying training system. This training system is under the charge of Nineteenth Air Force, which runs 19 training locations and conducts more than 490,000 flying hours annually (Strang, 2015). Next, we discuss the enlisted aircrew training system and the officer pilot training system, focusing on the SUPT segment of officer flying training. Other officer flying training pipelines (e.g., combat systems officer) were beyond the scope of this study.

Enlisted Aircrew Training

The Air Force's enlisted aircrew training system prepares airmen for a diverse set of enlisted aviator occupational specialties, all of which fall within the *operations* career group. These career fields are in-flight refueling (boom operators); flight engineers; aircraft loadmasters; airborne mission systems operators; flight attendants (not available to non-prior service airmen); airborne cryptologic language analysts; airborne intelligence, surveillance, and reconnaissance (ISR); special mission aviators, and remotely piloted aircraft (RPA) sensor operators.

Enlisted Student Population Sizes and Pipeline Lengths

As discussed in the previous chapter on enlisted technical training, the number of students in a training pipeline, differing course locations, and the length of time required to complete a pipeline are relevant for the design of the survey system. We examined the number of new airmen (less than one year of service) in enlisted aircrew AFSCs in FY 2016. The AFSC with the fewest entrants was airborne ISR operator (eight new airmen). The AFSCs with the greatest number of new airmen were the airborne cryptologic language analysts (181) and the RPA sensor operators (117). Table 3.1 provides this information for each enlisted aircrew career field available to non-prior service students. In sum, 554 new airmen were in enlisted aircrew occupations in FY 2016.

Table 3.1. Enlisted Aircrew AFSCs and Number of New Airmen in Each Group in FY 2016

AFSC and Title	FY 2016 Number of Airmen with Less Than One Year of Service
1A0X1 In-Flight Refueling	38
1A2X1 Aircraft Loadmaster	71
1A3X1 Airborne Mission Systems Operator	103
1A8X1 Airborne Cryptologic Language Analyst	181
1A8X2 Airborne ISR Operator	8
1A9X1 Special Mission Aviator	36
1U0X1 RPA Sensor Operator	117

SOURCE: RAND-generated based on raw FY 2016 data provided by the Air Force.
NOTE: Each individual within an AFSC will have a number in place of the "X" that represents the individual's skill or qualification level. The table displays only AFSCs available to non-prior service airmen.

We also reviewed the total number of planned pipeline days for enlisted aircrew training pipelines. Pipeline time includes the time spent at Lackland AFB in the technical training stage of the pipeline and the latter portion of IST in flying training (which may occur elsewhere), as well as any time in between courses and other delays. As with technical training, the actual length of these pipelines can vary depending on factors such as holiday leave, student injuries, time awaiting security clearances, and available training slots and timing (e.g., when courses at the Defense Language Institute are offered). We see variation in scheduled lengths by career, with the RPA sensor operator AFSC having the shortest training pipeline estimated at 15 weeks, and the airborne cryptologic language analyst pipeline estimated at 108 weeks. All of the other enlisted flying training pipelines available to non-prior service airmen were scheduled to take between about 24 weeks and 65 weeks for students to complete.

Enlisted Aircrew Training Locations and Pipeline Structure

Following BMT, enlisted aircrew students first complete an introductory aircrew fundamentals course and a basic course specific to their AFSC at Lackland AFB in San Antonio, Texas, under the command of Second Air Force. Upon successful completion of these basic courses, most students are awarded their AFSC, but before they can perform in their specialty, students disperse to various installations to receive flying training under the command of Nineteenth Air Force. With the exception of those who will work with remotely piloted aircraft, all enlisted aircrew undergo about four weeks of combat and water survival training at Fairchild AFB, typically after their basic coursework and before they begin training on the aircraft. Depending on the career field requirements, enlisted aircrew may undertake language at the Defense Language Institute or parachute training. All enlisted aircrew receive flying training tailored to the type of weapons system in which they will specialize (e.g., C-5 transport aircraft, HH-60 helicopter, MQ-1 remotely piloted aircraft). Flying training installations include Altus

AFB in Oklahoma, Little Rock AFB in Arkansas, Kirtland AFB in New Mexico, Lackland AFB and Randolph AFB in Texas (both part of Joint Base San Antonio), and Keesler AFB in Mississippi (AETC, 2014). The following is an example of an enlisted aircrew training pipeline.

Airborne Mission Systems Operator Pipeline

Airborne mission systems operators operate, maintain, report on, and test radar, communications, and electronic equipment. After BMT, students remain at Lackland AFB for technical training in aircrew fundamentals and basic airborne mission systems operator skills (see Figure 3.1). After earning the AFSC, students attend combat and water survival training at Fairchild AFB. Next, they transition to their first duty stations where flying training will qualify them on either the Airborne Warning and Control System (AWACS) or the Joint Surveillance Target Attack Radar System (JSTARS). In FY 2016, 103 new airmen were airborne mission systems operators.

Figure 3.1. Enlisted Airborne Mission Systems Operator Technical Training and Flying Training Pipeline, as of January 2015

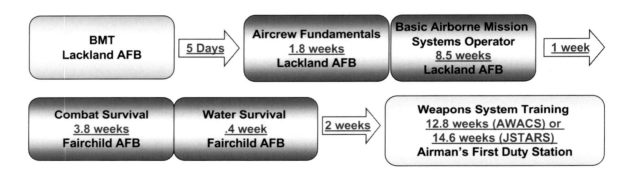

SOURCE: AETC, "Flying Training Pipelines," slides provided to authors, October 2, 2015a, slide 29.

Residential and Instructional Environments

The descriptions from Chapter 2 of the residential and instructional environments for enlisted students in technical training also apply to enlisted students in the flying training portion of their pipeline. However, flying training includes on-the-job training with functioning Air Force units. Thus, there can be more opportunities for travel and overnight stays away from base for these enlisted aircrew students learning to work onboard aircraft in flight, as they participate in flying training missions to gain real-world hands-on experience.

During enlisted aircrew flying training, students who are learning their weapons systems while at their first duty stations typically interact mostly with people assigned to their flights and then with those assigned to their squadrons.[1] First-term airmen could train alongside more experienced airmen who are changing AFSCs (e.g., maintenance personnel who have requested to move into an aircrew specialty). Thus, it is possible for NCOs and junior-enlisted personnel to train together in these units. Beyond fellow students and others in the flying training environment who outrank students, there are several positions of authority close to them in the chain of command with direct responsibility for their training. Flight commanders are officers with authority over the units responsible for day-to-day training of enlisted aircrew. Instructors are civilian or military personnel who evaluate student performance in the technical training and flying training courses. MTLs are NCOs who continue the work begun at BMT to help airmen adapt to Air Force standards and culture and can counsel or discipline airmen for violations. MTLs, flight commanders, and squadron commanders work together to promote and evaluate the performance of enlisted personnel during flying training.

Officer Flying Training for Pilots

Although AETC's first priority for this study was to focus on enlisted technical and flying training, AETC leadership also requested that we adapt the BMT survey for officer pilot training, which is one type of officer flying training. Prior to pilot training, officers will have been socialized into the Air Force. As mentioned previously, most Air Force officers receive their commission following successful education and training at the U.S. Air Force Academy, ROTC, or Officer Training School before advancing to specialized training for their career fields.[2] This training occurs at multiple bases across the country.

The Air Force's officer pilot training consists of two series: SUPT and Euro-NATO (North Atlantic Treaty Organization) Joint Jet Pilot Training (ENJJPT). SUPT trains students to become pilots of manned aircraft. These officers already have college degrees; the "U" in SUPT refers to students as "undergraduates" because they have not yet graduated from pilot training and received their pilot wings, or aeronautical rating. Graduate pilot training continues to develop new pilots' skills in operating the specific aircraft that they will fly in the operational Air Force. Additionally, a more experienced pilot may enter graduate flying training pipelines to learn to fly a different aircraft. The second series (ENJJPT), located at Sheppard AFB in Texas, is similar to SUPT, but the schedule is slightly different. Many of the students come from allied nations in NATO, and training is limited to bomber and fighter pilot training (Sheppard Air Force Base, 2012).

---

[1] Each numbered Air Force has several levels of subordinate units: wings, groups, squadrons, and flights. Wings are subordinate to numbered Air Forces, groups are subordinate to wings, squadrons are subordinate to groups, and flights are subordinate to squadrons. Squadrons are the basic unit of the Air Force and flights are the smallest subdivision. For more details, see Air Force Instruction 38-101, 2017.

[2] The exception is that some individuals with advanced specialized skills in professional fields such as law and medicine may enter by direct commission. According to the Air Force Personnel Center's IDEAS database, as of April 2016, the source of commission for active component Air Force officers was 43 percent from Air Force ROTC, 23 percent from U.S. Air Force Academy, 17 percent from Officer Training School, and 16 percent from direct commission.

Most of the day-to-day flying training takes place at the squadron and flight levels. Civilian instructors typically teach the academic courses that are part of the SUPT curriculum. Instructor pilots teach the primary and advance flying training portion of the training where students learn to pilot trainer aircraft. These instructors typically are Air Force officers, but they may be civilian contractors or officers from another service branch (e.g., Army officers training Air Force students to become helicopter pilots). Some of the Air Force instructors will be first assignment instructor pilots (FAIPs). FAIPs are new pilots who were assigned to serve as instructor pilots immediately after completing their flying training, rather than moving on to a flying training unit and into the operational Air Force. FAIPs potentially could instruct students who were their peers at a previous installation (e.g., classmates at the U.S. Air Force Academy or fellow graduates from Officer Training School). Consequently, FAIPs may face challenges managing their new professional relationships with students who once were their peers. Instructors, flight commanders, and squadron commanders jointly evaluate the performance of students during flying training. These evaluations carry significant weight and largely determine whether students will continue into the next stage of their pipeline and their assigned aircraft.

Specialized Undergraduate Pilot Training

SUPT pipeline instructors provide initial skills training to officers to fly one of three groups of aircraft: (1) airlift; tankers; command and control, intelligence, surveillance, and reconnaissance (C2ISR); and special operations forces (SOF) fixed wing; (2) bombers and fighters; and (3) helicopters. The SUPT pipeline includes pre-SUPT screening, SUPT (consisting of academics, primary training, and advanced training), and post-SUPT training (bridge and operational training), as shown in Figure 3.2.

Figure 3.2. Stages Before, During, and After Officer Specialized Undergraduate Pilot Training

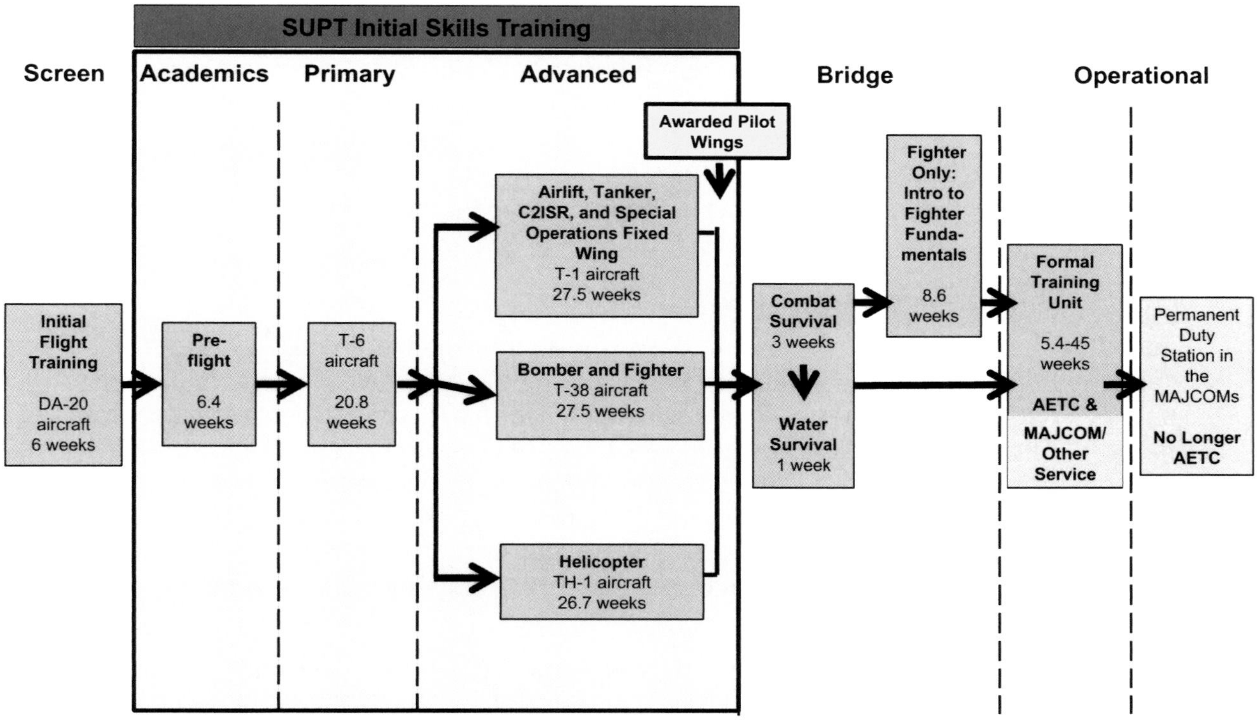

SOURCE: Adapted from Ausink et al. (2005) and updated with information on pipelines as of 2016 provided by AETC, U.S. Air Force.
NOTE: MAJCOM = major command.

Pre-SUPT Screening

Pre-SUPT screening is the initial course that all Air Force aviator candidates must attend. The course is six weeks long and is held in Pueblo, Colorado. This introductory course is where all active-duty, guard, and reserve Air Force officers aspiring to become pilots learn the basic flying skills. The course also provides personnel some initial flight experience on the DA-20 aircraft (see Doss Aviation, 2018, for further details). Successful candidates will then move to their assigned SUPT training bases.

SUPT

SUPT consists of three segments: academic training, primary flying training, and advanced flying training. However, not all students begin their pilot training immediately after arrival at their training base, because there are a limited number of each type of aircraft available and the Air Force's need for different types of pilots is constantly changing. The Air Force can place such students on "awaiting pilot training" status, during which the students assist units across the installation with tasks that are not directly related to their career fields as they await their turn to begin SUPT.

SUPT is the IST portion of flying training, which consists of the following:

19

- **Academic training.** Students first spend 6.4 weeks in pre-flight academics, typically taught by a civilian instructor.
- **Primary flying training.** Next, students enter primary training, a 20.8-week stage where students learn how to fly a Beechcraft T-6 Texas II. During primary training, instructor pilots exercise a significant level of authority over students. Instructor pilots evaluate the performance of their students, and flight commanders use this information to rank students. These rankings determine whether students will train on the T-1, T-38, or TH-1 during advanced flying training. Classes may consist of approximately 20 to 25 students.
- **Advanced flying training.** The advanced training stage involves students being divided into one of three tracks. The first track is training to fly airlift, tanker, C2ISR, or SOF fixed-wing aircraft. Students assigned to this track complete 27.5 weeks of training on the T-1. At the time of this study, T-1 classes were made up of about 12 to 17 students. The second track focuses on skills needed to fly bomber and fighter aircraft. It lasts 27.5 weeks and students fly a T-38 jet. Class sizes during this study were small: about five to nine students. The third track is for students assigned to helicopter undergraduate pilot training, which entails 26.7 weeks flying the TH-1 helicopter. Only four to five students at a time entered this track. It is possible for students to complete training in this advanced stage for one class of aircraft (e.g., bombers and fighters) but be tracked to fly another class of aircraft (e.g., airlifts or tankers) after completing the advanced stage. Class sizes can be adjusted based on the availability of training aircraft and the needs of the Air Force.

The Air Force has a rigorous process for selecting candidates to become students in SUPT. However, there are instances when students fail to complete their pilot training (Thomas, 2009). Most students who leave pilot training do so voluntarily (also known as "dropping on request"), but other reasons include medical issues, poor academic or flying performance, or a lack of adaptability (e.g., fear of flying, airsickness, or manifestations of apprehension). Students who fail a stage of SUPT for performance reasons may have the opportunity to repeat that stage (i.e., washback) or may transfer into a new career field.

Air Force policy outlines the procedures for assigning students to a track during advanced flying training and to their major weapons assignment in formal training units (AETC Instruction 36-2205, 2014). These procedures take into account the needs of the Air Force, availability of track and assignment slots for students, and student preferences. Instructor pilots make a training recommendation, the flight commander either concurs or does not concur with this recommendation, and then the flight and squadron commanders convene to assign students. The wing commander is actively involved in this process and has approval authority before forwarding assignments to the operations group commander.

Post-SUPT Training

Upon graduation from SUPT, new pilots will travel to Fairchild AFB in Washington state to spend three weeks completing combat survival training and one week completing water survival training. This intensive training program prepares students for survival under strenuous circumstances. Following survival training, new pilots proceed directly to a formal training unit, with the exception of those awarded a fighter pilot AFSC who must first complete the 8.6-week training course, Introduction to Fighter Fundamentals, at Randolph AFB in Texas, Sheppard AFB in Texas, or Columbus AFB in Mississippi. As new pilots move into the operational Air Force, they receive 5.4 weeks to 45 weeks of training with their formal training units. These units may operate under AETC or under one of the other Air Force MAJCOMs.

Flying Specialties and Time in the Training Pipeline

Officer AFSCs differ from those for enlisted personnel. There are approximately 149 AFSCs for officers (U.S. Air Force, 2012).[3]

In the pilot career field, officers learn to fly a particular type of aircraft: fighter, bomber, tanker, airlift, SOF fixed-wing, helicopters, or C2ISR aircraft. Officers preparing for other career fields will receive flying training appropriate for their needed expertise, and this training is also the responsibility of the Nineteenth Air Force. The air battle manager career field is responsible for managing the entire flight operation. Combat systems officers (CSOs), formerly known as navigators, have a range of responsibilities, including flight navigation, weapons systems, and electronic warfare of the aircraft. Students who are training to become CSOs receive their initial flying training in Pueblo, Colorado, and continue with combat and water survival training at Fairchild AFB in Washington. Then, students go to Naval Air Station Pensacola in Florida to complete their primary and advanced stages of training. Upon successful completion of these stages, students receive aircraft-specific training by AETC or another MAJCOM (Joint Base San Antonio, undated). RPA pilots receive training in one of two types of armed unmanned aerial vehicles (MQ-1 and MQ-9) or an unmanned surveillance vehicle (RQ-4). Students training to become RPA pilots have a unique pipeline; these students begin an introductory course on RPA flying, then continue with a course for RPA instrument qualifications, followed by another course on RPA fundamentals. These students then continue to the MAJCOMs for additional training on specific types of aircraft. Thus, although we considered whether we could include initial skills flying training for these other officer careers in our study, their pipelines differ enough from one another and the SUPT pipelines that additional research beyond our scope would have been necessary to include them.

---

[3] These AFSCs have four characters that provide information about the officer's skills (Air Force Instruction 36-2101, 2013). Consider AFSC "11B3" as an illustration. The first character is a number that can range from one to nine, representing the career group or identifier. These career groups and identifiers are the same categories as described in Chapter 2 for enlisted personnel. For our example, the first "1" represents the operations career group. The second character is a number that represents a utilization field. In our example, the second "1" represents the pilot career field. The third character is a letter that represents a functional area, which is "B" for bomber pilot in the example. The fourth character is a qualification level, which is "3" in our example, representing a 'qualified' level. When AFSCs are aggregated, the Air Force uses the "X" character to represent the qualification level because it will vary by individual. An individual officer's AFSC may also contain a prefix that indicates an ability, skill, special qualification, or system designator not limited to a particular AFSC. For example, "A" as a prefix to the four-character AFSC represents someone who is qualified as an operations warfare instructor. AFSCs may also contain a suffix (also called a "shred") representing positions that are associated with particular equipment. For example, "A" as a suffix is associated with the B-1 aircraft (Air Force Instruction 36-2101, 2013).

Conclusion

This chapter provided a review of the Air Force's training system for enlisted aircrew and officer pilots. It also provided some additional information on other officer flying training pipelines that were ultimately beyond the scope of this study. AETC's flying training system is expansive, representing 44 percent of the Air Force's total flying hours annually (Strang, 2015). However, the enlisted aircrew training is a relatively small program that prepares enlisted personnel for a diverse set of occupational specialties. The bulk of the flying training pipeline is SUPT for officers, which was the focus of our research on officers and target for the first officer pretest of the abuse and misconduct survey. In the future, AETC may wish to extend the survey system to other officer flying training pipelines.

Part II: Adapting and Pretesting the Survey Content and Administration

4. Adapted and New Survey Content

This chapter describes the basic structure of the new survey presented in Appendix C, noting where material was added to or adapted from the BMT survey (Keller, Miller et al., 2015) to fit the enlisted technical and flying training environments and officer SUPT. Multiple strategies were used to develop the survey content. The research sponsor requested new content to meet AETC's needs. We also reviewed relevant DoD, Air Force and AETC policy and studied technical training and flying training student and pipeline data. We built upon our previous review of civilian and military abuse and misconduct survey measures published in the academic literature that we conducted while developing the BMT survey. Subject-matter experts on the team, who already had a strong background in measurement of each domain, conducted literature reviews of the past five to ten years to identify any new measurement literature or confirm that there were no new developments.

We solicited input on the strengths and limitations of the BMT survey from AETC staff who have been analyzing that survey data and the leaders and service providers who had been receiving BMT survey results briefings. Throughout the project, representatives from the Occupational Analysis Division also provided insights on the training environments and suggestions for our survey drafts. We toured training areas and met with AETC leadership, instructors, MTLs, key staff (e.g., legal, medical, sexual assault response coordinator [SARC]), and students at AETC headquarters and three training bases to learn about schedules, equipment, and facilities in the training environment and to solicit detailed feedback on early survey drafts. Finally, we received helpful input on subsequent drafts from senior leaders and key staff at Second Air Force, Nineteenth Air Force, and AETC headquarters.

In response to our solicitation to AETC stakeholders to review the survey content, we received written and verbal comments through email, teleconferences, and in-person meetings between stakeholders and project staff. Their feedback was used to confirm the face validity of survey items and content, confirm that the abuse and misconduct items assessed behaviors that were clearly prohibited by military law or Air Force policy, ensure that diction was consistent with the environment, and correct items from the BMT survey that appeared to be ambiguous or poorly understood. All of these reviews were critical for ensuring our instructions and items were clear and appropriate for a variety of training environments. Then, as we describe in Chapter 5, we pretested the instrument with a sample of technical and flying training students before finalizing the content presented in Appendix C.

The overall design of the survey provides a framework for monitoring abuse and misconduct in six core domains:

- bullying and cyberbullying from other students
- maltreatment or maltraining by MTLs or instructors

- unprofessional relationships with MTLs, instructors, officers (for enlisted) or prior-service students or retrainees (for non-prior service enlisted)
- sexual harassment, gender discrimination, or sexual orientation discrimination by anyone
- sexual assault by anyone
- hazing by anyone.

In each of the six misconduct survey sections, students are asked to indicate the frequency with which they experienced a variety of specific behaviors within each misconduct domain. Reviewers of our survey drafts often suggested that we shorten the instrument, for example, by first asking students whether they were sexually harassed and then asking detailed follow-up questions only of the respondents who indicated they had been harassed. Unfortunately, the interpretation of such concepts as sexual harassment vary widely across individuals, and many people who have had experiences consistent with the legal or policy definition of sexual harassment, for example, do not label it as "sexual harassment" when asked. Had we structured the survey that way, we would likely underestimate the prevalence of misconduct.

In each section, after indicating the frequency with which they experienced each listed behavior, students are asked whether they were aware of other students experiencing the same behaviors, and whether they reported or told others about any incidents. Students who personally experienced an incident or were aware of an incident complete follow-up questions that assess the reasons they chose not to tell someone at AETC about the behavior or, if they did tell someone, additional details about their experiences (e.g., how seriously they felt their report was taken). They are also asked to provide additional details about the characteristics of the incident and of the person(s) who did it.

In addition to the misconduct domains, there are survey sections that collect basic information about the student's training and background, perceptions of the Air Force climate, and student access to and attitudes toward AETC feedback and support systems.

The remainder of this chapter provides a detailed description of the content of the technical training and flying training survey and how specific content was added or adapted from the BMT survey (available in full in Appendix C).

Informed Consent

The first survey screen displays the survey instructions and informed consent statement. The instructions and consent form could also be reviewed orally, either via a prerecorded video or by the survey proctor who is administering the survey. Providing the instructions both orally and in writing helps reach both visual and auditory learners and provides two opportunities for key points to be processed.

The informed consent describes the purpose of the survey and the confidential and voluntary nature of the survey. It emphasizes that students can opt to skip certain questions or the entire survey, and that there will be no negative consequences for declining to participate. It also emphasizes that this survey is not an official channel for reporting abuse or misconduct and provides students with information about how to file an official report or obtain support services.

After reviewing the consent material, students then indicate whether they consent to participate in the study. Students can select from three options: (1) consent to participate, and then complete the survey instrument; (2) decline to participate, but advance through the survey without providing responses so that it is not evident to other trainees that they have declined to respond (relevant for group administration settings); or (3) decline to respond, and exit the survey. For students who decline to participate, an optional question will appear that asks whether they would be willing to share why they do not want to complete the survey, with such options as "The survey is too personal," "I'm worried my privacy won't be protected," and "I don't believe it will make a difference." Students will be able to select all options that apply.

Training and Background Questions

The first section of the survey includes seven questions about students' training and background. Items assess military status (enlisted or officer), prior military service, training pipeline (flying or technical training), career group (asked of enlisted only, as the survey is not currently designed to include officers outside of SUPT), months in the training pipeline to date, and gender. This section also asks students to report all locations where they trained for their AFSC and to indicate their current training location. To avoid identifying students who train in small career fields at rarely visited installations, we recommend that the checklist of responses include only installations where more than 250 students train annually. An "other" option should be available for students who were at a base that trains fewer than 250 students annually. The list in the survey provided in Appendix C includes the locations where enlisted technical training and SUPT pilots most commonly train—however, it should be expanded as necessary to include all major training locations for the AFSC pipelines that AETC surveys.

Each set of questions provides necessary information about individual students and their training environments without reducing their confidentiality unnecessarily. Although a survey could include more-detailed questions about the demographic background of students (e.g., rank, race, sexual orientation), these additional questions would increase the possibility that others could identify who provided what answer. For example, students with rare demographic profiles (e.g., a Hispanic woman in an uncommon career field) may be uniquely identified by their demographics alone. That possibility could bias results of the survey if students believed that others could identify their answers based on the demographic questions they answered when they began the survey and, as a result, felt uncomfortable being open and honest about abuse and misconduct they witnessed or experienced.

We modified the gender question from the BMT survey because the then–Secretary of Defense had signaled the intention to end the ban on transgender service in the military. In consultation with other experts outside the project team, we carefully considered the relevance of gender roles and identity (e.g., man, woman) and biological sex (male, female) to this survey. We were also mindful that some individuals may not wish to choose between binary options, but that respondents might become identifiable by inference if very specific options were provided to accommodate minority populations (e.g., transgender male, gender fluid, agender). Ultimately, we decided to include a modified gender question at the beginning of the survey and ask about biological sex only as respondents enter the sexual assault section, where anatomically specific language is used to more clearly solicit information about potential incidents.

The modified gender item toward the beginning of the survey solicits respondents' own gender identity (rather than how others may view them) by asking, "How do you describe yourself?" Response options include "man," "woman," and "continue without answering this question." The latter applies not just to individuals with alternate gender identities but to anyone who prefers not to choose "man" or "woman" or not to reveal it on the questionnaire.

Later in the questionnaire, after a brief introduction to the sexual assault section indicating that upcoming questions will refer to specific body parts, the following item is displayed:

> Before we proceed, please help ensure that the computer displays the appropriate set of questions for you by indicating one of the following:
>
> - I am anatomically male.
> - I am anatomically female.
> - Continue without answering this question. I understand that I will see questions that refer to both male and female anatomy.

The wording helps ensure participants understand that there is a specific reason they are being asked for this information, yet still offers them the alternative not to reveal it and to see questions that they can understand in advance may not match their anatomy.

Specific Changes for the Technical Training and Flying Training Survey

The survey of BMT students includes only one demographic question: gender (Keller, Miller et al., 2015). Students in technical and flying training are more diverse in their military statuses, and therefore additional questions were necessary. For example, only new enlistees attend BMT, whereas the technical and flying training pipelines include enlisted personnel and officers, and prior service, retrainee, and non-prior service students. While BMT occurs only at Lackland AFB, technical and flying training occurs at multiple installations. For these reasons, we added new background questions to better capture the military diversity of the student population and some of the complexity of student training experiences.

Bullying

The bullying section of the survey measures bullying among students in the technical training and flying training environments. It includes two subsections: cyberbullying and offline bullying (i.e., bullying that takes place in person, on a phone call, or through other nonelectronic means of communication). Students are first provided with a definition of bullying we prepared (repeated exposure to negative acts over a period of time, in which a person has difficulty defending himself or herself) and are then asked to respond to a series of behaviorally specific items. The cyberbullying subsection asks students to think about how often they were "bullied via electronic methods of communication (text messaging, email, instant messaging, websites, social networking sites, etc.)." This section consists of six items (e.g., How many times did another student "send a message about you that was insulting or humiliating using electronic communication?" and "threaten you using an electronic communication?"). The offline bullying section consists of ten questions. Six of these items are parallel to questions asked in the cyberbullying subsection, but this subsection also includes behaviors that occur in-person but not in cyber settings (e.g., How many times did another student "steal something from you?" and "hit or kick you?"). For both sections, students are asked to indicate how many times another student engaged in each of the specific behaviors on a five-point scale with response options, including "never," "once or twice," "a few times," "weekly," and "daily."

Specific Changes for the Technical Training and Flying Training Survey

The Recruiting, Education, and Training Standards of Conduct (AETC Instruction 36-2909, 2013) establish the expectation of professional and respectful relationship among all individuals in the training environment, including among students. Because aspects of the BMT setting lend themselves to abuse and bullying among students (e.g., intensity of training, close interaction among students), a section of the BMT survey was developed to assess bullying among trainees (Keller, Miller et al., 2015). These same expectations also apply in the technical and flying training environments, and AETC is invested in also preventing bullying in these training environments.

The bullying section of the BMT survey includes six items designed specifically for the BMT training environment. Although there are many established bullying measures, many of these were designed for different populations (e.g., children and adolescents) or settings (e.g., workplace) (Keller, Miller et al., 2015). Therefore, these measures were used as a foundation for the development of items that were more applicable to BMT. There are three dimensions of bullying that are well-established in the literature: verbal bullying, physical bullying, and social exclusion or manipulation. The items developed for the BMT survey were designed to reflect these three dimensions (Keller, Miller et al., 2015). The six bullying items on the BMT survey are largely applicable to the technical and flying training environments. Three of these items (How many times did another student "steal something from you?", "threaten you?", and "hit or kick you?") were retained for the current version of the survey. Three were adapted with slight revisions. The item "Try to get you into trouble with an MTI" was revised to reference an instructor, and the item "Encourage other trainees to turn against you?" was revised to reference other students. In addition, "Try to embarrass you?" was revised to ask, "Try to put you in a humiliating situation, or play abusive pranks or tricks on you?" Finally, two items were added to parallel the new cyberbullying items and provide additional insights on bullying (described next).

In response to AETC's concerns that students could use social media to harass or insult one another, a new cyberbullying subsection was developed. It includes six items. Three of these items parallel the adapted BMT items for conventional bullying but are appended with the phrase "using electronic communication?" These items are: "Encourage other students to turn against you using electronic communication," "Threaten you using electronic communication," and "Try to get you into trouble with an instructor using electronic communication."

Three new items were developed based on published cyberbullying research. These items map to the factor structure of an established cyberbullying measure, which found that there were four cyberbullying factors: public humiliation, malice, unwanted contact, and deception (Doane et al., 2013). Three items were drafted to measure the first two factors (*public humiliation*: "Say something to you that was insulting or humiliating using electronic communication"; *malice*: "Send a message about you that was insulting or humiliating using electronic communication," or "Post something publicly about you that was insulting or humiliating using electronic communication"). The content of the *unwanted contact* factor overlapped with items in the Sexual Harassment section of this survey, and therefore we did not include new items to measure this factor. Finally, *deception* may be harder to detect (e.g., a student realizing that someone posting insulting comments was using a fictitious profile), and we were mindful of survey length; therefore, questions based on this factor were not included.

After developing the cyberbullying scale, corresponding versions of two items were added to the conventional bullying items ("Say something about you that was insulting or humiliating," "Send others a note or post something publicly about you that was insulting or humiliating?").

The second important change from the BMT survey pertains to the instructions that precede the bullying section. The BMT survey asked trainees to consider "things another trainee may have done while you were at BMT." Based on feedback from AETC leadership, training instructors and staff, and technical training and flying training students, we were concerned that the original instructions could inflate bullying estimates, as some of the behaviors listed can occur within normal peer relationships or conflicts. We turned to the research literature on bullying, which consistently described three elements that differentiate typical peer conflict from bullying: (1) the presence of a power imbalance; (2) repetitiveness of the victimization; and (3) that the behaviors happen over an extended period of time (Ybarra et al., 2012; Olweus, 2013; Nielsen, Matthiesen, and Einarsen, 2010). Moreover, in youth samples, failing to use the term "bullying" or to provide a definition can result in inflated prevalence rates (Ybarra et al., 2012). Therefore, we decided for this section to use the term "bullying" when asking about these behaviors and to provide a specific operational definition of bullying adapted from research on workplace bullying. The new introductory statement describes the three necessary characteristics of a power imbalance, repetition, and an extended period of time (Einarsen and Skogstad, 1996; Einarsen, 2000). In latter sections, we omitted similar prefatory terms that might lead to underestimation based on potentially flawed student understanding of, for example, what constitutes "maltraining," "unprofessional relationships," or "sexual assault." However, in this section, we expect popular understandings of the term "bullying" to more closely align with the construct we intend to measure.

Maltreatment and Maltraining

Maltreatment and maltraining refer to abuse of or use of impermissible training techniques toward students by MTLs or instructors. "Military personnel who are cruel toward, oppress, or maltreat persons subject to their orders are guilty of cruelty and maltreatment under Article 93, UCMJ [Uniform Code of Military Justice]" (AETC Instruction 36-2909, Second Air Force Supplement, 2015, p. 16). Because we include separate domains for hazing, bullying, sexual harassment, and sexual assault, our definition of maltreatment encompasses all other forms of instructor or MTL physical and verbal maltreatment of students that do not meet the definitions of these behaviors. Specifically, *physical maltreatment* is defined as "causing or engaging in unauthorized and unwanted physical contact with another or improperly depriving another of basic physical necessities" whereas *verbal maltreatment* "includes any language that degrades, belittles, demeans, maliciously embarrasses, or slanders an individual or group" (AETC Instruction 36-2909, Second Air Force Supplement, 2015, pp. 1–17). *Maltraining* is defined as "any practice not designed to meet a course training objective" (AETC Instruction 36-2909, Second Air Force Supplement, 2015, p. 16).

The survey includes 12 items to detect maltreatment and maltraining. Subscales include maltraining (three items), physical threats or force (five items), hostile comments (two items), privacy violations (one item), and encouragement of trainee mistreatment (one item). Respondents are asked to report the frequency (never; once or twice; a few times; weekly; daily) an MTL (if enlisted non-prior service student) or instructor engaged in any of these behaviors.

Specific Changes for the Technical Training and Flying Training Survey

The BMT survey includes 17 items. Six items from the original BMT survey were removed from the technical training and flying training survey (two items from the maltraining subscale, two items from the denial of services or rights subscale, and two items for privacy violation) and one additional item was added to the privacy violation subscale to reflect different maltreatment or maltraining scenarios that might occur in the technical and flying training environments. For example, the item "make you do PT [physical training], drill, or outside work detail in unsafe conditions" was removed because some career fields require training in unsafe conditions (e.g., Survival, Evasion, Resistance, and Escape [SERE] training) and students may not be aware of whether or not a particular environment is unsafe. In addition, slight changes were made to item wording to reflect differences between the BMT and the technical training environment (e.g., "trainee" was changed to "student," references to BMT were removed) or to correct inappropriate, ambiguous, or confusing wording based on feedback from AETC leadership or students. For example, we changed one item from "unfairly push you to quit or leave" to "single you out to quit or leave your training" because of concern that the word *unfairly* was overly subjective. We substituted "single you out" for "unfairly" to reflect disparate treatment, a more-objective criterion for maltreatment. Similarly, we added the word "inappropriate" to the item that read "use [inappropriate] physical force with you" to reflect the fact that training in many technical training career fields may require physical contact between instructors and students, including force, as part of training exercises.

Unprofessional Relationships

Unprofessional relationships are relationships between faculty and trainees that "detract from the authority of superiors or result in, or reasonably create the appearance of, favoritism, misuse of office or position, or the abandonment of organizational goals for personal interests" (Air Force Instruction 36-2909, 1999, p. 2).

The survey includes 15 items to detect unprofessional relationships. Items assess romantic, flirtatious, sexual talk (five items); personal or unofficial contact (one item); financial exchange (two items); and miscellaneous misconduct (seven items). Unlike sexual harassment, the romantic, flirtatious, and sexual talk described in the unprofessional relationship scale need not be unwanted or repeated. For example, although consensual sexual joking between a trainee and MTL is not classified as sexual harassment, it is still prohibited by Air Force policy. As with maltreatment and maltraining items, respondents are asked to report the number of times ("never," "once or twice," "a few times," "weekly," "daily") an officer (if enlisted), an MTL (if enlisted non-prior service student), or instructor engaged in any of these behaviors.

Specific Changes for Technical Training and Flying Training Survey

The BMT survey includes 16 items to detect unprofessional relationships. After reviews of policy documents and discussions with leadership and students, several changes were made to better reflect the technical and flying training environments. Two items were removed ("contact you through non–Air Force channels for personal reasons" and "invite you to a social gathering"), and one additional item was added to the scale ("offer you illegal drugs or prescription medication that had not been prescribed to you") to more accurately reflect risky behaviors that could be encountered in the technical training or flying training environments, including in the hours outside of training or away from base. Although the majority of items (ten) remained identical, small wording changes were made to clarify or update the remaining items. For example, the item "drink alcohol with you" was appended with the phrase "outside of Air Force–sponsored and commander-authorized events" to better reflect the greater autonomy afforded to students in technical training and flying training. Similarly, the item "meet you alone" was appended with the phrase "for personal reasons" to reflect the fact that one-on-one professional meetings between a student and an MTL or an instructor are permitted during technical training and flying training (but were prohibited during BMT).

Sexual Harassment, Gender Discrimination, and Sexual Orientation Discrimination

In 2014, RAND researchers updated DoD's Workplace and Gender Relations Survey (known as the "WGRA" for the active-duty population and "WGRR" for the reserve) to improve alignment between the survey measures of sexual harassment and gender discrimination and military equal opportunity (MEO) definitions of these offenses (Jaycox et al., 2014). The BMT survey predated this effort and, therefore, relied on an older sexual harassment measure that had been included in the previous versions of the Workplace and Gender Relations Surveys (Fitzgerald et al., 1999; Stark et al., 2002). To align measurement of sexual harassment and gender discrimination in the Air Force training environment to the measurement strategy used to estimate these violations across DoD, the sponsor requested that we update the technical training and flying training survey instrument to include RAND's 2014 modified measure of sexual harassment and gender discrimination.

The measure begins with 15 screening questions that assess a range of experiences that might qualify as either sexual harassment or gender discrimination. They include 11 screening questions that assess *sexually hostile work environments* (unwelcome sexual conduct or comments that are "explicitly or implicitly a term or condition of a person's job, pay, or career" or "unreasonably [interferes] with an individual's work performance or creates an intimidating, hostile, or offensive working environment" [10 U.S.C 1561[e] [1], 2006; DoD Directive 1350.2, 2003]). Examples of these types of experiences include unwanted sexual gestures, unwanted taking or sharing of sexually suggestive pictures or videos, and repeated attempts to establish a romantic or sexual relationship. Two screening questions assess *sexual quid pro quo harassment*, which refers to "any use . . . of any form of sexual behavior to control, influence, or affect the career, pay, or job of a member of the armed forces" (10 U.S.C 1561 [e][2], 2006). Together, sexually hostile work environments and quid pro quo offers make up the violations that are categorized as "sexual harassment." The screening questions also include two items that could indicate that gender discrimination has occurred—that is, unlawful discrimination on the basis of gender "that is not otherwise authorized by law or regulation" (DoD Directive 1350.2, 2003).

In addition to the 15 items from the modified Workplace and Gender Relations Survey, we added another item to the technical training and flying training survey. This new item assesses discrimination based on sexual orientation and matches the structure of the gender discrimination item. It reads, "Since the beginning of [technical/flying] training, do you think someone from work mistreated, ignored, excluded, or insulted you because of your sexual orientation?"

Sexually Hostile Work Environment

If a respondent indicates experiencing any of the 11 screening items assessing sexually hostile work environments, he or she is classified as experiencing a *problematic workplace environment.* To be classified as experiencing a *sexually hostile work environment,* he or she must indicate (via follow-up questions) that the behavior either (1) persisted after the person exhibiting the behavior knew the respondent or other people wanted it to stop or (2) was sufficiently severe that, in the respondents' opinion, most other military members of the respondents' gender would have found it offensive (Jaycox et al., 2014). Only students who report that a problematic workplace behavior occurred receive the follow-up items assessing persistence and severity.

Sexual Quid Pro Quo

Two screening questions assess the respondent's belief that a workplace benefit (or avoidance of a workplace punishment) was contingent on their sexual behavior. Responding "yes" to either question classifies the respondent as experiencing a *problematic workplace behavior*. Subsequent follow-up questions are used to rule out instances in which respondents report that they have no direct evidence that a workplace benefit was being offered in exchange for sexual behavior (e.g., when the respondent's belief was a based on a rumor about the individual). Respondents who indicate a form of direct evidence are classified as having experienced a *sexual quid pro quo* (Jaycox et al., 2014).

Sexual Harassment

Respondents are classified as having experienced *sexual harassment* if they are categorized as experiencing either a sexually hostile work environment or a sexual quid pro quo (Jaycox et al., 2014).

Gender Discrimination

If a respondent endorses either of the two screening items that assess possible instances of gender discrimination, he or she is classified as experiencing a *problematic workplace environment*. To be classified as experiencing *gender discrimination*, he or she must indicate (via follow-up questions) that there were work-related negative outcomes associated with the behavior (i.e., that it harmed or limited their career) (Jaycox et al., 2014).

Sexual Orientation Discrimination

If a respondent endorses the screening item that assesses possible instances of sexual orientation discrimination, he or she is classified as experiencing a *problematic workplace environment*. To be classified as experiencing *sexual orientation discrimination*, he or she must indicate (via follow-up questions) that there were work-related negative outcomes associated with the behavior (i.e., that it harmed or limited their career) (Jaycox et al., 2014).

Specific Changes for the Technical Training and Flying Training Survey

For the technical training and flying training survey, consistent with AETC's request, we have included the DoD-endorsed measure of sexual harassment and gender discrimination. This measure differs from the BMT survey measure of sexual harassment with respect to the number of items, the response options, and item wording. The types of behaviors that are assessed on the screening questions generally overlap.

The new measure differs most substantially in the inclusion of follow-up questions that gather the necessary information to make a more-definitive statement about whether the behavior rose to the level of an MEO violation. For example, the BMT survey assessed whether someone "displayed, used, or distributed sexist or suggestive materials." A respondent who has had this experience can be accurately described as someone who had experiences *consistent with* or *suggestive of* sexual harassment, but we cannot be sure whether the experience rose to the level of sexual harassment as it is legally defined. The DoD-endorsed measure collects the necessary additional information by requiring that the respondent indicate that they were personally "uncomfortable, angry, or upset" in response to the sexually explicit materials, and, furthermore, that the experience was either persistent (continued after the offender was asked to stop) or severe (a reasonable person would find the events offensive). This additional information collection allows the survey to provide estimates of both *inappropriate workplace behavior* (i.e., the events occurred but may not have met every legal criterion) and *sexual harassment* (i.e., the events occurred and they met the legal criteria that define sexual harassment). This is important to highlight because even if some incidents do not necessarily meet research, policy, or legal criteria for such terms as "sexual harassment" or "gender discrimination," their occurrence may still indicate problematic behavior in the training environment that AETC would want to prevent or address.

Sexual Assault

As part of the RAND Corporation's 2014 update of DoD's biennial Workplace and Gender Relations Survey, the DoD survey measure of sexual assault was also revised. At the request of AETC leadership, we have included this measure in the updated technical training and flying training survey. The measure is designed to assess

> rape and sexual assault offenses [including] unwanted penetration, however slight, of the vulva, anus, or mouth, or touching of body parts, with intent either to gratify a sexual desire or to abuse, humiliate, or degrade (except for experiences involving penetration with a penis, in which case evidence of intent is not required). The UCMJ provides a list of coercive offender behaviors that are sufficient to demonstrate that the sexual contact was criminal, including the use of force, threats, by drugging the victim or assaulting them while unconscious, by fraudulently claiming the contact served a legitimate professional purpose, by falsely claiming to be someone else, or by having sexual contact with someone who is incapable of providing consent (e.g., due to impairment by any drug or intoxicant or due to mental disease or defect). (Jaycox et al., 2014)

To match the complex legal definitions included in Article 120, the survey instrument uses a three-stage measurement strategy to assess (1) whether the person has had a sexual experience that matches the possibly criminal acts described in the UCMJ; (2) the contact occurred "with an intent to abuse, humiliate, harass, or degrade any person or to arouse or gratify the sexual desire of any person"; and (3) whether one of the UCMJ-defined coercive offender behaviors was used (e.g., force, threats, drugs) (Jaycox et al., 2014).

Six initial screening items assess "unwanted sexual experiences" that may or may not rise to the level of a sexual assault (e.g., "Within [a given time frame], did you have any <u>unwanted</u> experiences in which someone put any object or any body part <u>other than a penis</u> into your [vagina,] anus, or mouth?"). Students who respond "yes" to any of the screening items are classified as having an "unwanted sexual experience" but may or may not be classified as experiencing a sexual assault. Subsequent items assess whether the intent was to abuse or degrade them or to satisfy a sexual desire. Events that did not occur for a sexual or degrading purpose are not classified as a sexual assault (e.g., legitimate medical exam). Finally, if the purpose was sexual or degrading, the student is asked to indicate the behaviors the offender used. The list of 13 options corresponds to specific elements in the definitions of sexual assaults (e.g., "used physical force to make you comply," "did it when you were passed out, asleep, or unconscious"). Students who indicate that they have had an unwanted sexual experience, that it was done for an abusive or sexual purpose, and that the offender behavior matched a behavior included in the UCMJ are subsequently categorized as having experienced a sexual assault.

The DoD measure of sexual assault does not include an assessment of noncontact events, such as exposure or exhibitionism. To ensure these events would be captured in the new survey, we retained the following item from the BMT survey: "[Since the beginning of technical training/flying training], did anyone show you private areas of their body or make you show them private areas of your body when you didn't want to?" *Private areas* were defined to include "buttocks, inner thigh, breasts, groin, anus, vagina, penis, or testicles." This question does not include follow-up items.

Specific Changes for the Technical Training and Flying Training Survey

The DoD-endorsed measure of sexual assault differs from the BMT survey measure of sexual assault with respect to the number of items and item wording. The types of behaviors that are assessed in the screening questions generally overlap. The new measure differs most substantially in the inclusion of follow-up questions that gather the necessary information to make a more-definitive statement about whether the behavior rose to the level of a sexual assault. Both survey instruments provide information about whether respondents have experienced *unwanted sexual contact*, but the newly implemented instrument also provides information about whether respondents have experienced *sexual assault* as it is legally defined. Again, even if an event does not meet the legal threshold for sexual assault, it may still cross the line in terms of behaviors that AETC would consider contrary to Air Force values and good order and discipline.

Note About Survey Branching

The recommended measure of sexual assault requires survey software that can support complex branching. During the pretest, this capability was not available—therefore, we pretested the seven screening items only. We recommend that the full instrument, including follow-up items (Appendix C), be included when survey software is available to support them.

Hazing

Recently, cases of alleged hazing across the Services have contributed to a renewed congressional interest in eliminating this behavior (Keller, Matthews et al., 2015). As part of this effort, the Deputy Secretary of Defense issued a memorandum that provided guidance for the services regarding how to prevent and address hazing (Deputy Secretary of Defense, 2015). This memorandum contained a new definition of hazing that was the foundation for the hazing definition in the new DoD Instruction on harassment from early 2018:

> Hazing. A form of harassment that includes conduct through which Service members or DoD employees, without a proper military or other governmental purpose but with a nexus to military Service, physically or psychologically injures or creates a risk of physical or psychological injury to Service members for the purpose of: initiation into, admission into, affiliation with, change in status or position within, or a condition for continued membership in any military or DoD civilian organization. Hazing can be conducted through the use of electronic devices or communications, and by other means including social media, as well as in person.

> Hazing is evaluated by a reasonable person standard and includes, but is not limited to, the following when performed without a proper military or other governmental purpose:

(1) Any form of initiation or congratulatory act that involves physically striking another person in any manner or threatening to do the same;

(2) Pressing any object into another person's skin, regardless of whether it pierces the skin, such as "pinning" or "tacking on" of rank insignia, aviator wings, jump wings, diver insignia, badges, medals, or any other object;

(3) Oral or written berating of another for the purpose of belittling or humiliating;

(4) Encouraging another person to engage in illegal, harmful, demeaning or dangerous acts;

(5) Playing abusive or malicious tricks;

(6) Branding, handcuffing, duct taping, tattooing, shaving, greasing, or painting another person;

(7) Subjecting another person to excessive or abusive use of water;

(8) Forcing another person to consume food, alcohol, drugs, or any other substance; and

(9) Soliciting, coercing, or knowingly permitting another person to solicit or coerce acts of hazing. (DoD Instruction 1020.03, 2018, pp. 11–12)

The new policy further clarifies the following:

- Hazing does not include properly directed command or organizational activities that serve a proper military or other governmental purpose, or the requisite training activities required to prepare for such activities (e.g., administrative corrective measures, extra military instruction, or command-authorized physical training).
- Service members may be responsible for an act of hazing even if there was actual or implied consent from the victim and regardless of the grade or rank, status, or Service of the victim.
- Hazing is prohibited in all circumstances and environments including off-duty or "unofficial" unit functions and settings (DoD Instruction 1020.03, 2018, p. 12).

At the time of this study, incidents of hazing were not tracked at the DoD level (Keller, Matthews et al., 2015). Rather, each service maintained limited information on incidents of hazing. Due to the limited information collected, little is known regarding the frequency and severity of hazing across the services or in the Air Force, in particular. We drew from previous studies on hazing to develop the initial pretest items. Due to the limited research on military hazing, most of this research addresses hazing incidents in high schools, colleges, and among sports teams. Thus, feedback on draft items that we received from AETC leaders, instructors, and students was particularly valuable in ensuring that our measure was appropriate for these particular settings.

Earlier research suggests that many people do not know the definition of hazing (e.g., U.S. General Accounting Office, 1992). Therefore, using the word "hazing" within survey items, without provision of a definition that participants can read and understand, can result in unreliable and biased responses. To reduce this measurement error within surveys, the hazing literature suggests instead asking survey participants to consider whether they have experienced particular hazing behaviors (Keller, Matthews et al., 2015). Although hazing behaviors can be context-specific, with different groups performing different hazing acts, several broad dimensions can be captured when assessing distinct behaviors. These include physical abuse, psychological abuse, coerced abuse of others, coerced self-abuse, substance abuse, and sex-related acts (Allan and Madden, 2008; Hoover and Pollard, 2000; Waldron and Kowalski, 2009). In designing a new survey section on hazing for the technical training and flying training survey, we developed items to assess each of these dimensions. One exception is that hazing-related sexual assaults were excluded from the hazing assessment, because they are assessed in the survey section on sexual assault instead. For students who have experienced a sexual assault, the survey includes a follow-up item to establish whether the incident was hazing related.

The hazing section includes 24 items and asks students to indicate whether each behavior took place "as part of joining your career field" by selecting "no" or "yes." Example items include: "As part of joining your career field, did anyone persuade or force you to act in a demeaning or embarrassing way outside of your official training activities?" and "As part of joining your career field, did anyone press or punch an object into your skin (for example, wings, badges, or medals)?"

Specific Changes for the Technical Training and Flying Training Survey

The BMT survey does not contain a hazing assessment. To ensure the Air Force has visibility of hazing that may occur in technical and flying training, the measure described above was developed specifically for the technical training and flying training survey.

Assessing Hazing within SERE and Battlefield Airmen Training

In most cases, survey items measuring abuse and misconduct should generalize well across occupational specialties. However, interpretation of some survey items may be more difficult for a subset of Air Force specialties due to their unique training, which may include intense physical training, preparation to handle stressful conditions in real mission environments, and training that requires instructors to use physical contact with trainees (e.g., dunking during water skills training). In most other specialties, such behaviors by instructors would be considered maltreatment or maltraining and would be a clear violation of Air Force policy. However, for the subset of specialties, such as SERE specialists and battlefield airmen, these training methods are an important part of trainees' preparation to succeed in real mission environments.

Battlefield airmen comprise several specialties and are organized, trained, and equipped to provide expertise in ground combat environments. Specifically, battlefield airmen perform missions in the following areas: joint fires integration, tactical airlift operations, special operations, weather support operations, and personnel recovery (PR) operations. To prepare for these missions, battlefield airmen are carefully selected and trained to meet the physical and psychological demands not only in typical ground combat environments but also when operating in the "most austere conditions for extended periods" (Air Force Policy Directive 10-35, 2009). Consequently, training is extremely tough, physically and mentally, and is designed, in part, to teach trainees that there are real consequences for their actions. Errors during training may result in additional physical exercises for students but could result in mission failure and even loss of life in an actual mission environment. Although training instructors must adhere to clearly documented training guidelines, including specifying the reason for any additional physical exercises, trainees may not initially appreciate or recognize the relevance of these training techniques.

To address the unique nature of these training pipelines, specific items on the survey were reviewed to minimize confusion about whether the behavioral items measuring bullying, hazing, maltraining, and maltreatment could be legitimate or official elements of training. In addition to redesigning survey items to clearly differentiate authorized training from abuse and misconduct, we solicited input from Air Force leadership and trainees to ensure accurate interpretations of survey responses. Nonetheless, AETC will need to continue to be mindful of possible question misinterpretation among students completing highly physically and psychologically demanding training, such as SERE training.

Assessment of Attention to the Survey

Each survey domain contains a series of questions assessing negative experiences during training. Most students will not have experienced any abuse or misconduct during training and will subsequently respond "never" or "no" to a long series of items. In this situation, there is a risk of inattentive responding whereby students begin to simply select "never" without reading or fully understanding each question. To check for this behavior, each abuse domain includes an item that asks students to select an uncommon response. For example, one item states: "Please select 'Daily' for this item to help us confirm that students are reading these items." This data point will help administrators to distinguish the students who are responding hastily without full consideration (i.e., selected "never" to every item) from students who had answered carefully and truly had no abuse experience (i.e., selected "never" to all but the screening item, to which they responded "daily"). We recommend that students who respond incorrectly to a reading assessment item be treated as missing on the given abuse domain. For students who respond incorrectly to the reading assessment on three or more abuse domains, we recommend that they be marked as missing for the entire questionnaire, as the accuracy of their responses is questionable.

Abuse and Misconduct Follow-Up Questions

Characteristics of the Misconduct

Within each of the six sections on misconduct, all students who indicated that they had experienced any the specified inappropriate behaviors or who were aware of other students being abused in the training environment received a series of follow-up questions about the event(s). Students who indicated that they did not experience and were not aware of other students experiencing the misconduct assessed in a given section were automatically skipped to the next survey section.

Some of the abuse and misconduct follow-up items on their characteristics were modeled after a similar set of items included in DoD's Workplace and Gender Relations Survey (Rock et al., 2011; Defense Manpower Data Center, 2014). For the BMT survey, we modified the original DoD items and responses. At a minimum, all six misconduct sections included follow-up items that assessed the number of perpetrators, installation where the misconduct occurred, and whether the student told another student about his or her experience.

For the bullying section, the bully was predefined as another student, and therefore no further question was necessary to establish their position in the organization. For all other misconduct sections, the organizational position was assessed. For maltreatment and maltraining, enlisted students are asked to indicate whether the person who did it was an MTL or an instructor. Officers in SUPT are asked to indicate whether the instructor who did it was a First Assignment Instructor Pilot. For unprofessional relationships, these same questions were repeated, but an additional response category ("officer") was added for enlisted students. For sexual harassment, sexual assault, and hazing, the list of responses was expanded to include non-prior service student, prior-service student, retrainee (for enlisted), MTL (for enlisted), instructor, someone else in the chain of command, other U.S. military personnel not listed above, military personnel from other country, civilian, and do not know or other. Officers in SUPT who selected "instructor" were asked whether the instructor was a First Assignment Instructor Pilot.

The bullying and maltreatment/maltraining sections did not include any additional characteristic items. Each of the remaining misconduct sections included at least one characteristic item that was unique to the particular type of misconduct. The unprofessional relationships assessment focused on actions by MTLs, instructors, and officers (if the student was enlisted). A follow-up item captures unprofessional behaviors by retrainees and prior-service students against non-prior service students. The sexual harassment section included an item that assessed the gender of the perpetrator(s). The sexual assault section included characteristic follow-up items that assessed the number of sexual assaults that occurred, whether the sexual assault was hazing related, gender of the perpetrator(s), where it occurred, and support services received. The hazing section included a follow-up item to assess the degree to which the student participated willingly or was socially, verbally, or physically pressured to participate in the hazing.

Note that, for students who had the misconduct occur more than once, the survey instructions guide them to consider only the most-serious event or the event that had the greatest effect on them. Although some students will have experienced more than one event, asking details on each of the multiple events would substantially lengthen the survey and could potentially identify victims to other trainees in the room because they would have a longer completion time. We believed that AETC leadership would have a greater need for documentation of the most-serious events, and, therefore, we chose to focus on the most-serious events in the follow-up questions.

There were minimal changes to this section relative to the BMT survey. Given that technical and flying training occur at multiple installations and that students transition between those installations, we added a single item to assess the installation at which the worst (or only) incident occurred.

Reporting and Telling Others About the Misconduct

Individuals who experience negative events, such as bullying, sexual harassment, or sexual assault, may face considerable barriers to reporting those events. Victims may be uncomfortable making a report, not want anyone to know about the incident, or fear that their confidentiality will not be protected (Jaycox et al., 2015). The 2014 RAND Military Workplace Study results showed that among sexual assault victims who chose to report the assault, 52 percent of women and 55 percent of men experienced professional retaliation (e.g., denied promotion), social retaliation (e.g., ignored by coworkers), or administrative actions (e.g., placed on a medical hold) (Jaycox et al., 2015). For these reasons, some researchers and victim advocates have argued that a victim who chooses not to report the perpetrator has made a rational choice in which he or she believes that the negative consequences associated with reporting outweigh the potential personal benefit (Herbert and Dunkel-Schetter, 1992; Ullman, Foynes, and Tang, 2011). At the same time, a system as a whole (e.g., the AETC training environment) benefits from victims who report their experiences. Only after a victim (or a confidante or witness) officially reports an event can leadership intervene to remove the accused from the environment and implement policies to reduce the risk of future assaults. Thus, it is important to understand the barriers that prevent some victims from reporting negative events and, for those victims who do report these events, the nature of their experiences with the reporting system.

Thus, the reporting section of the survey assesses the decisions and experiences of any student who either disclosed or chose not to disclose that he or she had experienced bullying, maltreatment or maltraining, unprofessional relationships, sexual harassment, sexual assault, or hazing. To assess bystander reporting, students who indicated that they were aware of another student who had experienced one of these events were also surveyed about their disclosure decisions and experiences. Items include an assessment of

- whether the student told someone about the incident
- how the student disclosed the incident (e.g., told an instructor, told someone else in the chain of command, wrote it down on paper and put it in a critique box)
- students who chose not to disclose the incident and their barriers to disclosure (e.g., "I didn't think I would be believed"; "I was afraid reporting might cause trouble for my flight")
- students who chose to tell someone about the incident and

  - how seriously they felt their report was taken
  - what happened after they disclosed the misconduct (e.g., "the behavior continued or got worse")
  - what happened after they reported (e.g., "the person who did it or their friends tried to get even with me for reporting"; "the person I reported it to praised me for reporting")
  - if they had it to do again, whether they would still report the incident ("Yes" or "No").

Converting this section from the BMT survey to use in the technical training and flying training environments required minimal revisions. Examples of alterations include changing references to "MTIs" to "MTLs," updating the titles of student leaders (e.g., "bay chief"), and including a wider range of reporting channels that are more readily available to students outside of BMT (e.g., staff member at the Airman and Family Readiness Center).

Perception of Leadership Climate

Organizational climate focuses on how individuals experience and make sense of an organization. Specifically, organizational climate involves perceptions of policies, practices, and procedures that are rewarded, supported, and expected. The importance of the organizational context in understanding workplace phenomena is well established, and, in particular, research has indicated the importance of organizational climates in shaping behavior (Ostroff, Kinicki, and Tamkins, 2003). For example, research on safety climates within organizations has found a relationship with the number of accidents that take place (Christian et al., 2009) and whether individuals are likely to report an accident (Probst, Brubaker, and Barsotti, 2008). Researchers have also examined the existence of climates for sexual harassment and the extent to which individuals perceive that the organization tolerates sexual harassment and implements related policies and procedures designed to prevent it (e.g., Culbertson and Rodgers, 1997; Hulin,

Fitzgerald, and Drasgow, 1996; Williams, Fitzgerald, and Drasgow, 1999). One meta-analysis found that organizational climate for sexual harassment was the strongest predictor of whether sexual harassment took place in the organization (Willness, Steel, and Lee, 2007).

Drawing on established measures of climate and factor analyses of tested items, we developed separate scales of four items each that assess perceptions of the squadron climate for each of the abuse and misconduct domains for the BMT survey (Keller, Miller et al., 2015). In that study, the factor analyses demonstrated that separate scales for squadron climate on each domain were needed, rather than a single general scale for climate, because trainee perceptions of their leadership varied by type of abuse and misconduct. During technical training and flying training, students may train within more than one squadron over the course of their pipelines, and therefore these items were revised to reference "Air Force [technical/flying] training leadership" rather than "squadron leaders." Example items include "Air Force [technical/flying] training leadership makes honest efforts to stop sexual harassment" and "Air Force [technical/flying] training leadership encourages the reporting of sexual harassment." Students are asked to rate these statements according to a five-point response scale ranging from "strongly disagree" to "strongly agree."

Feedback and Support Systems

The survey concludes with a section to assess feedback and support systems available to report misconduct and abuse. Four subsections assess different aspects of the feedback and support systems available in the technical training and flying training environments. First, students are asked how easy or difficult they feel it would be to arrange to speak personally with various Air Force personnel (e.g. instructors, Office of Special Investigations [OSI], a chaplain) about problems similar to those mentioned in this survey. Responses include "very easy," "easy," "neither easy nor difficult," "difficult," "very difficult," and for locations where there are vacancies or the organization is structured differently, "doesn't currently apply: we don't have one." Students are then asked whether they would recognize critical personnel by sight, as an indicator of the presence of those leaders and support personnel among students in the training environment. Students are then asked to report their perceptions of what instructors (and MTLs, if enlisted non-prior service students) would do if they knew a student was being abused or mistreated. Four items are asked separately for MTLs and instructors. Example items include "make honest efforts to stop it" and "expect the student to handle it," with students asked to rate these statements on a five-point response scale ranging from "strongly disagree" to "strongly agree."

To contain survey length, some pretest items from this section are not recommended for inclusion in the final survey. One set of items had asked about whether training leaders inspire students (e.g., training leadership inspires them to "do the right thing, even when no one is looking"). Additionally, we removed eight items assessing affective commitment to the Air Force (i.e., students' positive emotional attachment to or identification with the Air Force). Sentiments during initial skills training could be misleading if interpreted as a measure of future behavior, and the recommended survey does include one item assessing organizational commitment on the basis of the training experience (i.e., "Overall, my commitment to the Air Force has strengthened through technical [or flying] training").

Finally, the survey assesses students' perceptions of the availability of support from fellow students and individuals inside and outside the chain of command (e.g. "I have a fellow student I can count on to look out for my well-being"), as well as their attitudes toward and willingness to use hotlines or critique or drop boxes as a feedback mechanism.

These questions were largely adopted from the original BMT survey. To adapt to the technical and flying training environments, references to additional Air Force personnel were included, such as student leaders (e.g., red or teal rope), chief MTLs, instructors, and MTL flight chiefs. In addition, items were added to the survey to assess the extent to which students are socialized into airman values and hold positive views toward the Air Force.

Self-Reported Honesty

The survey concludes with an item that asks students to indicate how open and honest they felt they could be when responding to survey items. Response options include "not at all open or honest," "somewhat open and honest," and "completely open and honest." Although all feasible steps should be taken to ensure that students feel comfortable providing fully accurate descriptions of their training experiences, it is likely that these measures will not be successful for a small subset of students. This item allows survey administrators to detect those students who, by their own self-reporting, may have submitted responses that were not accurate. We recommend that students who indicate that they were "not at all open or honest" be excluded from survey analyses. The proportion and type of students who select this response should also be tracked over time to assess the success of system measures to reassure students about the confidentiality of the survey and to detect any changes in students' willingness to respond honestly. This item may also serve as a general indicator of trust in the training environment.

Additionally, the survey includes items that will help AETC identify participants who were not reading the items closely (i.e., items that ask respondents to select a certain option) or who were not comfortable being open and honest on the survey, so that those respondents can be screened out and possibly analyzed separately prior to reporting survey results to leadership.

Survey Access

Two optional questions at the end of the survey are designed to provide the means to analyze whether responses vary by means used to access the survey. If students have both a common access card (CAC) and non-CAC option or the choice of using a personal computer, tablet, smartphone, or a military device, these questions could be included. With a sufficient number of similar respondents in a subgroup (e.g., all SUPT students in a given year), it could be informative to explore whether any access modes are associated with greater comfort in being open and honest, as assumptions may or may not be borne out.

Conclusion

When implemented, the survey will collect the data necessary to assess the prevalence and probability of reporting bullying, cyberbullying, maltreatment or maltraining, unprofessional relationships, sexual harassment, gender discrimination, sexual orientation discrimination, sexual assault, and hazing. As shown in Table 4.1, seven misconduct domains have been adapted from or added to the original BMT survey for use in technical training and flying training environments to monitor abuse and misconduct. The survey will also provide critical visibility of the characteristics of misconduct, barriers to reporting, support systems, and climate.

Table 4.1. Number of Items in Each Misconduct Domain and Revisions from Original Basic Military Training Survey

	Number of Items	Revisions Relative to BMT Survey		
		Revised Items	Added Items	Dropped Items
Cyberbullying	6		✓	
Bullying	10	✓	✓	
Maltreatment or maltraining	12		✓	✓
Unprofessional relationships	15	✓	✓	✓
Sexual harassment, gender discrimination, and sexual orientation discrimination	16–56[a]		✓	✓
Sexual assault	7–82[a]		✓	✓
Hazing	24		✓	

[a] Variation is due to follow-up items that are assessed only if initial screening items are answered affirmatively.

5. Survey Pretest Methods

We conducted a pretest of the survey instrument and survey administration methods with students in both technical training and flying training environments. We administered the pretest using methods under consideration for the final survey with respect to timing of the pretest, the participants, and the survey mode. For example, because AETC will be administering future iterations, the survey was programmed on an AETC server dedicated to collecting, storing, and protecting survey data.

Subsequent chapters address our recommendations for future administration, while this chapter describes pretest methods and the relevant factors we uncovered in the process that informed our survey system recommendations. We also used the pretest to confirm that questions were understandable, that response options were complete, and whether any survey questions could be eliminated or shortened without losing important information. Finally, we used pretest data to estimate the average survey completion time and to determine the influence of survey administration mode on responses and willingness to participate. The following sections describe the administration of the pretest, including (1) *where* the pretest took place, (2) *when* students completed our survey pretest and *who* participated, (3) *how* the survey was administered, and (4) *how* the survey pretest results were used.

Where the Survey Pretest Took Place

We designed the survey to eventually be administered at all technical and flying training locations at regular intervals. For the survey pretest, it was not necessary nor feasible to survey the entire technical and flying training populations across all training sites. The pretest instead surveyed a sample of students at five training locations: Fairchild, Keesler, Lackland, Laughlin, and Sheppard AFBs.

Factors Considered in Choosing Locations to Survey

Diversity of student experiences and student population size. During BMT, trainees have a relatively standardized experience. All complete their training on the same base, using the same infrastructure, over an eight-week period. However, after students graduate, they move on to more heterogeneous training experiences that vary based on career field. Ultimately, the survey system will need to be as inclusive as possible of students completing training at all training sites. Therefore, to pretest the survey, we selected sites that afforded the opportunity to capture a diversity of student experiences, while maintaining efficiency by targeting locations with large student populations.

Technical feasibility and opportunities. When selecting locations for the survey pretest, we also considered the available information technology (IT) infrastructure. Ultimately, the survey system will be implemented at locations with varied IT capabilities—from limited IT resources to state-of-the-art IT infrastructure. For the BMT survey, we recommended that the ideal feasible IT environment was a large computer lab that allowed CAC-less access to the survey to preserve both confidentiality and trainee perceptions of confidentiality. Through extraordinary efforts and special computer network configurations, AETC was able to configure new facilities to provide this type of survey environment. However, obtaining those permissions and building that type of capability across all or even most IST training locations are not likely feasible for this extension of the survey system. Therefore, for this pretest, we compared survey functionality within an ideal IT system versus alternative, pragmatic delivery systems (i.e., web-based delivery on machines requiring a CAC for access). We considered pretesting an administration strategy that invited students to take their survey on their own time, through their own devices, but this was not possible given the software and network security configurations at the time.

Technical Training Pretest Locations

For the technical training pipelines, we conducted the survey pretest at Sheppard AFB, Keesler AFB, and Lackland AFB. We selected Sheppard AFB and Keesler AFB because, as noted in Chapter 2, the average daily student censuses are large. Because only a subset of all students were invited to complete the pretest (i.e., only those nearing completion of their pipeline on the pretest dates), the large populations at Keesler and Sheppard ensured that adequately sized samples of students were available to participate.

Our rationale for including Lackland AFB was twofold. First, Lackland has a large average daily student census, similar to Keesler and Sheppard. In addition, Lackland has the unique IT infrastructure system developed for the BMT survey (as noted earlier). This infrastructure allowed us to better understand the potential influence of requiring a CAC for survey access (see Chapter 8).

Flying Training Pretest Locations

We selected Laughlin AFB and Fairchild AFB as the two flying training locations for the pretest. Laughlin AFB in Texas was an attractive location for the pretest because it trains the greatest number of SUPT students. In addition, students who complete their primary pilot training at Laughlin are also tracked to fly the T-1 and T-38 aircraft during their advanced training and will complete that advanced training at Laughlin. Thus, conducting the pretest at Laughlin gave us the opportunity to sample students completing primary training and students completing advanced SUPT training at a single location.

We selected Fairchild AFB in Washington state as the second flying training pretest location because of the target of opportunity it presented: All enlisted aircrew and all officers in the SUPT pipeline complete combat and water survival training at this location immediately following completion of their AFSC-awarding course. Thus, we were able to include students who had just arrived from more bases than we were able to visit. The survey questions for these students asked about their experiences in their training pipelines *prior* to their arrival at Fairchild. These students were surveyed at the end of their first week at Fairchild, before they began field exercises and SERE training, in order to avoid student temptation to also include incidents that occurred at Fairchild during SERE training.

When in the Training Pipelines the Pretest Was Administered

For the pretest, we invited enlisted technical training students who were nearing completion of a pipeline that was less than six months in length. For the officer SUPT students, we pretested students near the end of primary training and near the end of advanced flying training. This timing allowed students to report on nearly all training experiences during their pipelines and captured students at a similar time point as recommended for the final survey system. Although we aimed to invite a *census* of all students nearing completion of the identified stages of training *at the time of the RAND site visit,* this was not possible given logistical constraints (e.g., student schedules, availability of computer labs). Still, from December 2016 to February 2017, we scheduled six site visits at times that maximized the number of eligible students. We coordinated with a point of contact at each site to identify dates when the team could deliver the survey to a subset of students who were approaching or had just passed the identified training milestone. In part, the selection of dates was dependent on the availability of a facility for survey administration, and the identification of groups of students whose schedules could accommodate the pretest. We requested that Air Force training leaders or instructors provide students with the information they needed to be able to attend a voluntary survey administration session. The sessions were held in computer labs or classrooms, and students took the surveys via Air Force computers connected to an Air Force network. During the pretest administration, AETC leadership said they would suspend their requests for enlisted students to participate in other surveys with potentially overlapping content.

Who Participated in the Pretest

Of the students who attended a survey session, 777 responded to the first survey question assessing their consent to participate. Of these students, 75 (10 percent) did not consent to participate; all or nearly all of whom were enlisted students. (Seventy-three were enlisted students based on our invitations; two students who declined to participate at Fairchild could have been either enlisted flying training students or officers.) Of the 777 who responded, 98 students (12 percent) were excluded because (1) they were ineligible to participate (e.g., students from militaries of allied nations, students who had too recently arrived at training), (2) they failed to read the survey carefully (as indicated by failure to mark the response option requested in screening items), or (3) they self-reported that their answers were not at all open and honest. Most of these exclusions were due to ineligibility: A survey built into the end of a training pipeline would avoid the inclusion of recent arrivals.

The final analytic sample of students who consented to participate included 604 students (516 enlisted students and 88 officers) from Fairchild, Keesler, Lackland, Laughlin, and

Sheppard AFBs. Among the 516 enlisted participants, 76 percent were men, 23 percent were women, and 1 percent did not indicate a gender. Additionally, 93 percent were non-prior service airmen. As shown in Figure 5.1, the pretest analytic sample was diverse in terms of respondent career group and training location; however, it was not feasible within this study to include students from across all IST pipelines, so some career groups (e.g., medical) and locations (e.g., Goodfellow AFB in Texas) were not represented.

Figure 5.1. Career Group and Survey Location of Enlisted Participants in the Pretest Analytic Sample

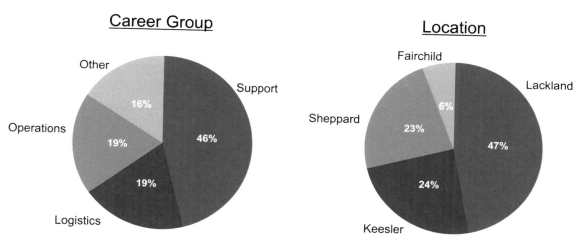

Among 88 officers who participated in the survey pretest, 91 percent were men, 7 percent were women, and 2 percent did not indicate a gender. All officer students in our analytic sample were in SUPT, which is in the operations career group: 67 percent were completing their primary pilot training, and 33 percent were completing or had just completed their advanced pilot training. Fifty-three percent of students were surveyed at Laughlin AFB, while 47 percent were surveyed at Fairchild AFB.

Given the selection of students, this pretest represents only a snapshot of responses for a nonrepresentative sample of students in technical and flying training. Although the pretest results were critical for instrument development, they do not offer a benchmark for the misconduct experiences of the entire population of technical training and flying training students.

How the Survey Pretest Was Administered

One important goal of the pretest was to determine how different modes of administration affect responses on the survey. Therefore, to the degree possible, we used the pretest as an opportunity to vary certain aspects of the administration, solicit student preferences, and, ultimately, describe the effect of these decisions on survey participation and responses.

Time was set aside in students' schedules to participate, and training leaders or instructors informed them of the survey purpose, times, and location. Participation in the confidential survey was completely voluntary. Only RAND staff administered the surveys: no training leaders, instructors, or other staff were permitted to be in the room during the survey. RAND team members administered the survey pretests in classrooms and computer labs. Students completed the survey on Air Force computers connected through an Air Force network to a survey hosted on an Air Force website. Students were required to login to the computers with their CAC, with the exception of some students at Lackland, where there is infrastructure to support a non-CAC mode of administration. Students were not asked to enter such identifying information as names or contact information—in fact, they were expressly asked not to enter such information.

At Lackland, we conducted a small experiment that systematically varied whether students completed the survey on military computers that (1) required CAC access or (2) did not require CAC access. Given this unique infrastructure at Lackland, we invited students there to participate in the pretest and randomly assigned them to either a computer lab that did not require a CAC be inserted in order to use the computers or a lab with computers that require a CAC. Comparing responses across the two groups (which should have similar rates of maltreatment experiences) allowed us to assess the degree to which a CAC requirement influences responses and potentially suppresses (or does not suppress) the rate at which students disclose misconduct.

How the Survey Pretest Results Were Used

Pretest results informed the design of the final survey. The pretest version offered many opportunities for students to highlight items that were incomplete or unclear. These included "other" write-in response options to alert us to overlooked response options and open-ended questions assessing misconduct that currently was not included on the survey but should be. A final open-ended item also allowed students to point out survey questions or sections that were confusing or hard to answer and to provide suggestions for improving them. We also invited students to offer comments informally at the end of the survey session, and some took the opportunity to share their thoughts verbally before departing.

We have confidence in the face validity of the survey questions based on responses from our sample. The write-in responses suggested that students were usually able to find their responses among the options provided, and that students generally did not have complaints about the clarity of the instructions or survey questions. Results from the pretest showed that groups of questions assessing the same general construct were correlated with one another in the expected direction. To build on these findings, we recommend that the Air Force continue to monitor the reliability and validity of survey questions. It is possible that future generations of airmen could perceive questions or instructions in different ways.

Finally, the pretest version also included several questions about how different situations might influence students' decision to participate in a future survey like the one they had just taken (e.g., mode of survey administration, time built into training schedule for participation). Those results were used to inform the survey system recommendations reported in the following chapters.

Conclusion

In this chapter, we described the methods used to pretest the survey, including the research sites, when the pretest took place, who participated, how the survey pretest was administered, and how the results were used. Based on analyses of the pretest results, the final recommended survey presented in Appendix C does not vary substantially from the pretest version of the survey. The primary differences are that

- items included only for pretest purposes were removed (e.g., options to provide written comments, measuring attitudes toward future survey participation)
- a few items were trimmed because the construct was measured just as well with fewer items (e.g., six items toward the end of the survey regarding attitudes toward using critique/drop boxes were reduced to three)
- skip patterns and items that could not be programmed for the pretest were returned to the final survey
- a few items that were not central to the main survey purpose were removed to shorten average survey administration time to keep it to approximately 20 to 25 minutes. For example, an eight-item scale toward the end of the survey that addressed commitment to the Air Force was removed. We retained one item regarding perceptions of whether commitment to the Air Force was strengthened through technical training or flying training.

Pretest results relevant for the development of the recommended survey system are included in the subsequent chapters, along with the recommendations they informed.

Part III: Survey System Recommendations

6. When to Administer the Survey

We considered two primary options for the timing of the survey: (1) administer the survey at a single point in time (e.g., an annual survey that is fielded in June) or (2) connect survey administration to a milestone in the training pipeline (e.g., the end of a course). In this chapter, we review both options, discuss the advantages and disadvantages, and, ultimately, recommend that the survey be administered near graduation or after six months of training (whichever comes first). However, surveying a snapshot of students on base at a single point in time remains a legitimate alternative. Both options would underrepresent students who leave technical training or flying training without graduating—therefore, an alternate survey strategy for this group is discussed.

Snapshot of Students

The first option would be to administer the survey at a single point in time and capture a snapshot of all technical training and flying training students at that point. This method focuses on the training environment as a whole at a point in time, but captures students at a variety of points in their training pipelines. The approach is illustrated in Figure 6.1 by using notional technical training pipelines—which, as described in Chapters 2 and 3, vary in length, timing, frequency, and location. In Figure 6.1, the colored boxes represent required courses of various lengths, and color changes within an AFSC pipeline represent a change in installation. The people symbols represent the survey sample, which, in this case, would be drawn from across the pipelines, all in the month of June.

Figure 6.1. One Option Administers the Survey at a Single Point in Time

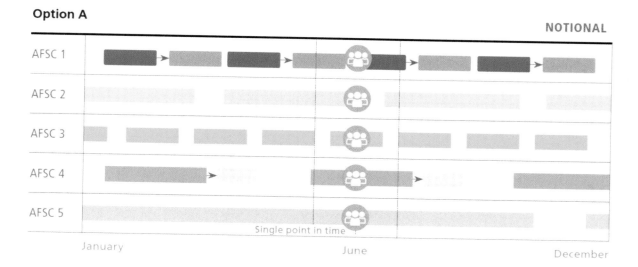

53

Administering the survey as a snapshot at a single point in time has a number of advantages. The survey could provide an estimate of unit or installation climate for all students at a single point in time, under a common group of installation leaders and service providers. This could be helpful if a problem were more environmental across students at a given location rather than tied to any pipeline-specific timing or activities. This approach could also standardize the influence of AETC-wide policy changes, announcements, new initiatives, or other factors that might influence incidence rates or reporting decisions, whereas end-of-course surveys might capture students in some pipelines before such changes and some students afterward.

Administering the survey at a single point in time would also capture more variety in terms of time in training; some students would be in their first week of training and others would already have completed several months of their training pipelines (as shown in Figure 6.1). By asking students to indicate how long they have been in training or at a certain installation, it would be possible to describe temporal patterns to the prevalence of behaviors (e.g., Are certain types of misconduct more common when a student has just arrived at an installation? Are other types of misconduct more common later?). However, the more time has passed after an experience, the more students may be challenged to recall it or how they felt about it at the time. Thus, the information provided by those who started their training pipelines more than six months before the time of the survey may not be as accurate as that provided by students with solely more recent experiences. Although the snapshot method is cross-sectional in nature, it would be possible for AETC to monitor certain behaviors over time by examining changes from survey to survey at that same point in time each year or every six months.

Finally, this type of survey effort would be periodic rather than ongoing. There would be a preparatory period for the survey (e.g., contacting training leadership, altering training schedules, establishing survey sites and administrators), then a defined time set aside for survey administration (e.g., a month), followed by a period of data analysis and report preparation. With the snapshot approach, we would recommend surveying no more than twice per year. Reports could be produced once or twice a year.

There are also some challenges that would need to be addressed with a snapshot approach. For example, it would be advisable to establish a minimum time on installation for survey eligibility, as it might not be worth students' time or training disruption to survey them about their experiences after only a few days in training. Additionally, because students taking the survey will have been at a given installation for varying lengths of time, it would be important to measure students' training time on the date they complete the survey and account for this variation if any cross-site comparisons are desired. As schedules and pipelines will vary from year to year, it will also be important for analyses to control for how long students have been in training when comparing a single installation's rates over time.

With this approach, AETC would need to define the window in which the survey would be administered (e.g., one week, one month) to avoid inadvertently omitting students in pipelines with gaps between cohorts or who are away on training missions. Several factors would go into the decision of how long the window for survey administration should stay open. If the survey must be accessed through an Air Force computer, AETC will need to ensure the survey is open long enough to afford sufficient opportunity for all students to access computing facilities. If a census is to be surveyed, it might be challenging in some locations to set aside and staff computer labs or classrooms to permit all students to participate. If the entire population will be surveyed, then administrators would also need to consider the peak load that the existing IT systems can support.

Finally, AETC leaders would need to determine how frequently to administer the survey. Administration once a year might make it challenging to adequately represent students in small, frequent short-term classes and prevent timely visibility of a significant rise in problematic behavior or attitudes or potential impact of a policy or program change. Twice a year would provide more frequent and timely information. However, in an environment with consistently few problems from year to year and no significant policy, personnel or program revisions, once a year may be sufficient. AETC could always insert an extra survey administration if leaders became concerned about a rise in misconduct or wanted to gauge the potential impact of an initiative in a more timely manner.

Connecting the Survey to the Training Pipeline

The second option would be to connect the survey administration to a milestone within the training pipeline itself—for instance, by surveying students at the end of the AFSC awarding course, as shown in Figure 6.2. Using the same notional pipelines as in Figure 6.1, in this example, the survey is administered at the end of the training pipeline, or, in the case of particularly long pipelines, the survey may also be administered at the midpoint.

Figure 6.2. A Second Option Connects the Survey to the Training Pipeline

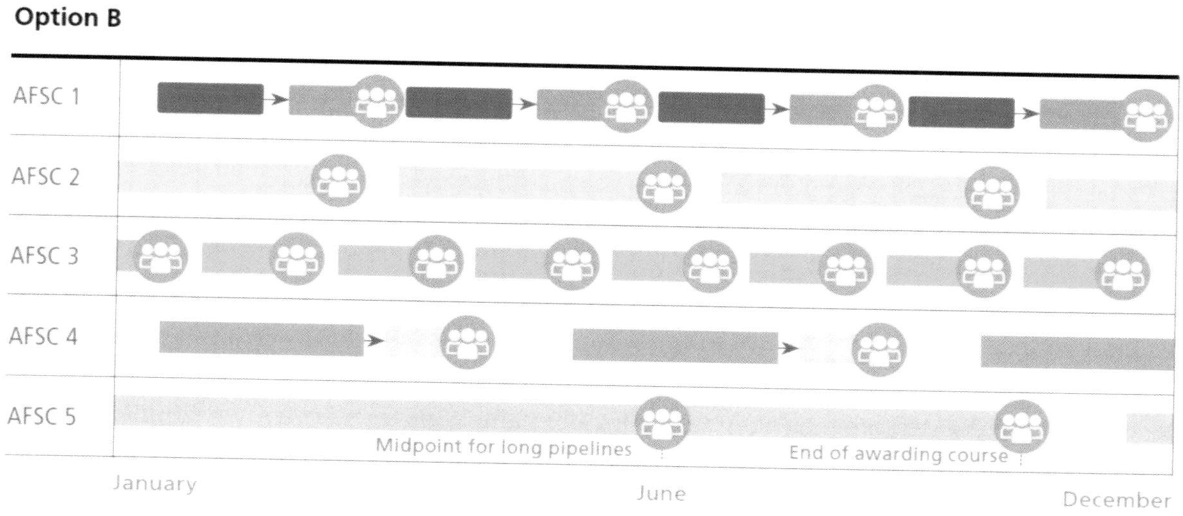

There are a number of advantages to this method frequently recommended in our meetings with AETC leadership, instructors, and students. First, by administering the survey at a standard point in the training pipeline, all students in a given career field are reflecting on a standardized training segment (e.g., the first course, the entire pipeline). Using the snapshot method, students could be at any stage in their training. This strategy connected to the pipeline would permit comparisons between students who are at a comparable stage of training, whether comparing rates over time at a single base or, as in the case of SUPT, comparing students in the same types of training pipelines located at different installations.

One of the most important advantages of this second method is that the routine timing makes it possible for survey administration to be incorporated into standard course proceedings (e.g., accompanying end-of-course exams or evaluations or during out-processing proceedings). Institutionalized timing and resources in the standard training schedule avoid coordination challenges that would be necessary to successfully execute periodic administration in the training environment. Administering the survey using this approach could also be less disruptive timing for training courses than a snapshot approach, which would either require training leaders to arrange an alternate training schedule across the base (perhaps interrupting training at inopportune moments) or students to participate during their own time.

In contrast to the periodic snapshot survey, the pipeline-associated survey supports continuous monitoring of the training environment. As a result, it also enables more frequent updates to leadership and more immediate feedback on new initiatives, should they be requested.

Connecting the survey to a training milestone also has challenges that would need to be managed. A primary challenge to connecting the survey to the pipeline is determining the ideal administration time. There are several factors that might influence this decision. First, the survey could be administered early during the training pipeline, when leadership is concerned that students may be most vulnerable. However, because there may be other points of vulnerability during the training pipeline, administering the survey too early might result in later events going undetected. A second option would be to survey students at regular points (e.g., every two months). Although this would provide more accurate estimates of the frequency of incidents, challenges include survey fatigue, potential reductions in response rates, and burden on the training schedule. A third option would be to survey all students at the end of their respective training pipelines. This could be simpler from a logistical perspective, but this option presents analytic challenges because of the variable length of pipelines. Although most technical training pipelines last less than six months, certain specialties have significantly longer training pipelines (e.g., pararescue training is 30 months on average). For students in longer training pipelines, we have concerns about the accuracy of student recall and the potential for underreporting. In addition, by the time that leadership learns about problematic behaviors occurring in longer training pipelines, the climate, instructors or leadership for that stage may have already shifted. Therefore, a fourth option would be to survey students at one standardized point during the pipeline, with the goal of balancing the desire to observe as much of training experience as possible while also minimizing the memory drop-off for major life events, which typically occurs after seven months (Raphael, Cloitre, and Dohrenwend, 1991).

Administering the survey at the end of a pipeline does not remove variability in pipeline length but would establish a minimum time in training (approximately six weeks). However, just as with the snapshot approach, data analyses will need to account for those differences.

Recommendation to Link Survey Timing to the Training Pipelines

After considering both options, we recommend connecting survey administration to milestones within the training pipelines. Once implemented, we believe routine administration at a standardized point in time is more likely to be successfully executed than periodic efforts to mobilize personnel across the training bases. Second, ongoing administration to all students reaching the relevant training milestone provides leaders with the option for more frequent or quick-turn reports should they wish for more timely feedback on an issue of concern or new initiative. Third, this approach allows for deliberate selection of when in the training to solicit student feedback on their experiences, so that all students in each career field are providing an assessment based on a common stage in their training.

For students in enlisted technical training and flying training, we recommend surveying students at the end of their training pipeline or at approximately six months, whichever comes first (see Figure 6.3).

Figure 6.3. Survey Enlisted Students at the End of the Pipeline or About Six Months

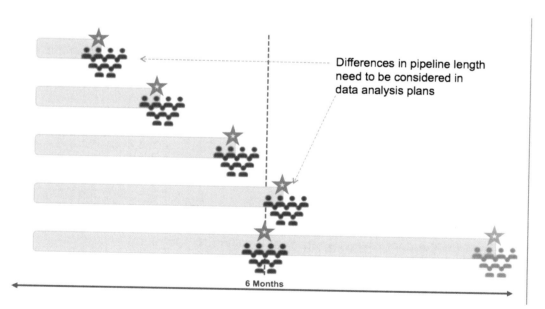

Research suggests that accuracy of recall for life events, even significant traumas, declines substantially seven months after the event (Raphael, Cloitre, and Dohrenwend, 1991). Because

57

most enlisted technical training pipelines are shorter than six months, accuracy of recall is not a significant concern. However, surveying students in longer pipelines at six months will circumvent concerns about recall. Thus, for the vast majority of students, the survey will capture their entire IST experience. For the pipelines that are longer, the survey will capture their early training experience, a time period during which students may be most vulnerable to misconduct. If AETC leadership becomes concerned about misconduct occurring later in any of the lengthy pipelines, they have the flexibility to deploy the survey again to follow up on the issue.

Students training for enlisted aircrew AFSCs could be surveyed at the end of the flying training phase of their training and permitted to indicate their experiences in both the technical training phase and the flying training phase (just as other enlisted students can report on experiences at multiple locations). The results for the technical training phase of enlisted aircrew training could be analyzed and reported separately from their subsequent flying training experiences given that different chains of command oversee each.

For SUPT students, we recommend a modified survey administration schedule (see Figure 6.4). Because the undergraduate pilot training pipeline is much longer than other pipelines, and because it occurs in distinct phases, we recommend that SUPT students be surveyed twice. The first survey would be administered at the end of their primary training, which would reflect the time awaiting pilot training (which could be brief or longer than a year), pre-flight academics (about 1.5 months), and T-6 training (about 5 months). We recommend that the primary training survey be scheduled before decisions about advanced training tracks are made, in case satisfaction with that decision colors the ratings of flying training leadership. The second survey would be administered at the end of advanced training (about 7 months later) and should occur before decisions about aircraft assignments are announced, again so satisfaction with those decisions does not alter student ratings of flying training leadership. This timing was suggested by leaders, instructors, and students as one that would make sense both in terms of the time in each training segment and the natural break in instructors and classmates that occurs between primary and advanced training.

Students Who Do Not Complete Their Training

For all enlisted and SUPT students who leave training without graduating, we recommend that they be invited to take the survey before their exit. These surveys should include an indicator that they were completed by nongraduates so they can be aggregated and analyzed separately from graduates. It is important to include students who did not complete training because it is possible that abuse or misconduct was a factor in their failure to complete.

Figure 6.4. Survey Officer SUPT Students at the End of Phases One and Two

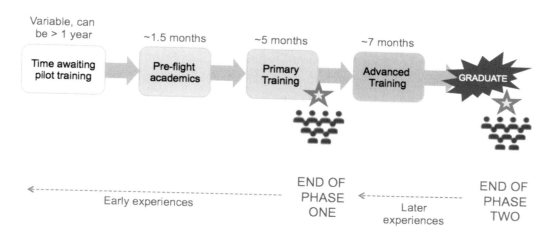

In sum, creating such a survey system enables leadership to learn about incidents of abuse and misconduct during technical training and flying training. Second, the results enable leadership to compare students at the same points in their training from one year to the next— thereby providing a mechanism to determine whether interventions and policy changes to mitigate abuse or misconduct were effective. However, the single-snapshot-in-time approach remains a legitimate alternative should AETC leadership determine it is more feasible or better aligned with their goals than the pipeline-milestone approach.

Deconflicting with Other Surveys in the Environments

In addition to participating in the proposed survey, trainees may be asked to participate in several other survey research efforts led by DoD or the Air Force. These efforts vary along different dimensions, including when they are administered and the topics addressed in each survey. To ensure maximum utility of the currently proposed survey effort, we reviewed additional surveys that may be administered during technical or flying training to assess potential overlap with the current survey effort. We specifically considered the Defense Equal Opportunity Management Institute's (DEOMI's) Organizational Climate Survey (DEOCS), DoD's Workplace and Gender Relations Survey, the Air Force Community Feedback Tool (formerly the Air Force Community Assessment Survey), the Air Force Total Force Climate survey, criminal activity surveys administered by OSI, and end-of-course surveys administered during technical training and flying training. Appendix A provides a description of each effort.

AETC is unlikely to be able to influence the timing of the Workplace and Gender Relations Survey and DEOCS, which have schedules set by DoD policy.[7] However, there may be

---

[7] Many technical training and flying training students are not eligible to participate in the WGRA, which only samples service members with at least five months of service at the time of survey administration.

opportunities to influence sampling plans for the Air Force–controlled surveys to reduce the survey burden carried by technical training and flying training students. The most critical deconflicting will be with AETC end-of-course surveys. For example, after the BMT survey system was implemented, Keesler AFB implemented an interim survey of misconduct as part of end-of-course surveys of technical training students at Keesler. This brief survey has been a critical source of information for Keesler technical training leadership while they waited for development of a commandwide survey. If and when this survey system is implemented, we recommend that the end-of-course misconduct surveys be phased out so that Keesler students are not asked to report misconduct through two separate AETC survey efforts.

Conclusion

Given AETC priorities and practical concerns, we recommend building the survey into the training pipeline. This allows the survey to

- serve as an alternate feedback system for all students
- be incorporated into standard course schedules
- support comparisons of average annual responses from students in the larger pipelines (e.g., security forces) who were surveyed at the same point in their training.

For non-prior service enlisted students, we recommend surveying them at the end of their training pipeline or at approximately six months, whichever comes first. This timing will

- capture their earliest technical training experiences and, for many, their entire experience
- avoid significant concerns with accuracy of recall
- allow for a more timely leadership response to emerging problematic trends
- not preclude deploying the survey again toward the end of lengthy training pipelines, particularly those lasting a year or longer.

Students training for enlisted aircrew AFSCs should be asked to include experiences in both the technical training and flying training phases of their pipelines, so that leadership has visibility of both types of environments. Results can be sorted so that experiences during technical training at Lackland AFB can be distinguished from those occurring afterward.

Because the officer undergraduate pilot training pipeline is much longer than most other pipelines we examined, and because it occurs in distinct phases, we recommend surveying officer SUPT students at least twice:

- at the end of their primary training (with the survey asking students to include the time waiting for pilot training and pre-flight academics, as well as their T-6 primary training)
- at the end of advanced training (approximately seven months later).

In each case, the survey should be administered before decisions about advanced training or aircraft assignments are made so that survey responses, particularly those pertaining to the flying training leadership, are not colored by satisfaction (or dissatisfaction) with those decisions.

In addition, we recommend that students who leave technical training or flying training without graduating be invited to take the survey prior to their exit. Those surveys should include an indicator that they were taken by nongraduates so they can be aggregated and analyzed separately from graduates.

Finally, we recommend phasing out any other AETC end-of-course misconduct surveys so that students are not asked redundant questions in the same period. However, other surveys could still encourage students to report misconduct through formal channels or seek assistance through service providers such as chaplains and health care professionals.

7. Who Should Participate in the Survey

This chapter reviews the strengths and weaknesses of two participant sampling strategies for the survey system. The first is probability or random sampling, where the researcher selects a random subset of a population to participate in the survey. The second technique is a census, in which everyone in the population is invited to take the survey. For this particular survey effort and setting, we recommend the latter, but we recognize that both techniques have strengths and limitations.

Probability Sample

Samples are subsets of a population. For this survey system, the population of interest will be students enrolled in Air Force technical training and flying training pipelines. AETC could sample these students using a variety of techniques. For example, analysts could use an equal probability sample where all students have the exact same chance of being part of the invited subset (Kalton, 1983, p. 7). Alternatively, analysts could select a stratified probability sample in which some students (e.g., women, students in courses with relatively few students) have a greater chance than others of being invited to complete the survey in order to increase the likely number of surveys obtained from small subgroups.

Advantages

Probability samples have several advantages. First, samples can be cost-effective and reduce the human resources invested in the student time to take the survey. In part, this explains why many surveys administered by or for the U.S. military use probability samples.[8] Fewer personnel need to take time away from work to participate, and it requires fewer resources to mail (and in some cases, email) a survey invitation to a sample rather than a census. For surveys administered in person, there are fewer survey sessions requiring staffing and fewer facilities, computers, and servers need to be devoted to the effort.

Second, probability samples can reduce the number of surveys in which personnel are asked to participate and thus can potentially increase willingness to participate in the surveys they are invited to complete. Military personnel may be asked to take several different surveys each year (Miller and Aharoni, 2015). If only a small sample of students needs to complete the survey, it reduces the survey burden for the majority of students who are not invited to participate. During the survey pretest, we received informal feedback from some students who were concerned about the number of surveys, particularly misconduct surveys, that the military asks them to complete.

---

[8] Some examples include the Workplace and Gender Relations Surveys, Post-Election Voting Survey of Uniformed Service Members, and the DoD Status of Forces Surveys.

Additionally, on the survey pretest 36 percent of students said they would be less likely to participate in a survey like this one if they had taken another Air Force survey in the past month.

Disadvantages

Probability samples are not without limitation. Within the context of enlisted IST, it may be easier to send an entire class to a computer lab than to solicit participation from a sample of students. Many enlisted students in technical training do not yet have access to their official email account, so email invitations are not always a suitable option for reaching a sample. AETC administrators could distribute lists of selected airmen to the training units and request that they notify the selectees about the survey, but that would require identifying special staff for the duty to avoid placing the responsibility into the hands of the individuals that students are asked to report about or evaluate (e.g., MTLs, instructors, service providers). Alternatively, asking all students to report to the survey room only to dismiss nonsampled students would make it highly visible who was selected to participate and who was not.

Some students may wonder why they were selected to take the survey instead of their peers (e.g., does leadership suspect or know something happened to them?) or why they were not selected (e.g., were local leaders afraid they might say something negative?). That is, even when students are randomly sampled, there is no guarantee that students will believe they were randomly selected. These misconceptions could lead students to decline to participate in the survey or to provide answers they believe are desirable by their leaders, biasing the results. Also, where students are tightly scheduled, those selected might be at a disadvantage if they are taking the survey while fellow students are receiving additional instruction or opportunities to study or rest.

In addition, the design of a quality probability sample requires time, effort, and specialized expertise. To implement the approach over the long term, the Air Force would need to hire or assign a scientist with expertise in survey sampling to manage the sampling portion of the survey system. Even for a relatively straightforward equal probability sample administered only once or twice a year, such expertise would be necessary for creating a sampling design, conducting nonresponse analyses, and constructing sampling weights. Such efforts could be costly for AETC in the long term.

Census

Unlike a sample, a census is a complete enumeration of individuals within a population. For a milestone-connected survey system, a census would involve inviting every student at a particular point in their training pipelines to participate (e.g., every student graduating from their training pipelines). For the snapshot approach, a census would involve inviting all students who are present at a training location at a particular point in time.

Advantages

There are several advantages to a census that align well with AETC leadership's motivations for developing it. First, a census would allow the survey to serve as an alternate channel for students to anonymously disclose misconduct to leadership—every student would have this opportunity available to them. Furthermore, a census could have the added benefit of promoting Air Force values and standards of conduct. Reading the survey questions could reinforce students' knowledge of acceptable and unacceptable behaviors in the Air Force. In addition, the survey content provides reminders of the many leaders and support staff in the training environment that students may contact to report misconduct or seek assistance.

A census also provides more of an opportunity to observe low-frequency events (e.g., sexual assault) than a probability sample.[9] For example, the 2014 RAND Military Workplace Study estimated that 0.3 percent of active-duty Air Force men and 2.9 percent of active-duty Air Force women experienced a sexual assault in the previous year (Jaycox et al., 2014). Based on these estimates and results from the BMT survey, we expect that the percentage of students who experience certain types of abuse and misconduct will be particularly low. A census will allow AETC to estimate these percentages with greater precision compared with a sample.

Additionally, if every student is invited to complete the survey, it will not be necessary to develop a sampling strategy or construct sampling weights (although response weights may still be required). As suggested above, logistically it may be simpler to have flight leaders arrange for students in their flights to attend a survey session as part of the day's schedule than to arrange for selected individuals to participate. Furthermore, if there were a "bad actor" among the training leadership, it may be harder for that individual to prevent an entire class from taking the survey, and to do so unnoticed, than to prevent only a few students selected in a probability sample.

Finally, the larger sample size implied by a census would increase AETC analysts' ability to summarize misconduct at lower levels of aggregation, while still protecting students' confidentiality. Thus, it would increase the likelihood that analysts could report the results by gender, geographical location, career group, or career field. For example, if few women are training in a particular career field, and only a couple of these women are included in the survey sample, then there would be a risk that someone might infer their identities if results were reported by gender for that career field. In comparison, by including everyone in the survey, the number of people who fall into each specific category is higher, which helps to protect confidentiality for all participants. Put simply, a census helps to protect the confidentiality of students while increasing the likelihood that information about subsets of students is still reportable. That capability would be particularly important for career fields that enroll small numbers of students.

---

[9] While a census increases capacity to capture rare events (e.g., sexual assault), a full census may be unnecessary to estimate the percentage of students who experience more common types of misconduct (e.g., bullying).

Disadvantages

However, there are several disadvantages to a census. A complete enumeration of all students in the Air Force training pipelines means that many more students would be invited to respond to a survey that requires about an average of 25 minutes to complete. Significant effort would be required to adapt training schedules to accommodate the surveys, to staff the survey sessions, and to ensure that facilities, computers, and networks are available and accessible. Finally, it would be even more crucial to deconflict surveys with overlapping content to avoid oversurveying students, as more students will be affected by it than if a sample were drawn.

Recommendation for a Census Approach

We recommend a census for the survey system. Table 7.1 summarizes the pros and cons of a sample versus a census for the technical training and flying training settings. Arguably, two of the most important concerns in administering this survey are whether students feel comfortable taking the survey and whether the survey has the capacity to capture rare events like sexual assault. With a sample, students may conclude that they were purposefully selected to answer the survey, leading them to opt out of participation or give socially desirable answers to survey questions. A census would allow the survey to serve as an alternate, anonymous reporting channel for abuse and misconduct, and the act of reading the survey items could reinforce students' understanding of proper conduct and values in the Air Force. Additionally, the survey introduction and closing statements reiterate the myriad channels available for reporting abuse and misconduct or seeking support services, such as counseling or medical care. Given the advantages of a census, we recommend that all students be invited to participate in the survey.

Table 7.1. Advantages and Disadvantages of a Probability Sample and Census for Surveying in Technical Training and Flying Training Environments

Approach	Advantages	Disadvantages
Probability sample	• Help reduce survey burden • Less demand for computers and space • Takes fewer students away from training	• Expert effort needed to repeatedly draw samples and develop estimates • Effort to contact individual students and make arrangements for some to participate • Fairness, potential concerns about being singled out or excluded • Greater limitations on ability to report out results by lower levels of aggregation (e.g., location, career field) • Less likely to detect rarer behaviors (e.g., sexual assault)
Census	• Survey serves as an alternative confidential reporting channel for all students • Simpler to schedule moving a whole class to a survey location rather than pulling and managing a sample • Reading survey items about prohibited behaviors may promote understanding of standards and values among new airmen • Greater opportunity to detect low-frequency events • Improves ability to report out results by lower levels of aggregation (e.g., location, career field) • Provides more statistical power	• Facilities and staff needed to provide every student the opportunity to participate • May be more disruptive because all students are expected to attend the survey session

Conclusion

For a periodic, scientific evaluation of AETC technical training and flying training environments as a whole, a probability sample may be the most efficient and practical survey recruitment strategy. However, given AETC's intention for the survey to support ongoing monitoring of the environment, desire to be able to detect rare events such as sexual assault, interest in breaking the reportable results out by location or pipeline, and practical constraints of the training environments, we recommend inviting all students to participate in the survey.

8. Confidentiality and Maximizing Survey Participation

This chapter discusses strategies to maximize survey participation and promote open and honest survey responses, which are informed by our experience with the survey pretest and students' responses to questions on the topics. Confidentiality plays a key role in both of those aims. Additionally, to explore the potential influence of requiring a CAC for survey access on students' response patterns, we report the results of an experiment exploring the influence of CAC requirements on survey responses.

Strategies to Maximize Survey Participation

To obtain accurate estimates of misconduct, it will be important to maximize the survey response rate (i.e., the percentage of invited students who complete the survey). This is particularly important given research suggesting that participants may be concerned about disclosing sensitive information online (Allen and Roberts, 2012; Evans and Mathur, 2005), and challenges soliciting survey participation from the youngest, most junior-ranking military personnel (Miller and Aharoni, 2015). If only a small percentage of students participate, doubt about survey results will rise. For example, if only 20 percent of students participate, leaders may wonder whether only those students who had experienced abuse or misconduct completed the survey, and therefore biased the results. Alternatively, they could wonder whether many students who had experienced abuse or misconduct were afraid to participate and indicate their experience even on a survey promising confidentiality. To provide AETC with evidence-based guidance about the reasons that students choose not to participate and develop recommendations to increase survey participation without undue influence, we included four measures of survey participation in the survey pretest.

Willingness to Participate

The first measure is willingness to participate, which is the percentage of invited individuals who consented to participate in the pretest of the misconduct survey. For this survey, 90 percent of students who attended a survey session chose to participate. That percentage is higher than other web-based Air Force and DoD surveys, which have junior enlisted response rates that range from 5 percent to 25 percent (Miller and Aharoni, 2015). This suggests that an AETC survey system that relied on similar administration procedures as the pretest procedures could reasonably expect a high response rate well above other Air Force surveys. Of course, if administration procedures shift (e.g., toward self-initiated completion during students' personal time), then response rates are likely to also shift.

The 75 students who declined to participate[10] were asked whether they would be willing to share the reason or reasons they did not want to complete the survey, and they were able to select as many options as applied to them. Figure 8.1 displays the results. Among the 10 percent of students who declined to participate, many (41 percent) preferred not to respond to this question. Among the most common reasons were that the students believed that the survey did not apply to them (21 percent), did not like taking surveys (19 percent), and did not have enough time (17 percent).[11] When students choose not to participate in a misconduct survey because they believe it does not apply to them, it introduces the risk of overestimating misconduct in the training environment. In this case, only 2 percent of students who attended a survey session declined for this reason, which suggests that introduced bias was minimal. In response to these concerns, we revised the survey introduction to clarify that, even if a student is unaware of any problems in the training environment, their input on this survey can help the Air Force understand student perceptions of the available reporting channels and support systems in the training environment. Any survey invitation may wish to emphasize the same. In the final version of the survey we have retained these questions about the preference not to participate and added two options about whether leaders or other students in the training environment discouraged them from participating. In the future, it will be important to continue to monitor response rates and reasons for declining to understand the extent to which a bias may be introduced.

---

[10] Seventy-three of the 75 students who declined to participate were enlisted students, as they participated at locations where only enlisted were invited. Two students who declined to participate at Fairchild could have been either enlisted flying training students or officers. We do not have information about the gender of those who declined.

[11] The choice of "not having enough time" was surprising in the pretest context, as all students had been allocated 45 minutes in their schedules to attend the survey session. However, it was also clear that some students had not fully understood that they would be expected to remain in the survey session for the scheduled period, which we have now further clarified in the informed consent statement.

Figure 8.1. Reasons Among Students Who Declined to Participate

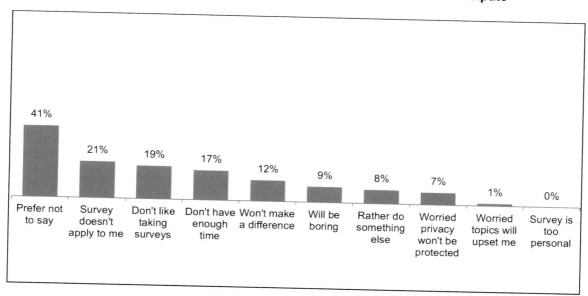

SOURCE: RAND Technical Training and Flying Training Proper Conduct Survey.
NOTE: *n* = 75 students.

In addition to the metrics we used to assess pretest participation, we also assessed willingness to take a similar survey in the future. If students are unwilling to take the survey more than one time, then their lack of participation in subsequent administrations of the survey may bias results. Additionally, this finding could speak to students' beliefs of the potential costs or value of participating. Figure 8.2 shows that approximately one-third of students indicated that they would be "not at all likely" or "somewhat unlikely" to take a follow-on survey in six months. One-quarter indicated that they were "neither likely nor unlikely" to participate in the future.

Figure 8.2. Student Responses to the Question, "If the Air Force Sends You a Survey Invitation for a Follow-On Survey in Six Months to Help It Ensure a Safe and Productive Work Environment, How Likely Is It You Would Participate?"

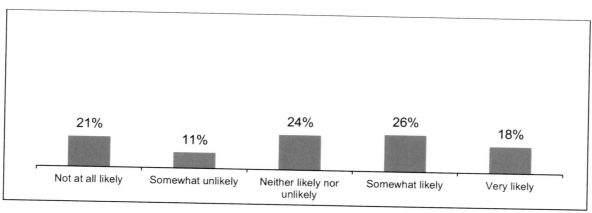

SOURCE: RAND Technical Training and Flying Training Proper Conduct Survey.
NOTE: *n* = 537.

To develop recommendations for improving survey participation, we assessed the factors that would influence students' willingness to participate. Specifically, the pretest included the item, "Please indicate whether the following would influence your decision to participate in a future survey like this." Table 8.1 presents those factors in the order of the most commonly endorsed conditions that students said would make them more likely to take a future survey similar to this one. The top influencer was participation time built into the schedule; 63 percent of respondents indicated that this factor would make their participation more likely. Forty-three percent of students said that encouragement by their flight commander or chief would increase their likelihood of taking the survey. Finally, nearly 30 percent of students indicated that taking the survey on their personal computer or mobile device would make their participation more likely (however, 55 percent of students said this option would not influence their decision). The circumstances that the greatest proportion of students indicated would make them *less* likely to participate were being asked to complete the survey on their own time (52 percent), having taken another Air Force survey in the past month (36 percent), or being invited by email to participate (22 percent).

Table 8.1. Top Conditions for Increasing Future Survey Participation, as Reported by Students

Condition	More Likely	Would Not Matter	Less Likely
Participation time is built into schedule	63%	31%	7%
Flight commander or chief announcement and encouragement	43%	44%	13%
Can take survey on personal computer or mobile device	29%	55%	16%
Invited by email to participate	20%	58%	22%
Have to take survey on military computer	19%	63%	19%
Asked to complete survey on own time	14%	34%	52%
Taken another Air Force survey in past month	6%	59%	36%

SOURCE: RAND Technical Training and Flying Training Proper Conduct Survey.
NOTE: n = 511–514.

Based on these data, we recommend that the Air Force build time into student schedules to take this survey rather than requesting that they complete it during their personal time. By including the survey in a formal schedule, the Air Force will likely improve the willingness of their students to complete this survey and give it their full attention. However, we recommend allowing only students and a civilian survey administrator in the survey room—therefore, no authority figures would be present while participants respond to sensitive questions about abuse or misconduct, reporting such behaviors, and leadership climate.

When the survey is administered in a group setting, we recommend that students be required to stay in the room for a predetermined period of time (approximately 45 minutes). All students should stay for the entire survey session to protect the confidentiality of students who may take longer to complete the instrument because their experiences generate follow-up questions. Requiring students to stay for the full session also ensures that students are not inadvertently incentivized to rush through the survey. Suggesting that students bring study material to the survey session could help them make good use of their time once they have completed the survey, and it could reduce the likelihood that students will be tempted to distract others or watch them complete their surveys.

Scheduling training time to accommodate survey sessions will need to occur pipeline by pipeline. Based on comments by Air Force training leaders and instructors, we expect this task will be challenging; many pipelines have little unscheduled time or are non–Air Force led (e.g., training for medical AFSCs). Support and communication from leadership that these survey sessions are important and valued may help to facilitate this task, and guidance or coordination from AETC headquarters also may be needed.

In addition, on the basis of pretest data, we also recommend that flight commanders and flight chiefs announce the survey beforehand, communicating the importance of the survey and encouraging their students to participate. This recommendation would also support a broader goal of ensuring that students and their leaders know about the purpose of this survey and understand how their participation can help to inform policy decisions and improve the training environments.

Willingness to Proceed to the End of the Survey

The more information students are willing to provide on the survey, the more leadership can learn from them. To learn more about willingness to complete the entire survey, we tracked the percentage of students who started this survey but then stopped before reaching the end. There were 105 students who did so (15 percent). Figure 8.3 displays the cumulative percentage of students who started but discontinued participating before reaching a given section. The graph shows minimal drop-off for most sections of the survey, including all of the misconduct sections. When surveys include sensitive topics, examination of drop-off patterns can provide an indication of sections that respondents found troubling or offensive. For example, if a large percentage of students had dropped during the sexual assault section, it could indicate that these questions were difficult for students to view. We did not find any evidence of this; the drop-off rate was consistent across sections (1 percent), which suggests that students did not find any particular misconduct section any more or less troubling than others. Six percent of students stopped taking the survey during the section with closing questions. Within this closing section, there were no drop-offs for the question on how open and honest they had been. Instead, the drop-offs increased to 14 percent when asked about whether they would be willing to take this survey again in six months and then reached 15 percent for questions on the factors that would influence their future participation in surveys. Drop-off could be related to the amount of time students had already devoted to the survey or to the perceived importance of these last questions. We cannot be certain about what caused the increase in drop-offs for these questions, but note that these questions are not included in our recommended final survey instrument.

71

Figure 8.3. Cumulative Percentage of Students Who Stopped Taking the Survey Before Completing Each Section

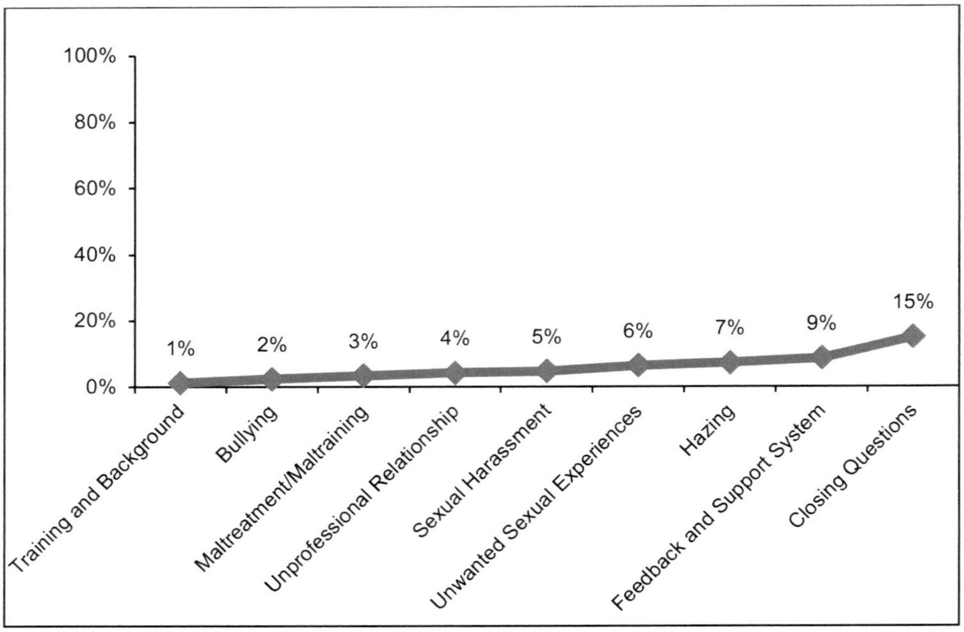

SOURCE: RAND Technical Training and Flying Training Proper Conduct Survey.
NOTE: n = 105.

Willingness to Be Open and Honest When Responding

A closing question at the end of the pretest survey asked students how open and honest they felt they could be while completing the survey ("not at all," "somewhat," or "completely"). As shown in Figure 8.4, the majority of students (80 percent) reported that they were "completely open and honest"; 19 percent reported that they were "somewhat open and honest"; and 1 percent reported that they were "not at all open and honest."

Figure 8.4. Student Responses to the Question, "How Open and Honest Did You Feel You Could Be When Answering These Survey Questions?"

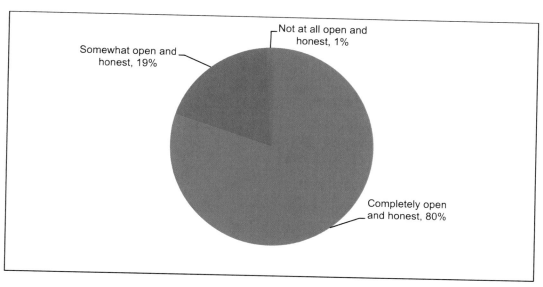

Not at all open and honest, 1%

Somewhat open and honest, 19%

Completely open and honest, 80%

SOURCE: RAND Technical Training and Flying Training Proper Conduct Survey.
NOTE: *n* = 524.

Although not all students who provide dishonest or misleading survey responses will choose to be honest in their response to this particular question, some will. Therefore, this question allows survey administrators to screen out some (although not all) surveys with inaccurate data. For students who self-report that they were "not at all open and honest," we recommend that their surveys be removed from the analytic data set. All other analyses in this document excluded students who reported that they were not at all open and honest during the survey pretest.

Continuing to track this metric over time will provide leaders with a sense of the degree of student trust in the survey system and a window into the quality of students' data for survey administrators. If the percentage of students reporting that they could not be open and honest rises substantially, it would be important to explore why students are uncomfortable being candid so that leaders can implement strategies to address their concerns (e.g., through focus groups with subsequent classes of students—not the respondents who stated their discomfort).

Maintaining Confidentiality

Some students may be more honest about their experiences when they believe their responses are anonymous or confidential. As AETC looks to implement this survey on a large scale in the future, individual survey responses indicating a specific case of misconduct should never be forwarded to squadron commanders or OSI representatives for investigation. This protection of the survey data is essential to ensure the confidentiality of student responses and maintain student trust and openness. We also recommend that open-ended items (those that solicit written responses) not be included in the final survey. Although written comments can be informative and valued by Air Force leaders, the proposed survey in Appendix C does not solicit them to help preserve the confidentiality of the survey tool and avoid students potentially identifying themselves or a suspected offender through this channel.

Additional factors may influence students' perceptions of the confidentiality of the survey. For instance, an externally hosted survey may appear to be more confidential than an Air Force–hosted survey. However, external survey hosts often gather certain information automatically (e.g., internet protocol addresses, browser type, date, time stamp) (Allen and Roberts, 2012), and therefore inadvertently create identifiable data. Two other measures that may promote perceptions of confidentiality are ensuring that MTLs and instructors are not in the room during survey administration and having computer banks available that do not require a CAC. We examined this latter option more closely.

Influence of Computer Access Cards on Responses

When the BMT abuse and misconduct survey is administered at Lackland AFB, trainees complete the survey in one of two computer labs equipped to provide computer access without the use of a CAC. Allowing trainees to complete the survey on a machine that does not require a CAC assures them that the survey is truly confidential and that their responses cannot be linked back to them. During our pretest of the BMT survey, among trainees who reported they were either somewhat or completely open and honest on the test survey, 38 percent indicated that they would be very uncomfortable if they had to use their CAC cards to take the survey (Keller, Miller et al., 2015).

Creating this capability at Lackland was extremely difficult and labor intensive. This capability does not generally exist at other bases, and the time and resources necessary to establish it make it infeasible to expect that all training environments will have the capability to support non-CAC access to the survey. That is, we expect that most technical training and flying training students will be required to use their CACs to complete the survey on a military computer in the future—therefore, the concern is that this could bias survey results toward fewer reported incidents.

To better understand whether requiring students to use their CACs to access the survey biases students toward underreporting and, if so, to what extent, we conducted an experiment at Lackland AFB. The experiment systematically varied the type of computer lab in which students were randomly assigned to complete the survey. The majority of the students selected for participation at Lackland AFB were in the security forces career field (military police and force protection), but other pipelines were also included. Out of the 253 enlisted students invited to participate, approximately half ($n = 128$) were randomly assigned to complete the pretest survey in a computer lab that did not require their CACs, and half ($n = 125$) were assigned to a lab that requires use of a CAC card. Both computer labs were located in the same building and have identical floor plans and computer banks.

Once survey administrators had randomly assigned students to one of the two computer labs, they provided students with identical instructions and informed consent statements. After participants had proceeded through the main sections of the survey, they were asked in the closing questions whether they needed to use their CACs to access the survey. We did not ask this question at the beginning of the survey to avoid emphasizing to them whether a CAC was required or not and thus potentially biasing their responses to the subsequent questions. Therefore, one limitation of our experiment is that our analyses include only responses from students who consented to participate in the pretest, persisted to the last survey section, and indicated whether they had used a CAC or not. As such, we cannot speak to whether the CAC requirement influenced willingness to consent to participate in the survey or was associated with drop-off prior to the CAC question. However, because the two sets of students were randomly assigned to use or not use their CACs, and all other aspects of administration were identical for these two groups, we were able assess whether survey responses varied as a result of CAC requirements and, if so, to what extent.

Among the students who completed the survey, the proportion who indicated that they had experienced misconduct (on any of the six domains) did not differ significantly across students who used or did not use their CACs. The level of self-reported openness and honesty on the survey was also not significantly different across those who did or did not use their CACs. Finally, there was no statistically significant indication of students reporting more or less favorable perceptions of Air Force climate, leadership, or organizational commitment based on whether they were required to use a CAC or not. That is, across all assessed domains, we did not find evidence among this particular population that administering the survey in settings in which a CAC is required biased survey results among those willing to participate.

Given the significant effort required to enable students to use their CACs on the Air Force computers, however, we recommend that a non-CAC solution be made available in locations where such a solution is available or easily implemented (e.g., Lackland AFB). It also communicates to students that leadership is serious about safeguarding their privacy and that they can be confident that their survey responses will be confidential. However, given insufficient evidence to state that the survey will be biased if a CAC is required, we do not recommend that resources be invested in creating these solutions in locations where doing so would require considerable personnel time or resources— not without first evaluating whether the lack of differences between CAC and non-CAC users extends to those other locations, or whether a CAC requirement influences willingness to participate at all.

Conclusion

The survey pretest provided insight into ways to maximize survey participation, such as ensuring students understand how the survey applies to them (or the value of contributing to the community), building time into the training schedules for the surveys, and having flight leaders announce the survey and encourage participation. For the pretest, 90 percent of students who attended a survey session agreed to participate, and most students who began the survey persisted through until the end of the survey. Common reasons for declining to participate included perceived lack of relevance, lack of time, and dislike of taking surveys in general—however, 41 percent who declined had reasons they did not want to reveal.

Nearly all students felt they could be at least somewhat open and honest on the survey. In an experiment at one training base, we found no significant differences between the responses of students who used a CAC to access the survey relative to those who did not. It is possible that a CAC requirement may influence the decision to participate, but the experiment design did not allow us to test this. Nevertheless, if non-CAC survey options are available, they would help AETC avoid the labor involved with ensuring students are able to use their CACs and promote confidence among students in the confidentiality of the survey system.

9. Technical and Human Resource Challenges to Resolve Before Implementing the Survey System

This chapter discusses some of the technical and human resources issues that AETC will need to address before implementing the proposed system across technical training or flying training.

Mode of Administration

The content of the survey necessitated a complex design, including skip patterns dependent on student characteristics and their responses to misconduct items. We considered two primary options for mode of administration: a paper-based survey and a computer-based survey. We identified several logistical challenges associated with a paper-based survey that rendered this option infeasible, particularly given the scope of the pretest and eventual final survey. Use of a paper-based survey increases the likelihood of user error and data entry errors (American Psychological Association, 2009); is more time- and cost-intensive, particularly with respect to preparing and processing the surveys (Keller, Miller et al., 2015); and presents challenges when asking questions dependent on such complex branching as those in the present survey (Sexton, Miller, and Dietsch, 2011). Branching personalizes the survey to each student and reduces survey time by presenting only the questions relevant to the student. For example, officers do not need to see items specific to enlisted technical training, and students who did not experience a misconduct incident should not see items about whether they reported misconduct. As a result, we focused on various options for administering a computer-based survey.

Survey Software

The legacy software that AETC has for survey programming is decades out of date and lacks many standard features of contemporary survey programming software. As a result, it could not support all of the survey content that required branching. In particular, the legacy software made it impossible to program the full set of updated DoD Workplace and Gender Relations Survey measures of sexual harassment and sexual harassment, so we were unable to include the follow-up questions that assessed whether the behavior rose to the level of an MEO violation or UCMJ-defined sexual assault. AETC programmers invested substantial effort into programming from scratch the necessary work-arounds to allow the pretest effort to move forward, and their expertise and time were absolutely critical to the success of the pretest. Had they had access to a contemporary software platform, the effort would have been much more efficient.

To support the survey system moving forward, we recommend that AETC use a contemporary survey platform that will support all necessary features of the survey in a more-efficient manner. This shift would require reprogramming the existing survey but would offer multiple advantages. Most importantly, it would permit AETC to fully implement the DoD Workplace and Gender Relations Survey measures of sexual harassment and sexual assault, which could not be fully accommodated by the legacy software used to support the pretest. Up-to-date survey software would also improve the efficiency of AETC's skilled programming staff, expedite any future modifications to the survey, and provide expanded capabilities in the administration and management of the survey. Modern survey software also often offers features that support analysis and visual display of results (e.g., generating figures), which could facilitate timely and effective reports. Additionally, this software could be used across AETC for other survey efforts.

Computers and Networks for Survey Administration

We considered three main options for administering a computer-based survey: (1) a local Air Force server, in which the survey would be administered on a networked set of computers in close proximity to the server and connected directly to the server; (2) an Air Force network server that connects across bases computers with Air Force network access; and (3) an external online survey host (e.g., Qualtrics).

For computer-based administration, support via local Air Force servers presented a number of concerns. First, because there would be no centralized server, every survey location would need to maintain its own local server, which will require more effort to manage and support than a single centralized sever. For instance, any changes or updates to the survey would have to be implemented on all local servers in the system, which is both time- and resource-intensive. Second, backing up, obtaining and merging data from multiple local servers for centralized analysis and reporting would be challenging. Finally, it can be costly to purchase and maintain local servers and survey software. In contrast, surveys that are administered online, whether via an external host or through an Air Force network server, are more efficiently managed.

Therefore, we next identified various considerations that helped us to determine whether it would be preferable to administer the survey via an Air Force network server or on an external online host. For practical purposes, the pretest was hosted on an Air Force server with access restricted to two civilian Air Force IT specialists who programmed the survey and oversaw secure data transfer to RAND researchers. However, to inform possible AETC implementation, we describe the factors that we considered below.

Data Security

Given the sensitive nature of the survey, it is essential to maintain the security of survey data. Hosting the survey on an Air Force server is likely to maximize the data security. Data hosted externally may be more susceptible to interception by a third party (Nosek, Banaji, and Greenwald, 2002). In addition, surveys administered on externally hosted sites might maintain their data on a non-U.S.–based external server. By using an Air Force network server, the Air

Force controls where data are stored and how they are transferred. Use of an externally hosted server also presents certain contractual issues that could threaten data security. For instance, an external host may transfer ownership to another company or go out of business (Molnar and Schechter, 2010). That said, some reputable external hosts have data security measures in place that meet DoD standards. If an external host were used, it would be important to properly vet the organization and its security capability. In partnership with a trusted organization, the Air Force could arrange to have the externally gathered data transferred to an Air Force system for storage and use and periodically deleted from the external server.

The management of the survey data files should be coordinated to ensure that any connectivity or submission problems are identified quickly and rectified with minimal loss of data. This includes identifying where the survey data will be stored, designating sufficient secure data storage and backup, monitoring access, and observing the number of completed surveys to ensure they are matching expectations. During ongoing survey administration, the data files should be checked regularly to identify any issues with the survey software or with the transmission of files to the secure server.

Infrastructure and Technology Resources

The survey system will ultimately be implemented at locations with varying levels of IT resources. Planning for the pretest provided an opportunity to learn about the ways that a survey functions on different IT systems. For instance, one option for administration was to have students use Air Force computers connected to the survey via a kiosk version of the network so that a CAC would not be required for participation and no data would be saved locally. However, this was available at only one installation (Lackland AFB). Software and data security constraints meant that the surveys could not be installed on local computer networks at any of our sites—therefore, with the exception of Lackland participants, students needed to access the survey through Air Force computers that connected via an af.mil link and thus required use of their CACs.

An Air Force network and CAC requirement can present access challenges to transient enlisted students who will not necessarily be registered to use the computers on their training bases, may not yet have been scheduled to complete their mandatory information security training, or may have forgotten the CAC personal identification number (PIN) they have rarely, if ever, used at that point. For example, prior to the start of many of our survey sessions, we had to arrange for students to be able to reset their PINs for their CACs, as many of them had forgotten theirs. Resetting a PIN is not as simple as students clicking a "forgot my password" link online and following instructions. At one location, for example, it entailed arranging for an authorized staff member with access to a PIN-resetting machine arriving at the survey building an hour before the survey so students could line up and have their PINs reset in time for the survey. Thus, requiring a CAC for survey participation can present a major challenge— regardless of whether it could potentially bias student responses toward underreporting or discourage them from participating (as discussed in Chapter 8).

Other infrastructure-related considerations include the existence of rooms with large computer banks, the logistics of finding and reserving such a room, or survey access on personal devices. To ensure that the survey administration is efficient for both administrators and students, adequate numbers of working computers should be designated for survey sessions. If active Air Force network access is required, someone must confirm that the selected computers are connected to the network prior to scheduled sessions. Requesting that students wait for available computers, either because there are not enough available computers or existing computers are not functioning properly, may discourage participation.

Where feasible, installation of privacy screens on computers may promote greater openness in reporting sensitive information by providing students with greater confidence that others beside or behind them will be unable to view their screens.

Human Resource Challenges

The recommended survey system is a significant undertaking that will require considerable staff support from AETC. We recommend that the Air Force have a full-time civilian behavioral or social scientist to work at AETC headquarters to manage survey administration, analysis, and reporting. This position should be staffed with a researcher with relevant expertise who should be provided with the necessary resources to ensure success. Specifically, this entails the capacity to continue to monitor the climate and evaluate the appropriateness of survey items for pipelines that were not included in the pretest. This staff person should have the skills to analyze survey data, triangulate the results with other technical training and flying training data or information, and prepare survey result reports and briefings. The tasked staff person should have access to leadership to provide immediate feedback on meaningful changes in abuse or misconduct indicated by the survey and be able to advise leadership on survey results and response strategies.

In addition, we recommend that a project team be assembled and include staff who can identify pipeline administration strategies and manage student participation in the survey. Similarly, the project team should identify the appropriate point in each pipeline to administer the survey and work to seamlessly integrate the survey into the pipeline schedule. Given that pipelines differ both in length and in training requirements, the survey should be introduced at the appropriate time in each pipeline to allow comparisons across students at a comparable stage in their training with minimum disruption to the training environment. Moreover, to promote open and honest participation, we recommend civilian survey administrators who are not in a position of authority over the students and are not any of the individuals referenced in the survey (e.g., not the SARC who serves the student population).

Management of the survey should also encompass management of survey administration to encourage high rates of participation. This includes coordinating survey times around other student obligations, ensuring students will be able to find the survey administration site, reminding students in advance to check their PINs and to bring their CACs, and, if necessary, reminding them of the survey administration schedule.

We recommend that open-ended items *not* be included in the survey in order to protect confidentiality. If AETC does opt to include qualitative data collection, significant labor resources should be allocated for this task during survey administration planning. If assigned with the collection of such data, the survey lead (the behavioral or social scientist) should manage the cleaning, coding, and categorizing of such data.

Conclusion

To support an abuse and misconduct survey system, we recommend that the survey be computer administered via online connections to a central server. Survey software updates will be necessary to fully program and efficiently support the survey, and all IT solutions should consider and protect response confidentiality. Finally, at least one full-time behavioral or social scientist located at AETC headquarters should oversee the survey.

10. Recommendations for Analyses and Reporting

This chapter offers recommendations for analyzing and reporting the survey data. These include strategies to preserve the confidentiality of the survey system, detect differences between subgroups or changes over time, and place the results in broader context.

Managing Results to Preserve the Confidentiality of the Survey System

A critical element of the system design for this survey is confidentiality of the individual responses. To avoid undermining the survey's added value to leadership, individual survey findings of misconduct should not be forwarded to squadron commanders or OSI representatives for follow-up investigation. Instead, the survey can be used to prompt other forms of action, such as further exploration of cultural or other institutional factors that may contribute to abuse and misconduct or discourage official reporting and help-seeking. For example, leaders could hold focus groups or town halls with MTLs, instructors, or students to present or discuss results of concern, or chaplains or first sergeants could more discreetly raise certain topics when making general inquiries about the well-being of students. However, no students should be withheld from progressing through or out of their pipelines in order to accomplish this, as that pattern could also lead to hesitation to indicate problems through the survey. Without confidentiality, the survey loses its value in providing visibility to leaders on misconduct that students were not willing to reveal through official reporting channels. The survey instructions do remind students of their official reporting channel options, should they be willing to come forward.

To further protect confidentiality, no data should be presented on groups with fewer than ten individuals. When group sizes drop below ten, it will be necessary to combine similar pipelines, classes, or training locations or to continue collecting data over a longer period until the necessary number of additional respondents has been collected.

Additionally, reports to leadership should include information about student participation, as these details can serve as indicators of trust in the confidentiality of the survey system and trust in members of the training environments. Participation information would include how many students declined to participate, reasons for not participating, and how open and honest students felt they could be when answering questions.

Comparing Subgroups or Rates Over Time

Results can be reported separately for enlisted and officers, for men and women, for different bases, or for different pipelines. Group comparisons will be impacted by the number of respondents. Two factors are at work here, so we conducted analyses to determine the minimum sample sizes that are adequate for (1) delivering stable estimates of misconduct and (2) protecting the confidentiality of all students in that group. Often, there is a tension between the end user (who may prefer to learn about survey rates at fine levels of analyses—for example, rates among women in each career field while they were training at each installation), statistical power considerations (a relatively large sample is required to be confident about each estimated rate of misconduct), and confidentiality considerations (groups must be large enough that the data cannot be used to identify any given person in the group based on his or her answers).

Ultimately, AETC leaders will want to understand whether an observed rate of misconduct is different from one time point to the next (e.g., in 2016 relative to 2017) or in one group relative to another group (e.g., men relative to women, Lackland relative to Keesler). To make these kinds of comparisons, it is necessary to have a large enough sample of students who complete the survey to be confident that a difference between groups would be observable. Appendix D provides more-specific guidelines on the types of comparisons that might be possible given sample sizes and prevalence of abuse and misconduct.

Differences in pipeline lengths also need to be considered in data analyses plans to avoid misleading comparisons of incident rates across widely differing periods.

Triangulating Data and Placing Results in Context

Incidents indicated through the survey should be compared with rates of incidents reported to leadership or service providers to examine how much underreporting may be occurring and to help provide insights on areas of concern, such as reasons for not reporting. In addition to reported incidents, potentially relevant data that could complement the survey data include injury and illness rates, counseling referrals, rates of attrition and recycling, and results from other student surveys. Other types of relevant information may include

- changes in relevant policy
- changes to training pipelines and programs
- staffing changes (e.g., changes in rank, gender, or number of instructors)
- changes in student admissions (e.g., population size, demographics).

This approach would allow interpretation of any observed changes in survey responses with changes in other areas of the training environments and would help to provide an assessment on the effects of implemented policies and changes in procedures. This information combined with survey information may also be relevant for interpreting other training trends, such as rates of attrition.

Analyzing the Data and Preparing Reports

In the previous chapter, we recommended that AETC have at least one full-time civilian behavioral or social scientist with relevant expertise and resources to manage the survey at AETC headquarters. Responsibilities would include continuing to evaluate the appropriateness of the survey items to those pipelines not included in the pretest, analyzing the surveys and triangulating the results with other training data, alerting leaders of meaningful changes in abuse and misconduct, preparing survey reports and briefings, and advising leadership on interpretation of results and response strategies.

Although a detailed analysis plan is out of the scope for this report, we provide a few general recommendations. First, prior to reporting any survey data, survey validity checks should be conducted to confirm the quality of the data. The analyst should provide reports of survey results every six months to establish a stable baseline and then annually. If there have been relevant policy changes or meaningful spikes in abuse and misconduct, AETC can also choose to request more frequent reports as needed. Reports should not be exhaustive in nature; rather, they should use graphics and figures to highlight for leadership the key takeaways from the latest set of surveys, with additional detail available as backup slides or appendixes or provided upon request. Reports should be shared with AETC leadership who should consider releasing findings to key stakeholders such as instructors and MTLs and soliciting their input in developing any necessary courses of action. Sharing selected results with students would also be a helpful way to signal transparency and willingness to consider student input. Overall, dedicated personnel with methodological and substantive expertise will be able to report the results in a way that can help AETC staff to avoid misinterpreting data (e.g., presuming there are measurable differences based on "eye-balling" the results) and extract the greatest value from the survey system.

Conclusion

AETC sought a confidential survey that would complement existing reporting and feedback channels about abuse and misconduct in the training environments. Without confidentiality, this survey loses its critical ability to provide visibility of behaviors that students are unwilling to reveal through official reporting channels. The surveys do remind students of their official reporting channel options, should they be willing to come forward, but no one should attempt to discern which individuals completed which surveys or forward individual (rather than aggregate) responses to squadron commanders or OSI representatives for follow-up investigation. The survey can prompt other forms of action, as noted earlier, such as further exploration of cultural or other institutional factors that may contribute to abuse and misconduct or discourage official reporting or help-seeking behaviors.

If AETC leadership wishes to compare incident rates across training pipelines, differences in pipeline lengths must be considered to avoid misleading comparisons across widely differing periods.

The survey results should be triangulated with other technical training and flying training data, such as formally reported incidents, injury and illness rates, counseling referrals, rates of attrition and recycling, and results from other student surveys. Survey results could also be used to spark further explorations into problems areas: For example, leaders could hold focus groups or town halls, or chaplains or first sergeants could more discreetly raise certain topics when making general inquiries about the well-being of students.

The survey results should be presented in context with other information that might be relevant for interpreting the results. This could include policy changes, changes to training pipelines and programs, staffing changes, and changes in student admission policies or practices.

11. Conclusion

This report documents the development of a proposed survey system to enhance AETC's ability to monitor abuse and misconduct in selected technical training and flying training pipelines. The confidential survey system includes a survey instrument (Appendix C), as well as recommendations about survey administration, data analyses, and reporting results to leadership. Although students who are willing to report abuse and misconduct already have many formal channels through which they can alert leadership or seek assistance, this unique, confidential system provides visibility of behaviors students are not willing report, as well as insight into reporting decisions, experiences, and the training environments. Reading survey questions may also reinforce Air Force training about the types of behaviors that are unacceptable and the many places airmen can turn for assistance.

Limitations

Should AETC choose to adopt some or all of the proposed survey system, the limitations of this study should be considered. We solicited input from leaders and staff across Air Force–led technical training and flying training, and we pretested the survey with a diverse subset of students. However, certain locations or pipelines not included in our pretest may have local practices, terms, or understandings that are not sufficiently captured by the present instrument. Additionally, some of the proposed administration methods may not be as feasible in non–AF-led environments.

Therefore, AETC should actively seek input across the pipelines regarding any potential need for revision in order to match the setting, particularly in the first year the new survey is administered or as the survey is deployed into new settings. For example, in training locations run by other organizations (e.g., Army base, Defense Language Institute), there may be other reporting channels or other names for the types of channels listed in our survey. We focused on enlisted training pipelines available to non-prior service students, and because prior-service airmen or retrainees may also be in some of those courses, the survey is already designed to include those students. However, we have not examined the training pipelines available only to retrainees or prior-service airmen (e.g., chaplain assistant, MTL) and thus cannot speak to whether additional modifications would be necessary. Similarly, the technical training and flying training environments for officers outside of SUPT may call for further adaptation or consideration of the optimal timing for survey administration.

Additionally, because the existing Air Force software available for the survey pretest lacked some features of modern survey software, a few of the more complex survey branching features could not be employed and tested, such as those used to determine whether incidents might meet the legal thresholds for sexual harassment or sexual assault. Therefore, we recommend that the survey is programmed using modern survey software, and that the survey data analysts use early survey data to evaluate item performance, drop-off rates, and time to survey completion to ascertain whether there are any required adjustments, such as removing other content to keep the survey within the targeted average response time.

Recommendations

Throughout this report, we reviewed options for administering the survey and provided recommendations for the overall survey implementation. We summarize the key elements of the recommended survey system below:

- When should the survey be administered?
  - Survey enlisted students in technical training or flying training at the end of their training pipelines or at approximately six months, whichever comes first.
  - Survey SUPT students at the end of primary training but prior to decisions about advanced training tracks; then again at the end of advanced training but prior to decisions about aircraft assignments.
  - Survey students who leave training without graduating prior to their exit.

- Who should participate in the survey?
  - Conduct a census of training students at the selected points in their pipelines.
  - Invite and permit all students to participate; however, participation should be voluntary.

- How should the survey be administered?
  - Ask flight commanders and chiefs to announce the survey and encourage participation.
  - Communicate how leaders have used results in the past.
  - Build survey time into student schedules and avoid scheduling it at the same time as competing activities, such as meals or commander's calls.
  - Allow only students and a civilian survey administrator in the room during the survey, so no authority figures are present.
  - Coordinate administration with other surveys to reduce survey fatigue.
  - Explore feasibility of not requiring a CAC or Air Force network access for survey participation to eliminate the labor needed to set up such access for this transient population of new airmen.
  - Explore options for taking the survey on personal computers or devices, which could still be executed during a scheduled survey participation period.
  - If Air Force computer network access is required, ensure sufficient availability of computer rooms and computers with Air Force network access across installations.
  - Ensure that students know how to find the survey session rooms.
  - Explore feasibility of installing privacy screens.

- How should results be reported?

- Have a full-time, civilian behavioral or social scientist with relevant expertise and resources manage the survey analyses and survey reporting.
- Provide reports of survey results every six months to establish a stable baseline and then annually and as needed.
- If groups sizes are adequate (see Appendix D), report results separately for enlisted and officers, men and women, different bases, and different pipelines.
- To protect confidentially, do not report separate results for any groups with fewer than ten individuals.
- Report results from pipelines with too few students to report separately in a timely manner by grouping them with other classes in the same training location or career group.
- Triangulate survey results with other data on abuse and misconduct (e.g., official reports, injuries, attrition) to examine potential underreporting and to help provide insight on how to address areas of concern identified by the survey.
- Present survey results in context, to include relevant information that may explain changes in the results over time (e.g., policy changes, staffing changes).

Conclusion

We have proposed a confidential survey system intended to solicit open and honest feedback from Air Force technical training and flying training enlisted students and officer SUPT students about incidents of abuse and misconduct in the training environment, attitudes toward and experiences with reporting incidents, and attitudes toward AETC leadership, feedback and support systems. The system is intended to provide greater visibility of events that may not be reported through official channels. It can identify barriers to official reporting so that command can address them. The survey also solicits information to identify key characteristics associated with incidents (e.g., location, type of people involved)

The survey is not intended as an investigative tool. To avoid undermining the intent of the survey, no one should ever to try to deduce who filled out any particular survey. Meaningful spikes in misconduct should prompt an assessment of changes in the climate, leadership, or student body to learn about possible causes. For example, a civilian behavioral or social scientist hired to lead the survey effort could conduct focus groups, or leaders could hold town halls with students and flight leaders to learn more about the current climate.

The survey can also serve to reinforce among respondents the types of behaviors that are not acceptable within the Air Force and to remind them of the diverse array of options within the Air Force that they have for reporting incidents or seeking help. If implemented, the survey would benefit from additional testing to confirm that it is functioning as intended, including as it is extended to enlisted training pipelines not included in the survey pretest. Moreover, the instrument will likely need additional adaptation if extended to other officer flying training pipelines (e.g., combat systems officer) or officer technical training pipelines, as these environments may differ from those considered in this study. However, most of the content on abuse and misconduct, reporting channels, reporting attitudes and experiences, and leadership climate should translate to other environments.

Appendix A. Air Force and DoD Surveys That Assess Misconduct

Technical training and flying training students may be asked to participate in other Air Force and DoD surveys that have content that overlaps with the proposed survey system. To the extent possible, it will be important to deconflict these surveys to prevent duplication. These efforts vary along different dimensions, including when they are administered and the topics addressed in each survey. Throughout the survey development process, we were often asked how this survey differed from others and whether there was sufficient lack of overlap to warrant adding another survey. To clarify, this appendix provides a brief description of other surveys in the environment.

DEOCS

The DEOCS is an anonymous online survey, administered by DEOMI, that unit commanders and directors throughout DoD may request be administered to their unit. DoD Directive 1350.2 and a DoD memorandum have established that commanders of units with 50 or more people must conduct a climate assessment within 120 days after taking command and must report the results and analysis of annual climate surveys to the next level in their chain of command (DoD Directive 1350.2, 2003; DoD, 2013). To be able to generate a DEOCS report, however, a minimum of 16 responses from within the unit is required. Thus, commanders of units with less than 16 people may not request this survey for their unit (DEOMI, 2015a).

The DEOCS addresses organizational effectiveness and equal opportunity (EO) issues, and it may be administered to both military and civilian personnel. The core DEOCS survey contains approximately 95 items, and commanders may add ten locally developed questions and five short-answer questions (DEOMI, 2016). In addition to ten demographic items, survey sections within the core DEOCS instrument assess perceptions of organizational effectiveness, EO/equal employment opportunity (EEO)/fair treatment, sexual assault prevention and response, and discrimination/sexual harassment. Locally developed questions are designed or requested by commanders and can address a multitude of topics, including perceptions of the physical environment (e.g., parking availability), autonomy and innovation, and family support (DEOMI, 2015b).

Several items used in the DEOCS assess topics that are also addressed in our current survey effort for AETC. For example, within the organizational effectiveness section of the DEOCS, participants indicate their agreement with the item "Discipline is administered fairly" (1 = strongly disagree, 2 = disagree, 3 = agree, 4 = strongly agree). A similar item in the maltreatment/maltraining section of the current survey asks, "During [technical training/flying training], did an instructor discipline only you when others made the same mistakes?" (1 = never, 2 = once or twice, 3 = a few times, 4 = weekly, 5 = daily). Similarly, within the EO/EEO/Fair

Treatment section of the DEOCS, participants indicate agreement with the item "Sexist jokes are not used in my work area" (1 = strongly disagree 2 = disagree 3 = agree 4 = strongly agree). A similar item in the current survey asks, "During [technical training/flying training], has anyone, male or female, repeatedly told sexual stories or jokes that were offensive to you?"

Although survey items across the efforts may address similar concepts, the DEOCS focuses on shared perceptions of policies and practices within units (DEOMI, 2016), while the RAND survey focuses on monitoring and reporting of abuse and misconduct during training. Thus, rather than addressing perceptions, the current effort focuses on experienced events and reporting behaviors, and it specifically focuses on events that occurred during training. The current survey, therefore, primarily uses a series of items addressing the specific experiences and behaviors of individuals, whereas the DEOCS primarily utilizes items addressing individuals' opinions. Further, the DEOCS must be requested by unit command. By contrast, it is intended that the current survey be administered regularly, rather than only upon command request. Finally, the DEOCS assesses some topics that are not assessed in the current survey effort, including racial discrimination and religious discrimination. However, the current survey effort more thoroughly assesses reporting and responses to reporting than the DEOCS.

WGRA

Another survey administered to active-duty military personnel across DoD is the WGRA, the active-duty version of the Workplace and Gender Relations Survey. Under Public Law 104-201, the military must conduct a survey of the gender relations experienced by the active-duty force. DoD's WGRA fulfills this requirement. Since 2002, the WGRA has been conducted six times, in 2002, 2006, 2010, 2012, 2014 (as a part of the RAND Military Workplace Study), and 2016. This anonymous survey is administered by the Defense Manpower Data Center and addresses topics involving workplace gender relations, including the experience of gender discrimination, sexual harassment, and sexual assault.

As discussed in Chapter 4, the technical training and flying training surveys will adopt with only minor alteration the WGRA measures of sexual harassment, gender discrimination, and sexual assault as the strategy to assess these types of misconduct. The purpose is to support ongoing leadership monitoring of the training environment and of the potential impact of interventions targeting abuse and misconduct. There is some risk that a subset of technical training and flying training students would be asked to complete the survey developed for AETC and to participate in the WGRA. The WGRA is administered every two years to a sample with the purpose of estimating the prevalence of these behaviors across the services. In 2016, the WGRA was administered between July 22 and October 14 (Davis et al., 2017). Only service members who have served for five months or longer are invited to participate in the WGRA.

Air Force Community Feedback Tool (formerly Air Force Community Assessment Survey)

The Air Force sponsors a web-based survey effort designed to address installation-specific community needs and to inform support activities and resource allocation (Miller and Aharoni, 2015). The survey had been administered approximately every two years to a sample of active-duty Air Force members and their spouses, reservists and their spouses, and civilian employees. Recently, the survey had also been administered to Air National Guard members and their spouses (Reid, 2013). The 2013 version of the Air Force Community Assessment Survey was intended to take approximately 30 to 45 minutes for participants to complete, and the survey addressed multiple topics, including personal and family adjustment, posttraumatic stress, help-seeking stigma, and community well-being (Air Force Magazine, 2013).

Unlike the current effort, the Air Force Community Assessment Survey was not designed to address the training-specific experiences of students or recent graduates and their reporting attitudes and behaviors. It is also administered with less frequency than intended for the current effort. Compared with the current effort, this less frequent administration reduces the ability of the Air Force Community Assessment survey to regularly inform training commanders of more recent issues and concerns with incoming students.

In 2017, the Air Force launched a dramatically revised survey, rebranded as the Air Force Community Feedback Tool. RAND researchers designed, administered, analyzed, and reported the results of that tool. The primary purpose remains providing installation-level results to inform leadership and service provider efforts to promote the welfare of the local Air Force community. Although all airmen—including students—are eligible to participate, the survey content focuses little on incidents of abuse and misconduct, and results reports do not provide separate results for students. These data are complementary with AETC's data, as they include the broader community members' perceptions of leadership and military resources available to help members with their problems and needs.

Air Force Total Force Climate Survey

The Air Force Total Force Climate survey is another Air Force–specific survey effort. This is a census-based online survey, designed to be administered every two years to active-duty Air Force, Air National Guard, and Air Force Reserve airmen and Air Force civilian employees (U.S. Air Force Personnel Center, 2015; Miller and Aharoni, 2015). It is administered during a common window of time across the Air Force. The survey takes approximately 20 minutes to complete and addresses perceptions on various work-related topics, including resources, job satisfaction, unit performance, and leadership.

Unlike the current effort, the survey focuses on perceptions and opinions on multiple topics, rather than specific experiences with abuse and misconduct. Rather than being provided to only students or recent graduates, it actually excludes students, as well as prisoners and personnel on medical hold, among others. The survey is also administered less often than the current effort. Thus, we see no conflicts between the administration of this survey and AETC's.

Criminal Activity Surveys

OSI may administer criminal activity surveys to Air Force personnel. OSI conducts criminal investigations of potential felonies involving Air Force personnel. For example, OSI may investigate murders, sexual assaults, drug use or distribution, thefts, and assaults involving Air Force personnel. As we learned through representatives at AETC, OSI detachments may administer a criminal activity survey to Air Force personnel in units the detachments have jurisdiction over. These surveys are not anonymous and appear to assess Air Force personnel perceptions of safety at the base and in the local area. The questions contained within OSI detachment surveys and the mode of administration for these surveys (e.g., online versus paper-based) is not standardized across Air Force detachments. The survey length may vary, but these surveys appear to ask approximately 15 to 25 questions. In addition, the specific crimes assessed (e.g., drug use) vary across surveys according to OSI needs at the time.

Topics addressed within OSI detachments surveys may overlap with those addressed within the current survey effort. For example, a few of the AETC abuse and misconduct survey items rise to the level of crimes (e.g., physical assault, sexual assault). Additionally, many items within the current survey effort ask individuals to indicate their reporting behaviors and responses to reporting. Similarly, one item from an example OSI detachment survey shared with us asks, "Have you ever reported a crime? To whom? What was the response?" However, overall, there appear to be few similarities between the current survey effort and the types of surveys administered by OSI detachments in these training areas. Available OSI detachment surveys utilize open-ended questions that may address general perceptions of crime in the area, perceived effectiveness of the local OSI detachment, likelihood of reporting general criminal activity, and perceptions of drug use on base. By contrast, the current survey effort uses closed-ended items, is designed to maintain the same questions across survey administrations, addresses experiences with specific types of abuse and misconduct (including those that fall well below OSI's threshold), and specifically focuses on experiences during training.

End-of-Course Surveys

End-of-course surveys are administered to airmen who are completing a course or training pipeline. At the end of a technical training or flying training course (and thus potentially multiple times in a pipeline), students are asked to complete a course critique survey. These surveys address perceptions and experiences specific to training, including perceptions of and recommendations for instruction. For example, a previous end-of-course survey for flying training included the following open-ended question: "Did the academic instruction received at the beginning of the course translate well to the flightline and prepare you to succeed?" In addition, an example end-of-course item from a technical training course is "Test questions adequately measured my knowledge of course objectives" (1 = strongly disagree, 2 = disagree, 3 = agree, 4 = strongly agree, 5 = not applicable). Complete examples of end-of-course feedback surveys were available in AETC Instruction 36-2640 (2014).

Unlike the current survey effort, these end-of-course surveys were not designed to address experiences with abuse and misconduct during training. Rather, the surveys focus on the training content, testing content and timing, instructor provision of training, and perceptions of facilities. Further, unlike the current survey effort, the questions included in specific end-of-course critiques can vary across commanders. Although the Air Force provides guidance regarding these surveys (e.g., AETC Instruction 36-2640, 2014; AETC Instruction 36-2205, 2014), individual commanders can determine the content and mode of administration. Second Air Force did add a few general questions about whether students had witnessed or been the victim of various types of abuse and misconduct, including sexual assault, and whether they reported or would be willing to provide details on any they did witness or experience. If the current survey effort is adopted, those newer questions can be phased out to avoid redundancy and potential competition for student feedback, although AETC may still want to use the opportunity to remind students of their reporting options.

Appendix B. Enlisted Occupational Specialties Available to Non-Prior Service Students

To illustrate the diversity of Air Force enlisted technical training and flying training pipelines, Table B.1 displays the enlisted occupational specialties, or AFSCs,[12] that are available to non-prior service students and the number of new airmen holding those AFSCs in FY 2016. The student population in the technical training and flying training pipelines for these specialties may include some prior service students and retrainees who are changing AFSCs, but the majority of students are non-prior service students. AFSCs with the largest numbers of new airmen include career fields such as security forces (2,782), aircraft armament systems (674), munitions systems (650), tactical aircraft maintenance (581), aerospace propulsion (550), materiel management (521), and aerospace medical service (521). Although the first enlisted aircrew AFSC courses are officially technical training (overseen by Second Air Force), those AFSCs are awarded upon completion of courses in the latter flying training stage (which is overseen by Nineteenth Air Force). Those aircrew AFSCs fall in the operations career group and begin with "1A" and "1U."

---

[12] The Air Force assigns an alphanumeric code to personnel that represents their occupational specialties (AFSCs). There are approximately 100 careers available to entry-level enlisted personnel (U.S. Air Force, 2015a, 2015b). Using AFSC 2T372 to illustrate the classification system, the first character is a number between one and nine, representing the career group or identifier. In the example, the first "2" represents the logistics career group. The second letter represents a career field, which, in this case, is "T" for transportation and vehicle management. The third number specifies the career subdivision, which, in our example, is "3" for vehicle management. The fourth number specifies the skill level for the AFSC; in the example, "7" references the craftsman level. Skill level will vary as the person in a given career field advances in skill; thus, for the remainder of the report, we use an "X" in place of the fourth number to represent possible variation in skill levels. Finally, the last digit represents a specific career field, which is "2" for special vehicle maintenance in our example. In some cases, the AFSC will have a prefix representing specialized qualifications (e.g., "T" for formal training instructor) or a suffix for positions associated with particular equipment or functions (e.g., "A" for special vehicle maintenance of fire trucks).

Table B.1. Career and Identifier Groups, Enlisted AFSCs Available to Non-Prior Service Airmen, and the Number of New Enlisted Airmen in Each Group for FY 2016

Career or Identifier Group	AFSC and Title	FY 2016 Number of Airmen with Less Than One Year of Service
1XXXX (Operations Specialties)	1A0X1 In-Flight Refueling	38
	1A2X1 Aircraft Loadmaster	71
	1A3X1 Airborne Mission Systems Operator	103
	1A8X1 Airborne Cryptologic Language Analyst	181
	1A8X2 Airborne ISR Operator	8
	1A9X1 Special Missions Aviation	36
	1C0X2 Aviation Resource Management	179
	1C1X1 Air Traffic Control	393
	1C2X1 Combat Control	44
	1C3X1 Command Post	131
	1C4X1 Tactical Air Control Party	124
	1C5X1 Command and Control Battle Management Operations	100
	1C6X1 Space Systems Operations	72
	1C7X1 Airfield Management	62
	1C8X1 Ground Radar Systems	66
	1C8X2 Airfield Systems	76
	1N0X1 Operations Intelligence	281
	1N1X1 Geospatial Intelligence	229
	1N2X1 Signals Intelligence Analyst	216
	1N3X1 Cryptologic Language Analyst	293
	1N4X1 Fusion Analyst	282
	1P0X1 Aircrew Flight Equipment	216
	1T0X1 SERE	29
	1T2X1 Pararescue	76
	1U0X1 RPA Sensor Operator	117
	1W0X1 Weather	227
	1W0X2 Special Operations Weather	4
	TOTAL	**3,654**
2XXXX (Logistics Specialties)	2A0X1 Avionics Test Station and Components	109
	2A2X1 SOF/PR Integrated Communication/Navigation/Mission Systems	66
	2A2X2 SOF/PR Integrated Instrument and Flight Control Systems	40
	2A2X3 SOF/PR Integrated Electronic Warfare Systems	38
	2A3X3 Tactical Aircraft Maintenance	581
	2A3X4 Fighter Aircraft Integrated Avionics	257
	2A3X5 Advanced Fighter Aircraft Integrated Avionics	128
	2A3X7 Tactical Aircraft Maintenance	281
	2A3X8 Remotely Piloted Aircraft Maintenance	59
	2A5X1 Airlift/Special Mission Aircraft Maintenance	521
	2A5X2 Helicopter/Tiltrotor Aircraft Maintenance	104
	2A5X3 Mobility Air Forces Electronic Warfare System	0
	2A5X4 Refuel/Bomber Aircraft Maintenance	497
	2A6X1 Aerospace Propulsion	550
	2A6X2 Aerospace Ground Equipment	364
	2A6X3 Aircrew Egress Systems	113
	2A6X4 Aircraft Fuel Systems	242
	2A6X5 Aircraft Hydraulic Systems	193
	2A6X6 Aircraft Electrical and Environmental Systems	336
	2A7X1 Aircraft Metals Technology	95
	2A7X2 Nondestructive Inspection	122
	2A7X3 Aircraft Structural Maintenance	262

Career or Identifier Group	AFSC and Title	FY 2016 Number of Airmen with Less Than One Year of Service
	2A7X5 Low Observable Aircraft Structural Maintenance	98
	2A8X1 Mobility Air Forces Integrated Communication/Navigation/Mission Systems	121
	2A8X2 Mobility Air Forces Integrated Instrument and Flight Control Systems	100
	2A9X1 Bomber/Special Integrated Communication/Navigation/Mission Systems	58
	2A9X2 Bomber/Special Integrated Instrument and Flight Control Systems	47
	2A9X3 Bomber/Special Electronic Warfare and Radar Surveillance Integrated Avionics	111
	2F0X1 Fuels	335
	2G0X1 Logistics Plans	66
	2M0X1 Missile and Space Systems Electronic Maintenance	64
	2M0X2 Missile and Space Systems Maintenance	49
	2M0X3 Missile and Space Facilities	52
	2P0X1 Precision Measurement Equipment Laboratory	74
	2R0X1 Maintenance Management Analysis	57
	2R1X1 Maintenance Management Production	64
	2S0X1 Materiel Management	521
	2T0X1 Traffic Management	216
	2T1X1 Vehicle Operations	314
	2T2X1 Air Transportation	531
	2T3X1 Vehicle and Vehicular Equipment Maintenance	189
	2T3X7 Vehicle Management and Analysis	55
	2W0X1 Munitions Systems	650
	2W1X1 Aircraft Armament Systems	674
	2W2X1 Nuclear Weapons	71
	TOTAL	**9,475**
3XXXX (Support)	3A1X1 Administration	328
	3D0X1 Knowledge Management	101
	3D0X2 Cyber Systems Operations	354
	3D0X3 Cyber Surety	114
	3D0X4 Computer Systems Programming	36
	3D1X1 Client Systems	476
	3D1X2 Cyber Transport Systems	381
	3D1X3 RF Transmission Systems	249
	3D1X4 Spectrum Operations	0
	3D1X7 Cable and Antenna Systems	61
	3E0X1 Electrical Systems	123
	3E0X2 Electrical Power Production	137
	3E1X1 Heating, Ventilation, Air Conditioning, and Refrigeration	126
	3E2X1 Pavements and Construction Equipment	142
	3E3X1 Structural	126
	3E4X1 Water and Fuel Systems Maintenance	152
	3E4X3 Pest Management	38
	3E5X1 Engineering	75
	3E6X1 Operations Management	75
	3E7X1 Fire Protection	258
	3E8X1 Explosive Ordnance Disposal	70
	3E9X1 Emergency Management	49
	3M0X1 Services	420
	3N0X2 Broadcast Journalist	41
	3N0X5 Photojournalist	78
	3N1X1 Regional Band	23
	3N2X1 Premier Band	7

Career or Identifier Group	AFSC and Title	FY 2016 Number of Airmen with Less Than One Year of Service
	3P0X1 Security Forces	2,782
	3S0X1 Personnel	331
	TOTAL	**7,153**
4XXXX (Medical)	4A0X1 Health Services Management	189
	4A1X1 Medical Materiel	92
	4A2X1 Biomedical Equipment	42
	4B0X1 Bioenvironmental Engineering	94
	4C0X1 Mental Health Service	68
	4D0X1 Diet Therapy	15
	4E0X1 Public Health	112
	4H0X1 Cardiopulmonary Lab	25
	4J0X2 Physical Medicine	17
	4M0X1 Aerospace and Operational Physiology	11
	4N0X1 Aerospace Medical Service	521
	4N1X1 Surgical Service	71
	4P0X1 Pharmacy	66
	4R0X1 Diagnostic Imaging	86
	4T0X1 Medical Laboratory	129
	4T0X2 Histopathology	8
	4V0X1 Optometry	15
	4Y0X1 Dental Assistant	181
	4Y0X2 Dental Laboratory	34
	TOTAL	**1,776**
5XXXX (Professional)	5J0X1 Paralegal	49
	TOTAL	**49**
6XXXX (Contracting and Financial)	6C0X1 Contracting	95
	6F0X1 Financial Management and Comptroller	115
	TOTAL	**210**
7XXXX (Special Investigations)	TOTAL	**0**
8XXXX (Special Duty Identifiers)	8D100 Language and Culture Advisor	1
	8G000 Honor Guard	68
	TOTAL	**69**
9XXXX (Reporting Identifiers)	9L000 Interpreter/Translator	0
	9S100 Scientific Applications Specialist	34
	9T000 Basic Enlisted Airman	7000
	9T100 Officer Trainee	23
	9T200 Precadet Assignee	170
	TOTAL	**7,227**

SOURCE: RAND-generated based on raw FY 2016 data provided by the Air Force.

Appendix C. Survey Instrument

This appendix contains the proposed survey instrument and the underlying rationale for an approach to numbering survey items that may not be readily apparent.

A Note on Item Numbering

For consistency across the abuse and misconduct sections, follow-up items about the same topic (e.g., where the abuse occurred) are always labeled with the same number. This strategy reduces risk of merging errors at the data cleaning stage.

For example, follow-up item number two (labeled as FU2 in the survey instrument) always assesses whether the offender was one person or multiple people, regardless of whether it appears in the bullying section (BFU2), sexual harassment section (SHFU2), or sexual assault section (SAFU2). Follow-up item five (FU5) is always the same item asking whether the respondent told another student about the incident; this is true whether it corresponds to a bullying event (BFU5), unprofessional relationship event (URFU5), or hazing incident (HFU5).

As a consequence of this numbering strategy, numbering may not be consecutive in each follow-up section. For example, the sexual assault domain includes a question that assesses the relationship between the student and offender (SAFU3). The survey does not ask this follow-up question in domains where the relationship is already known by definition. For example, bullying is defined as a student-on-student event, therefore we do not ask FU3 in the bullying section, and this number (BFU3) will be missing from the follow-up items on bullying.

The sexual assault section ordering is the least intuitive. It begins with SAFU9 and SAFU10, because these questions had not been asked in the previous sections (where the number conventions FU1 through FU8 had already been used). Because it conceptually made sense to ask these questions *before* the items included in previous sections, they appear first.

Throughout the survey, we chose numbering conventions that prioritized ease and accuracy in the survey cleaning and analysis phase over ease for the casual reader of the instrument presented in this appendix.

Technical Training and Flying Training Proper Conduct Survey

Prepared by the
RAND Corporation

This survey will be programmed and administered electronically, so the on-screen appearance of some questions will differ from that shown in this document (e.g., a question that includes a long list of items might be divided across two pages, or individual questions in a sequence might appear on separate pages rather than the same page).

Notes about survey administration appear in green.
Notes about survey programming appear in red.

Estimated average time to complete the survey is 20–25 minutes. Although the survey appears quite lengthy, most students will not see most questions (e.g., someone who has not been hazed will not be asked follow-up questions about the hazing experience).

Some students may need additional time, depending on their experiences. We recommend providing a total of 45 minutes to take the full survey.

Where it says "[Timeframe]" in the survey, the language will be programmed as follows:
- If technical training or enlisted flying training student (first two responses to TB1), then insert: "SINCE the beginning of technical training for this AFSC"
- If SUPT student and completing primary training (third response to TB1), then insert "SINCE you arrived at this base to attend flying training"
- If SUPT student and completing advanced training (fourth response to TB1), then insert "SINCE you began advanced flying training"

[technical/flying] =
- If TB1 = ("Enlisted aircrew/flying training" or "Primary pilot training" or "Advanced pilot training"), then insert "**flying**"
- If TB1 = "Enlisted technical training", then insert "**technical**"

Survey Administration Script for In-Person Administration

These instructions should be provided verbally before students open the survey on the computer.

Note to survey staff: As students arrive, (1) confirm that they are military personnel in the U.S. Air Force; (2) request that before beginning, they use the restroom, if needed, to minimize disruptions during the survey; and (3) ask them to turn off the ringers, alarms, media volume, and notification alerts on their cell phones, if they have them.

Begin with introductions by the survey staff, and then read the following aloud.

All U.S. Air Force military personnel who are students in your class are being invited to take this survey. If you are enlisted, you may recall taking a very similar survey at the end of BMT.

The purpose of this Air Force–sponsored survey is to provide you and other students a confidential way to let leadership know about any bullying between students, hazing, maltreatment, maltraining, unprofessional relationships, sexual harassment, or unwanted sexual experiences that happen during [technical training/flying training]. The survey also asks why students may or may not report these experiences. Your responses will help leaders understand what is going on in the training environment and where there might be problems so they can address them. Reading some of the questions may cause discomfort, particularly those on unwanted sexual experiences that may seem graphic. You may skip any of these questions that you do not wish to answer, but the more detailed your responses, the more your answers can help. Even if you are unaware of any problems in the training environment, your input on this survey can help the Air Force understand student perceptions of the available reporting channels and support systems in the training environment.

There is only one question on the survey that requires a response to proceed. It asks you to identify whether you are an enlisted Airman in technical or flying training or an officer completing primary or advanced flying training. A response is essential to be able to display the right sets of questions for you, and so that the results can be grouped properly before being reported to AETC leadership.

This survey is confidential. We are not asking for your name, identification number, or your contact information. We are taking additional steps to ensure confidentiality, such as:
- not storing your ID number, IP address, or CAC number
- restricting access to the survey data to the researchers only
- grouping responses together so individual students cannot be identified
- never disclosing individual survey responses, unless we face the highly unusual situation of being required to by a judicial process (such as a subpoena).

Although you may have been required to attend this survey assembly and remain here until the end of the session, **your participation in this survey is completely voluntary.** You may choose to decline to participate. If you decide to start the survey, you can still choose to stop taking it at any time. After the first survey question, you may skip any other questions you do not wish to answer—even every other question on the survey.

There is no penalty if you choose not to participate. You will not be kept from graduating or receive any type of punishment for not completing this survey. Participation will neither help nor harm your future assignments or promotions in the Air Force. Because your responses are confidential, you cannot be penalized for any of your answers.

To avoid distracting others taking the survey, please come down to the front of the room if you need to:

- ask a question about the survey
- get technical help for any problems with your computer or the survey
- receive medical attention.

One of the staff will escort you outside of the classroom to ask you about your concerns.

Also, if you have cell phones, please adjust your cell phone settings so no alarms, ring tones, vibrations, or other notification sounds disrupt the survey.

The survey should take less than 45 minutes to complete. When you have completed the survey, you may read or sit quietly, but please do not disturb others by talking.

We want to emphasize to you that this is not an official channel for reporting abuse or misconduct. If you would like to talk to someone about any abuse or misconduct in order to get help or file an official report, you should contact one of the following directly: someone in your chain of command, a chaplain, a medical provider, the sexual assault response coordinator (SARC), Office of Special Investigations, or Security Forces. Also, some training locations provide critique boxes that you can drop a note into.

Note that the language in this paragraph is required by the Air Force Survey Office: If you enter any written comments on this survey, do NOT provide names of individuals, units, or locations. Remember OPSEC guidance and do not discuss or comment on classified or operationally sensitive information. We cannot provide confidentiality for your comments if you state that you have engaged in, or plan to engage in, criminal misconduct or you threaten to harm yourself or others.

The chaplain and SARC can provide CONFIDENTIAL help following a sexual assault if you have not made an official report and do not want them to tell anyone else what happened.

If you have any questions about the purpose or content of the survey, please contact [insert name and contact information here for survey point of contact.]

Note to survey staff: In the oral instructions, explain here how students should access the survey (e.g., "Please click on the survey icon on your computer desktop—you may now begin").

Regardless of whether you intend to fill out the questionnaire or not, please open the survey on your computer—you'll see the instructions you just heard and then will be able to indicate whether you wish to participate.

Thank you.

Note to survey staff: To prepare for any emergencies or urgent needs, have on hand telephone numbers for medical personnel, computing support, the chaplain on duty, the SARC, and Security Forces.

Instructions and Consent

These instructions will be displayed in writing on the computer to reinforce the verbal delivery of instructions and give students the opportunity to review before agreeing to participate.

All U.S. Air Force military personnel who are students in your class are being invited to take this survey. If you are enlisted, you may recall taking a very similar survey at the end of BMT.

The purpose of this Air Force–sponsored survey is to provide you and other students a <u>confidential</u> way to let leadership know about any bullying between students, hazing, maltreatment, maltraining, unprofessional relationships, sexual harassment, or unwanted sexual experiences that happen during technical training or flying training. The survey also asks why students may or may not report these experiences. Your responses will help leaders understand what is going on in the training environment and where there might be problems so they can address them. Reading some of the questions may cause discomfort, particularly those on unwanted sexual experiences that may seem graphic. You may skip any of these questions that you do not wish to answer, but the more detailed your responses, the more your answers can help. Even if you are unaware of any problems in the training environment, your input on this survey can help the Air Force understand student perceptions of the available reporting channels and support systems in the training environment.

There is only one question on the survey that require a response to proceed. It asks you to identify whether you are an enlisted Airman in technical or flying training or an officer completing primary or advanced flying training. A response is essential to be able to display the right sets of questions for you, and so that the results can be grouped properly before being reported to AETC leadership.

This survey is confidential. We are not asking for your name, identification number, or your contact information. We are taking additional steps to ensure confidentiality, such as:
- not storing your ID number, IP address, or CAC number
- restricting access to the survey data to the researchers only
- grouping responses together so individual students cannot be identified
- never disclosing individual survey responses, unless we face the highly unusual situation of being required to by a judicial process (such as a subpoena).

Although you may have been required to attend this survey assembly and remain here until the end of the session, **your participation in this survey is completely voluntary.** If you decide to start the survey, you can still choose to stop taking it at any time. After the first survey question, you may skip any other questions you do not wish to answer—even every other question on the survey.

There is no penalty if you choose not to participate. You will not be kept from graduating or receive any type of punishment for not completing this survey. Participation will neither help nor harm your future assignments or promotions in the Air Force. Because your responses are confidential, you cannot be penalized for any of your answers.

Also, please adjust your cell phone settings so no alarms, ring tones, vibrations, or other notification sounds disrupt the survey.

The survey should take less than 45 minutes to complete. When you have completed the survey, you may read or sit quietly, but please do not disturb others by talking.

We want to emphasize to you that this is not an official channel for reporting abuse or misconduct. If you would like to talk to someone about any abuse or misconduct in order to get help or file an official report, you should contact one of the following directly: someone in your chain of command, a chaplain, a medical provider, the sexual assault response coordinator (SARC), Office of Special Investigations, or Security Forces. Also, some training locations provide critique boxes that you can drop a note into.

The chaplain and SARC can provide CONFIDENTIAL help following a sexual assault if you have not made an official report and do not want them to tell anyone else what happened.

If you have any questions about the purpose or content of the survey, please contact [insert name and contact information here for survey point of contact.]

Consent1. Please indicate whether you do or do not consent to participate in this survey:
○ I have read the above statement about this survey and volunteer to participate.
○ I don't want to participate in this survey, but I am in a group and don't want anyone to know that I am opting out. Please allow me to advance through the survey without filling any of it out.
○ I do not want to participate in this survey, and I would like to exit the survey now.

If student selects first response, skip to Section I. If student selects second response, TB1=enlisted technical training AND skip to TB2. If student selects third response, continue.

Consent2. We understand that you prefer not to participate, and we respect your decision. Would you be willing to share the reason(s) that you don't want to complete the survey? *Select all that apply.*

☐ The survey doesn't apply to me.
☐ The survey is too personal.
☐ I'm worried my privacy won't be protected.
☐ It will probably be boring.
☐ I'm worried the survey topics will upset me.
☐ I'd rather do something else.
☐ I don't have enough time.
☐ I don't believe it will make a difference.
☐ I don't like taking surveys in general.
☐ Leaders in the training environment discouraged me from participating.
☐ Other students discouraged me from participating.
☐ I prefer not to say.
☐ Other

[Skip to FinalScreen.]

Section I: Training and Background

Students will not see banner titles.

[Programming note: With the exception of TB1, students should be allowed to skip any questions or even all remaining questions on the survey. For all routing in the survey, a skipped question should be treated as if the student responded "no" or "never" to the question, unless otherwise indicated. For example, if they skipped all the "experience" questions in any domain, they should move forward in the survey as if they answered "never" to all of those questions.]

Before you begin the survey, we would like to ask you a few questions about your training and background so we can group your responses correctly and provide leadership with more effective feedback. The first question is the only question on the survey that require a response to proceed. Your responses enable the survey to display the right sets of questions for you. If you do not want to provide this information, you may close your browser to exit the survey now.

TB1. What training have you been completing?
- o Enlisted aircrew/flying training
- o Enlisted technical training
- o Primary pilot training
- o Advanced pilot training
- o *Add "Other officer flying training" here if survey expands to include it.*
- o *Add "Officer technical training" here if survey expands to include it.*

[Programming note: Students who select one of the first two responses are enlisted. Students who select any of the other responses are officers.]

TB2. Are you a . . .
- o Non-prior service student: You are entering military service for the first time.
- o Prior-service student: You previously separated from the military but are re-entering and retraining now.
- o Retrainee: You already had an Air Force Specialty Code (AFSC), never left the Air Force, and are currently retraining for a new AFSC or shred.
- o Prefer not to answer. [Programming note: if this option is selected, show the non-prior service student responses for the remainder of the survey]

TB3. [Ask Enlisted only] **For which career group are you training?**
- ○ Operations (AFSCs beginning with 1)
- ○ Logistics and maintenance (AFSCs beginning with 2)
- ○ Support (AFSCs beginning with 3)
- ○ Medical (AFSCs beginning with 4)
- ○ Acquisition (AFSCs beginning with 6)
- ○ Professional, special investigations, or special duty (smaller AFSCs beginning with 5, 7 or 8)
- ○ Other (AFSCs beginning with 9)

TB4. How many months have you been in [technical/flying] **training?** [Drop-down menu with integer values from 1 to "24 or more."]

TB5. On which installation are you currently training? [Drop-down menu with all training locations being surveyed]

TB6a. Did you train for this AFSC at any other installations? Please do not include [if Enlisted, display: "BMT,"] previous assignments or previous AFSC training.
- ○ Yes
- ○ No

[Ask only if TB6a = Yes] **TB6b. Where else did you train for this AFSC?** Please do not include [if Enlisted, display: "BMT,"] previous assignments or previous AFSC training. *Select all that apply.* Expand list as necessary to include all major training locations for AFSC pipelines being surveyed.
- ☐ Columbus
- ☐ Defense Language Institute
- ☐ Fairchild
- ☐ Goodfellow
- ☐ Keesler
- ☐ Lackland
- ☐ Laughlin
- ☐ Randolph
- ☐ Sheppard
- ☐ Vance
- ☐ Vandenberg
- ☐ Other

TB7. How do you describe yourself?
- ○ Man
- ○ Woman
- ○ Continue without answering this question

Section II: Bullying

Bullying involves situations in which a person is singled out and repeatedly exposed to negative acts (e.g., physical harm, ridicule) over a period of time. It often involves an imbalance of power, so a person may have difficulty defending himself or herself against the mistreatment.

Below is a list of things another student may have done to bully you [Timeframe]. For these questions, please don't consider anything that happened to other students. Think only about whether these things happened to you.

For this first set of items, think about how often you were bullied via electronic methods of communication (text messaging, email, instant messaging, websites, social networking sites, etc.).

[Timeframe], how many times did another student . . .	Never	Once or Twice	A Few Times	Weekly	Daily
CB1. Say something to you that was insulting or humiliating using electronic communication?	O	O	O	O	O
CB2. Send a message about you that was insulting or humiliating using electronic communication?	O	O	O	O	O
CB3. Post something publicly about you that was insulting or humiliating using electronic communication?	O	O	O	O	O
CB4. Encourage other students to turn against you using electronic communication?	O	O	O	O	O
CB5. Threaten you using electronic communication?	O	O	O	O	O
CB6. Try to get you into trouble with an instructor using electronic communication?	O	O	O	O	O
S1. Please select "A Few Times" for this item to help us confirm that students are reading these items. [Screening item]	O	O	O	O	O

For the next set of items, think about how often you were __bullied _offline_: in person, on a phone call, or through other nonelectronic methods of communication.__					
[Timeframe], **how many times did another student . . .**	*Never*	*Once or Twice*	*A Few Times*	*Weekly*	*Daily*
B1. Say something about you that was insulting or humiliating?	o	o	o	o	o
B2. Send others a note or post something publicly about you that was insulting or humiliating? For example, post a note on a locker, wall, or bulletin board.	o	o	o	o	o
B3. Encourage other students to turn against you?	o	o	o	o	o
B4. Try to put you in a humiliating situation, or play abusive pranks or tricks on you?	o	o	o	o	o
B5. Try to get you into trouble with an instructor?	o	o	o	o	o
B6. Steal something from you?	o	o	o	o	o
B7. Threaten you?	o	o	o	o	o
B8. Hit or kick you?	o	o	o	o	o
B9. Grab or shove you forcefully?	o	o	o	o	o
B10. Destroy your property?	o	o	o	o	o

BFU1a. Are you aware of students doing any of these bullying behaviors to <u>other</u> students [Timeframe]? *Select all that apply.*
- ☐ No.
- ☐ Yes, I saw this happen.
- ☐ Yes, a student told me this happened to them.
- ☐ Yes, an [if enlisted non-prior service student, then display "MTL,"] instructor, or other leader informed me of this happening.
- ☐ Yes, I heard about this happening from someone else.

[If "No," skip to question BC1. Else skip to BR1.]

BFU2. On the previous pages, you indicated that at least one of these bullying situations happened to you personally. How many people did these things to you?
- o One person
- o More than one person
- o I don't know

[Ask only if TB6a = Yes] **BFU4. At which installation were you assigned when this situation occurred?** *If it happened on more than one installation, select all that apply.* [Display only installations selected in TB5 and TB6b]

BFU5. Did you tell any other students about any of these situations that happened to you?
- o Yes, I told another student.
- o No, I did not tell another student.

BFU1b. Are you aware of students doing any of these bullying behaviors to <u>other</u> students [Timeframe]? *Select all that apply.*
[Note: Questions BFU1a and BFU1b are identical.]
- ☐ No.
- ☐ Yes, I saw this happen.
- ☐ Yes, a student told me this happened to them.
- ☐ Yes, an [if enlisted non-prior service student, then display "MTL,"] instructor or other leader informed me of this happening.
- ☐ Yes, I heard about this happening from someone else.

[GO TO QUESTION BR1.]

For the situations in this section that happened to you personally, or that you were aware of happening to another student . . .

BR1. Did you report any of the behaviors in this section to any of the sources below? *Select all that apply or indicate that you did not report any incidents.*

☐ I told [If enlisted, then display "a student in an Airman Leader position (for example, a bay chief, teal rope, or red rope)"; if officer, then display "a student in a leadership position, such as a Senior Ranking Officer"].

☐ [If enlisted non-prior service, then display: "I told an MTL."]

☐ I told an instructor.

☐ I told someone else in my chain of command.

☐ I told an officer or NCO outside of my chain of command.

☐ I told someone in Air Force law enforcement: Office of Special Investigations (OSI) or Security Forces (SF).

☐ I told the Inspector General (IG).

☐ I told the Equal Opportunity (EO) Office.

☐ I wrote it down on paper and put it in a critique box/drop box.

☐ [If technical training student, then "I used the 2 AF hotline to report it."

☐ I told a chaplain or chaplain assistant.

☐ I told the SARC (sexual assault response coordinator).

☐ I told an Air Force therapist or counselor.

☐ I told an Air Force doctor, nurse, or other medical professional.

☐ I told a staff member of the Airman and Family Readiness Center.

☐ Other

☐ I did not report any incidents.

IF THEY SELECTED "I DID NOT REPORT ANY INCIDENTS," GO TO QUESTION BR2 BELOW.	IF THEY SELECTED THAT THEY REPORTED TO ANY SOURCE, GO TO QUESTION BR4 BELOW.
BR2. Please select the items below that describe why you did not report any incidents. *Select all that apply. More options will be shown on the next page.* ☐ I knew someone had already reported it. ☐ I thought someone else would report it. ☐ I only heard about it, so I wasn't sure if it was true. ☐ I didn't think there was anything wrong with it. ☐ I don't believe people should tell on one another. ☐ I didn't think anything would be done if I reported it. ☐ I didn't want anyone else to know it happened. ☐ I didn't think it was serious enough to report. ☐ I didn't think I would be believed. ☐ I was afraid reporting might cause trouble for my flight or class. ☐ I thought that reporting might delay my graduation or moving to my first duty assignment. *Note: More options will be shown on the next page.* ********** PAGE BREAK **********	If you reported one incident, please answer the next questions about that one report. If you reported more than one incident, please think of the incident that you consider the most serious. **BR4. How seriously do you feel your report was taken?** ○ Very seriously ○ Somewhat seriously ○ Not very seriously ○ Not at all seriously ○ I don't know

Please select the items below that describe why you did not report any incidents. *Select all that apply.*

- ☐ I handled it myself.
- ☐ I decided to put up with it.
- ☐ I didn't want the person who did it to get in trouble for it.
- ☐ I knew of others who were treated poorly for reporting.
- ☐ I didn't think my report would be kept confidential.
- ☐ I wanted to report it anonymously but didn't know a safe way to do that.
- ☐ I was afraid of getting into trouble for something I shouldn't have been doing.
- ☐ I was afraid the person who did it or their friends would try to get even with me for reporting.
- ☐ I was afraid students would punish me or mock me for reporting.
- ☐ I was afraid instructors would punish me or mock me for reporting.
- ☐ [If enlisted non-prior service, then:] I was afraid MTLs would punish me or mock me for reporting.
- ☐ Other

GO TO THE NEXT PAGE (QUESTION BC1).

BR5. What happened with the behavior after you reported it?
- ○ The behavior didn't happen again.
- ○ The behavior continued or got worse.
- ○ I don't know: The behavior was happening to someone else.

BR6. What happened to you after the report? *Select all that apply.*
- ☐ I got support to help me deal with what happened.
- ☐ The person I reported it to praised me for reporting.
- ☐ I got in trouble for my own misbehavior or infraction.
- ☐ The person who did it or their friends tried to get even with me for reporting.
- ☐ Students tried to get even with me for reporting.
- ☐ Instructors tried to get even with me for reporting.
- ☐ [If enlisted non-prior service, then:] MTLs tried to get even with me for reporting.
- ☐ None of the above happened to me.

BR7. If you could do it over, would you still decide to report the incident?
- ○ Yes
- ○ No

GO TO THE NEXT PAGE (QUESTION BC1).

Climate for Bullying: Average Items to Form Scale

AETC Student Rules of Conduct state that students are required to act in a respectful, professional manner at all times, including when interacting with other students. This means that bullying behaviors are not acceptable. Examples of bullying include calling another student insulting names, hitting another student, and spreading lies about a student.

The following questions ask you about the extent to which rules against <u>bullying behaviors</u> are enforced during Air Force [technical/flying] training. **For questions about [technical/flying] training leadership, we are referring to those Air Force NCOs and officers with training leadership responsibilities (for example, squadron commanders, directors of operations, flight commanders, flight chiefs, superintendents, and first sergeants).** Please respond based on what you believe about your leadership, even if you do not have direct knowledge about their attitudes or actions on this specific type of behavior.

	Strongly Disagree	*Disagree*	*Neither Disagree nor Agree*	*Agree*	*Strongly Agree*
BC1. Air Force training leadership makes honest efforts to stop bullying.	○	○	○	○	○
BC2. Air Force training leadership encourages the reporting of bullying.	○	○	○	○	○
BC3. Air Force training leadership takes actions to prevent bullying.	○	○	○	○	○
BC4. Air Force training leadership would correct or discipline a student who bullies another student.	○	○	○	○	○

Section III: Maltreatment/Maltraining

Students will not see banner titles.

Below is a list of things an [if enlisted non-prior service, then "MTL or"] instructor may have done during [technical/flying] training. For these questions, please don't consider anything that happened to other students. Think only about whether these things happened to you.

[Timeframe], how many times did an [if enlisted non-prior service, then "MTL or"] instructor . . .	Never	Once or Twice	A Few Times	Weekly	Daily
M1. Single you out for discipline when others made the same mistake?	o	o	o	o	o
M2. Single you out to quit or leave your training?	o	o	o	o	o
M3. Assign you activities unrelated to training objectives or Air Force requirements (for example, asked you to do his/her personal errands)?	o	o	o	o	o
M4. Mishandle your property in response to an infraction (e.g., dump your things out of a bag or drawer)?	o	o	o	o	o
M5. Encourage you to mistreat another student?	o	o	o	o	o
S2. Please select "Weekly" for this item to help us confirm that students are reading these items. [Screening item]	o	o	o	o	o
M6. Call you insulting names (for example, "ugly" or "idiot")?	o	o	o	o	o
M7. Make negative comments about your race, ethnicity, religion, gender, or sexual orientation?	o	o	o	o	o
M8. Threaten to hurt you?	o	o	o	o	o
M9. Intentionally damage something of yours?	o	o	o	o	o
M10. When angry, hit or punch an object (for example, a wall, window, table, or other object)?	o	o	o	o	o
M11. Throw something at you with the intent to hurt you?	o	o	o	o	o
M12. Use inappropriate physical force with you (for example, hit, grab, or shove you)?	o	o	o	o	o

114

IF A STUDENT MARKED "Never" FOR ALL OF THE ABOVE ITEMS, GO TO QUESTION MFU1a BELOW. ↓	IF A STUDENT INDICATED THAT THEY EXPERIENCED AT LEAST ONE OF THE ABOVE ITEMS, GO TO QUESTION MFU2 BELOW ↓

MFU1a. Are you aware of any [If enlisted non-prior service, then "**MTLs or**"] **instructors doing any of these things to <u>other</u> students** [Timeframe]? *Select all that apply.*

☐ No.
☐ Yes, I saw this happen.
☐ Yes, a student told me this happened to them.
☐ Yes, an [If enlisted non-prior service, then "MTL,"] instructor or other leader informed me of this happening.
☐ Yes, I heard about this happening from someone else.

[IF "NO," SKIP TO QUESTION MC1. ELSE SKIP TO MR1.]

MFU2. On the previous page, you indicated that at least one of these situations happened to you personally. How many people did these things to you?
   ○ One person
   ○ More than one person

MFU3_enlist. [If enlisted non-prior service, then display:] **Were they a(n) . . . ?** *Select all that apply.*
☐ MTL
☐ Instructor

MFU3_officer. [If officer, then display:] **Was the instructor(s) a First Assignment Instructor Pilot (FAIP)?**
   ○ No
   ○ Yes

[Ask only If TB6a = Yes] **MFU4. At which installation were you assigned when this situation occurred?** If it happened on more than one installation, check all that apply. *[Display only installations selected in TB5 and TB6b]*

MFU5. Did you tell any other students about any of these situations that happened to you?
☐ Yes, I told another student.
☐ No, I did not tell another student.

MFU1b. Are you aware of any [If enlisted non-prior service, then "MTLs or"] **instructors doing any of these things to <u>other</u> students** [Timeframe]? *Select all that apply.*
[Note: Questions MFU1a and MFU1b are identical.]
☐ No.
☐ Yes, I saw this happen.
☐ Yes, a student told me this happened to them.
☐ Yes, an [If enlisted non-prior service, then "MTL,"] instructor or other leader informed me of this happening.
☐ Yes, I heard about this happening from someone else.

MR1. Did you report any of the [if enlisted, then "**MTL or**"] **instructor behaviors in this section to any of the sources below?** *Select all that apply or indicate that you did not report any incidents.*

- ☐ I told [If enlisted, then display "a student in an Airman Leader position (for example, a bay chief, teal rope, or red rope)"; if officer, then display "a student in a leadership position, such as a Senior Ranking Officer"].
- ☐ [If enlisted non-prior service, then display: "I told an MTL."]
- ☐ I told an instructor.
- ☐ I told someone else in my chain of command.
- ☐ I told an officer or NCO outside of my chain of command.
- ☐ I told someone in Air Force law enforcement: Office of Special Investigations (OSI) or Security Forces (SF).
- ☐ I told the Inspector General (IG).
- ☐ I told the Equal Opportunity (EO) Office.
- ☐ I wrote it down on paper and put it in a critique box/drop box.
- ☐ [If technical training student, then "I used the 2 AF hotline to report it."]
- ☐ I told a chaplain or chaplain assistant.
- ☐ I told the SARC (sexual assault response coordinator).
- ☐ I told an Air Force therapist or counselor.
- ☐ I told an Air Force doctor, nurse, or other medical professional.
- ☐ I told a staff member at the Airman and Family Readiness Center.
- ☐ Other
- ☐ **I did not report any incidents.**

IF THEY SELECTED "I DID NOT REPORT ANY INCIDENTS," GO TO QUESTION MR2 BELOW.	IF THEY SELECTED THAT THEY REPORTED TO ANY SOURCE, GO TO QUESTION MR4 BELOW.

MR2. Please select the items below that describe why you did not report any incidents. *Select all that apply. More options will be shown on the next page.*

- ☐ I knew someone had already reported it.
- ☐ I thought someone else would report it.
- ☐ I only heard about it, so I wasn't sure if it was true.
- ☐ I didn't think there was anything wrong with it.
- ☐ I don't believe people should tell on one another.
- ☐ I didn't think anything would be done if I reported it.
- ☐ I didn't want anyone else to know it happened.
- ☐ I didn't think it was serious enough to report.
- ☐ I didn't think I would be believed.

If you reported one incident, please answer the next questions about that one report. If you reported more than one incident, please think of the incident that you consider the most serious.

MR4. How seriously do you feel your report was taken?
- ○ Very seriously
- ○ Somewhat seriously
- ○ Not very seriously
- ○ Not at all seriously
- ○ I don't know

MR5. What happened with the behavior after you reported it?
- ○ The behavior didn't happen again.
- ○ The behavior continued or got worse.
- ○ I don't know: The behavior was happening to someone else.

- ☐ I was afraid reporting might cause trouble for my flight or class.
- ☐ I thought that reporting might delay my graduation or moving to my first duty assignment.

Note: More options will be shown on the next page.

********** PAGE BREAK **********

Please select the items below that describe why you did not report any incidents. *Select all that apply.*

- ☐ I handled it myself.
- ☐ I decided to put up with it.
- ☐ I didn't want the person who did it to get in trouble for it.
- ☐ I knew of others who were treated poorly for reporting.
- ☐ I was afraid the person who did it or their friends would try to get even with me for reporting.
- ☐ I didn't think my report would be kept confidential.
- ☐ I wanted to report it anonymously but didn't know a safe way to do that.
- ☐ I was afraid of getting into trouble for something I shouldn't have been doing.
- ☐ I was afraid students would punish me or mock me for reporting.
- ☐ I was afraid instructors would punish me or mock me for reporting.
- ☐ [If enlisted non-prior service, then:]I was afraid MTLs would punish me or mock me for reporting.
- ☐ Other

GO TO THE NEXT PAGE (QUESTION MC1).

MR6. What happened to you after the report?
Select all that apply.

- ☐ I got support to help me deal with what happened.
- ☐ The person I reported it to praised me for reporting.
- ☐ I got in trouble for my own misbehavior or infraction.
- ☐ The person who did it or their friends tried to get even with me for reporting.
- ☐ Students tried to get even with me for reporting.
- ☐ Instructors tried to get even with me for reporting.
- ☐ [If enlisted non-prior service, then:]MTLs tried to get even with me for reporting.
- ☐ None of the above happened to me.

MR7. If you could do it over, would you still decide to report the incident?

- ○ Yes
- ○ No

GO TO THE NEXT PAGE (QUESTION MC1).

Climate for Maltreatment/Maltraining: Average Items to Form Scale

Air Force policies establish approved training methods and appropriate interactions [If enlisted non-prior service, then "between MTLs and students or"] between instructors and students. [If enlisted non-prior service, then "MTLs or"] Instructors making students perform humiliating tasks, requiring physical exercise in unsafe conditions, threatening or hitting students, and using crude or offensive language are examples of policy violations that the Air Force calls maltreatment or maltraining.

The following questions ask you about the extent to which policies against <u>maltreatment and maltraining</u> are enforced during [technical/flying] training. **For questions about [technical/flying] training leadership, we are referring to those Air Force NCOs and officers with training leadership responsibilities (for example, squadron commanders, directors of operations, flight commanders, flight chiefs, superintendents, and first sergeants).** Please respond based on what you believe about your leadership, even if you do not have direct knowledge about their attitudes or actions on this specific type of behavior.

	Strongly Disagree	Disagree	Neither Disagree nor Agree	Agree	Strongly Agree
MC1. Air Force training leadership makes honest efforts to stop maltreatment and maltraining.	○	○	○	○	○
MC2. Air Force training leadership encourages the reporting of maltreatment and maltraining.	○	○	○	○	○
MC3. Air Force training leadership takes actions to prevent maltreatment and maltraining.	○	○	○	○	○
MC4. Air Force training leadership would correct or discipline an [If enlisted non-prior service, then "MTL or"] instructor who engages in maltreatment or maltraining.	○	○	○	○	○

Section IV: Unprofessional Relationships
Students will not see banner titles.

Below is a list of some other things an [If enlisted, "officer or"] [if enlisted non-prior service student, then "MTL or"] instructor may have done [Timeframe]. For these questions, please don't consider anything that happened to other students. Think only about whether these things happened to you.

[Timeframe], how many times did an [If enlisted, "officer or"] [if enlisted non-prior service student, then "MTL or"] instructor . . .	Never	Once or Twice	A Few Times	Weekly	Daily
UR1. Ask you to "just call me by my first name"?	○	○	○	○	○
UR2. Drink alcohol with you outside of Air Force–sponsored and commander-authorized events?	○	○	○	○	○
UR3. Offer you illegal drugs or prescription medication that had not been prescribed for you?	○	○	○	○	○
UR4. Flirt with you?	○	○	○	○	○
UR5. Give you more privileges than others even though you didn't earn them?	○	○	○	○	○
UR6. Share sexual jokes with you?	○	○	○	○	○
UR7. Meet you alone for personal reasons?	○	○	○	○	○
UR8. Talk about his or her sex life with you?	○	○	○	○	○
UR9. Talk about your sex life with you?	○	○	○	○	○
UR10. Talk about dating you?	○	○	○	○	○
UR11. Offer to give or loan you money or pay for something for you?	○	○	○	○	○
UR12. Ask you to give or loan them money or buy something?	○	○	○	○	○
S3. Please select "Daily" for this item to help us confirm that students are reading these items. [Screening item]	○	○	○	○	○

119

[Timeframe], **how many times did an** [if enlisted, "**officer or**"] [if enlisted non-prior service student, then "**MTL or**"] **instructor** . . .	*Never*	*Once or Twice*	*A Few Times*	*Weekly*	*Daily*
UR13. Use your cell phone or other personal property without your permission?	○	○	○	○	○
UR14. Have a romantic relationship with you?	○	○	○	○	○
UR15. Engage in any type of sexual activity with you?	○	○	○	○	○

[If enlisted non-prior service student, then]
URFU7a. Did a retrainee or prior-service student do any of these things to you? For example, flirt with you, loan you money, have a personal relationship with you?

☐ No
☐ Yes, a retrainee did.
☐ Yes, a prior-service student did.

URFU1a. Are you aware of an [if enlisted, "**officer or**"] [if enlisted non-prior service student, then "**MTL or**"] **instructor doing any of these things to other students** [Timeframe]? *Select all that apply.*

☐ No.
☐ Yes, I saw this happen.
☐ Yes, a student told me this happened to them.
☐ Yes, an [if enlisted non-prior service student, then "MTL,"] instructor or other leader informed me of this happening.
☐ Yes, I heard about this happening from someone else.

[IF "NO," SKIP TO QUESTION URC1. ELSE SKIP TO URR1.]

URFU2. On the previous page, you indicated that at least one of these situations happened to you personally. How many people did these things to you?
○ One person
○ More than one person

URFU3_enlist. [If enlisted, then ask:] **Were they a(n) . . . ?** *Select all that apply.*
☐ Officer
☐ [If enlisted non-prior service student, then] MTL
☐ Instructor

URFU3_officer. [If officer, then ask:] **Was the instructor(s) a First Assignment Instructor Pilot (FAIP)?**
○ No
○ Yes

[Ask only If TB6a = Yes] **URFU4. At which installation were you assigned when this situation occurred?** If it happened on more than one installation, check all that apply. *[Display only installations selected in TB5 and TB6b]*

URFU5. Did you tell any other students about any of these situations that happened to you?
○ Yes, I told another student.
○ No, I did not tell another student.

[If enlisted non-prior service student, then] **URFU7b. You indicated that an officer, MTL or instructor did one of these things to you.** For example, flirted with you, loaned you money, had a personal relationship with you.

Apart from that situation, did a retrainee or prior-service student do any of these things to you?
☐ No
☐ Yes, a retrainee did.
☐ Yes, a prior-service student did

	URFU1b. Are you aware of an [if enlisted, "**officer or**"] [if enlisted non-prior service student, then "**MTL retrainee or**"] **instructor doing any of these things to other students** [Timeframe]? *Select all that apply.* [Note: Questions URFU1a and URFU1b are identical.]
	☐ No.
	☐ Yes, I saw this happen.
	☐ Yes, a student told me this happened to them.
	☐ Yes, an [If enlisted non-prior service, then "MTL,"], instructor or other leader informed me of this happening.
	☐ Yes, I heard about this happening from someone else.
	GO TO QUESTION URR1.

For the situations in this section that happened to you personally, or that you were aware of happening to another student . . .

URR1. Did you report any of the [if enlisted, "**officer or**"] [if enlisted non-prior service student, then "**MTL or**"] **instructor behaviors in this section to any of the sources below?** *Select all that apply or indicate that you did not report any incidents.*

☐ I told [If enlisted, then display "a student in an Airman Leader position (for example, a bay chief, teal rope, or red rope)" If officer, then display "a student in a leadership position, such as a Senior Ranking Officer"].

☐ [If enlisted non-prior service student, then display: "I told an MTL."]

☐ I told an instructor.

☐ I told someone else in my chain of command.

☐ I told an officer or NCO outside of my chain of command.

☐ I told someone in Air Force law enforcement: Office of Special Investigations (OSI) or Security Forces (SF).

☐ I told the Inspector General (IG).

☐ I told the Equal Opportunity (EO) Office.

☐ I wrote it down on paper and put it in a critique box/drop box.

☐ [If technical training student, then "I used the 2 AF hotline to report it."]

☐ I told a chaplain or chaplain assistant.

☐ I told the SARC (sexual assault response coordinator).

☐ I told an Air Force therapist or counselor.

☐ I told an Air Force doctor, nurse, or other medical professional.

☐ I told a staff member at the Airman and Family Readiness Center.

☐ Other

☐ **I did not report any incidents.**

IF THEY SELECTED "I DID NOT REPORT ANY INCIDENTS," GO TO QUESTION URR2 BELOW.	IF THEY SELECTED THAT THEY REPORTED TO ANY SOURCE, GO TO QUESTION URR4 BELOW.
URR2. Please select the items below that describe why you did not report any incidents. *Select all that apply. More options will be shown on the next page.* ☐ I knew someone had already reported it. ☐ I thought someone else would report it. ☐ I only heard about it, so I wasn't sure if it was true. ☐ I didn't think there was anything wrong with it. ☐ I don't believe people should tell on one another. ☐ I didn't think anything would be done if I reported it. ☐ I didn't want anyone else to know it happened. ☐ I didn't think it was serious enough to report. ☐ I didn't think I would be believed. ☐ I was afraid reporting might cause trouble for my flight or class.	If you reported one incident, please answer the next questions about that one report. If you reported more than one incident, please think of the incident that you consider the most serious. **URR4. How seriously do you feel your report was taken?** 　○ Very seriously 　○ Somewhat seriously 　○ Not very seriously 　○ Not at all seriously 　○ I don't know

☐ I thought that reporting might delay my graduation or moving to my first duty assignment.

Note: More options will be shown on the next page.

********** PAGE BREAK **********

Please select the items below that describe why you did not report any incidents. *Select all that apply.*

☐ I handled it myself.

☐ I decided to put up with it.

☐ I didn't want the person who did it to get in trouble for it.

☐ I knew of others who were treated poorly for reporting.

☐ I was afraid the person who did it or their friends would try to get even with me for reporting.

☐ I didn't think my report would be kept confidential.

☐ I wanted to report it anonymously but didn't know a safe way to do that.

☐ I was afraid of getting into trouble for something I shouldn't have been doing.

☐ I was afraid students would punish me or mock me for reporting.

☐ I was afraid instructors would punish me or mock me for reporting.

☐ [If enlisted non-prior service student, then]I was afraid MTLs would punish me or mock me for reporting.

☐ Other

GO TO THE NEXT PAGE (QUESTION URC1).

URR5. What happened with the behavior after you reported it?

o The behavior didn't happen again.

o The behavior continued or got worse.

o I don't know: The behavior was happening to someone else.

URR6. What happened to you after the report? *Select all that apply.*

☐ I got support to help me deal with what happened.

☐ The person I reported it to praised me for reporting.

☐ I got in trouble for my own misbehavior or infraction.

☐ The person who did it or their friends tried to get even with me for reporting.

☐ Students tried to get even with me for reporting.

☐ Instructors tried to get even with me for reporting.

☐ [If enlisted non-prior service student, then:]MTLs tried to get even with me for reporting.

☐ None of the above happened to me.

URR7. If you could do it over, would you still decide to report the incident?

o Yes

o No

GO TO THE NEXT PAGE (QUESTION URC1).

Climate for Unprofessional Relationships: Average Items to Form Scale

Air Force policies state that [If enlisted, "**officers and**"] [If enlisted non-prior service student, then "**MTLs and**"] **instructors** are not allowed to develop friendships or romantic relationships with students or show favoritism to specific students. [If enlisted, then "Similarly, prior service enlisted students and retrainees are not allowed to develop friendships or romantic relationships with non-prior service students."] The Air Force deems these unprofessional relationships, even if they develop only through cards, letters, emails, phone calls, the Internet, or instant messaging. Examples of behaviors that violate Air Force professional-relationship policies include [If enlisted non-prior service student, then "MTLs or"] instructors giving individual students special privileges as well as [If enlisted non-prior service student, then "MTLs or"] instructors dating, drinking alcohol with, or sharing sexual stories with students.

The following questions ask you about the extent to which policies against <u>unprofessional relationships</u> are enforced at [technical/flying] training. **For questions about** [technical/flying] **training leaders, we are referring to those Air Force NCOs and officers with training leadership responsibilities (for example, squadron commanders, directors of operations, flight commanders, flight chiefs, superintendents, and first sergeants).** Please respond based on what you believe about your leadership, even if you do not have direct knowledge about their attitudes or actions on this specific type of behavior.

	Strongly Disagree	Disagree	Neither Disagree nor Agree	Agree	Strongly Agree
URC1. Air Force training leadership makes honest efforts to stop unprofessional relationships.	○	○	○	○	○
URC2. Air Force training leadership encourages the reporting of unprofessional relationships.	○	○	○	○	○
URC3. Air Force training leadership takes actions to prevent unprofessional relationships.	○	○	○	○	○
URC4. Air Force training leadership would correct or discipline someone who engages in an unprofessional relationship.	○	○	○	○	○

Section V: Sexual Harassment

Students will not see banner titles.

As requested by AETC, this section has minimally adapted the DoD-approved assessment instrument for sexual harassment. Because it is standardized for all DoD uses, changes should not be made to the items unless the change is absolutely critical.

In this section, you will be asked about several things that someone from work might have done to you that were upsetting or offensive, and that happened [Timeframe].

When the questions say "someone from work," please include any person you have contact with as part of your military duties. "Someone from work" could be a student, supervisor, someone above or below you in rank, or a civilian employee or contractor. They could be in your unit or in other units.

These things may have occurred on duty or off duty, on base or off base. Please include them as long as the person who did them to you was someone from work.

Remember, all the information you share will be kept confidential.

Programming note: Please place the "Someone from work" definition box above sexual harassment screening items.

"Someone from work" includes any person you have contact with as part of your military duties. "Someone from work" could be a student, supervisor, someone above or below you in rank, or a civilian employee /contractor. They could be in your unit or in other units. These things may have occurred off duty or off base. Please include them as long as the person who did them to you was someone from work.

	No	Yes
SH1. [Timeframe], did someone from work repeatedly tell sexual "jokes" that made you uncomfortable, angry, or upset?	○	○
SH2. [Timeframe], did someone from work embarrass, anger, or upset you by repeatedly suggesting that you do not act like a [If TB7= man, display: "man". If TB7= woman, display "woman". If TB7 = ("Continue without answering this question" or missing, then insert "man or woman"] is supposed to? For example, by calling you a fag, tranny, gay, dyke, or butch.	○	○
SH3. [Timeframe], did someone from work repeatedly make sexual gestures or sexual body movements (for example, thrusting their pelvis or grabbing their crotch) that made you uncomfortable, angry, or upset?	○	○
SH4. [Timeframe], did someone from work display, show, or send sexually explicit materials like pictures or videos that made you uncomfortable, angry, or upset?	○	○

SH5. [Timeframe], **did someone from work repeatedly tell you about their sexual activities in a way that made you uncomfortable, angry, or upset?**	○	○
SH6. [Timeframe], **did someone from work repeatedly ask you questions about your sex life or sexual interests that made you uncomfortable, angry, or upset?**	○	○
SH7. [Timeframe], **did someone from work make repeated sexual comments about your appearance or body that made you uncomfortable, angry, or upset?**	○	○
SH8. [Timeframe], **did someone from work either <u>take or share</u> sexually suggestive pictures or videos of you when you did not want them to?** [If SH8 = No, then skip to SH9]	○	○
SH8a. Did this make you uncomfortable, angry, or upset?	○	○
SH9. [Timeframe], **did someone from work make <u>repeated</u> attempts to establish an <u>unwanted</u> romantic or sexual relationship with you?** These could range from repeatedly asking you out for coffee to asking you for sex or a "hook-up." [If SH9 = No, then skip to SH10]	○	○
SH9a. Did these attempts make you uncomfortable, angry, or upset?	○	○
SH10. [Timeframe], **did someone from work intentionally touch you in a sexual way when you did not want them to?** This could include touching your genitals, breasts, buttocks, or touching you with their genitals anywhere on your body. [If SH10 = Yes, then skip to SH12, and PerceivedHostileWorkEnvironment = TRUE]]	○	○
SH11. [Timeframe], **did someone from work repeatedly touch you in any other way that made you uncomfortable, angry, or upset?** This could include almost any <u>unnecessary</u> physical contact including hugs, shoulder rubs, or touching your hair, but would not usually include handshakes or routine uniform adjustments.	○	○
S4. Please select "Yes" for this item to help us confirm that students are reading these items. [Screening Item]	○	○
SH12. [Timeframe], **has someone from work made you feel as if you would get some workplace benefit in exchange for doing something sexual?** For example, they might hint that they would give you a good evaluation/fitness report, a better assignment, or better treatment at work in exchange for doing something sexual. Something sexual could include talking about sex, undressing, sharing sexual pictures, or having some type of sexual contact.	○	○

SH13. [Timeframe], **has someone from work made you feel like you would get <u>punished or treated unfairly in the</u> <u>workplace</u> if you did <u>not</u> do something sexual?** For example, they hinted that they would give you a bad evaluation/fitness report, a bad assignment, or bad treatment at work if you were not willing to do something sexual. This could include being unwilling to talk about sex, undress, share sexual pictures, or have some type of sexual contact.	○	○
SH14. [Timeframe], **did you hear someone from work say that** [If TB7 = man, display "**men**", If TB7 = woman, display "**women**", <u>If TB7 = ("Continue without answering this question" or missing), display "**Airmen of your gender (man or woman)**"</u>] **are <u>not</u> as good as** [If TB7 = man, display "**women**", if TB7 = woman, display "**men**", <u>if TB7 = ("Continue without answering this question" or missing), display "**the opposite sex**"</u>] **at your particular job, or that** [If TB7 = man, display "**men**", if TB7 = woman, display "**women**", <u>If TB7 = ("Continue without answering this question" or missing), display "**they**"</u>] **should be prevented from having your job?**	○	○
SH15. [Timeframe], **do you think someone from work mistreated, ignored, excluded, or insulted you because** [If TB7 = man, display "**you are a man**", if TB7 = woman, display "**you are a woman**", <u>if TB7 = ("Continue without answering this question" or missing), display "**of your gender (man or woman)**"</u>]**?**	○	○
SH16. [Timeframe], **do you think someone from work mistreated, ignored, excluded, or insulted you because of your sexual orientation?**	○	○

[Follow-up items to the inappropriate workplace behavior screening items provide an assessment of whether the inappropriate behaviors meet DoD criteria defining sexual harassment or gender discrimination.]

[Ask if SH1=1 (Yes) else skip to SH2b]

SH1b. You indicated that, [Timeframe], someone from work made you uncomfortable, angry, or upset by repeatedly <u>telling sexual "jokes."</u>

Do you think they knew that you or someone else <u>wanted them to stop</u>? If it happened more than once or by more than one person, do you think any of them ever knew?
> Yes 1
> No 2
> [If SH1b=2 (No) then skip to SH1d]

SH1c. You indicated that, [Timeframe], someone from work made you uncomfortable, angry, or upset by repeatedly <u>telling sexual "jokes."</u>

Did they <u>continue</u> this unwanted behavior even <u>after</u> they knew that you or someone else wanted them to stop?
> Yes 1
> No 2
> [If SH1c=1 (Yes) then skip to SH2b, AND PerceivedHostileWorkEnvironment = TRUE]

SH1d. Do you think that this was ever severe enough that <u>most</u> [If TB7=Man, then insert <u>"men"</u>. If TB7=Woman, then insert <u>"women"</u>. If TB7 = ("Continue without answering this question" or missing, then insert <u>"people of your gender"</u>] in the military would have been <u>offended</u> by these jokes if they had heard them? If you aren't sure, choose the best answer.
> Yes 1
> No 2
> [If SH1d=1 (Yes) then PerceivedHostileWorkEnvironment = TRUE]

[Ask if SH2=1 (Yes) else skip to SH3b]
SH2b. You indicated that, [Timeframe] someone from work made you embarrassed, angry, or upset by repeatedly <u>suggesting that you do not act like a</u> [If TB7=Man, then insert "<u>man</u>". If TB7=Woman, then insert "<u>woman</u>". If TB7 = ("Continue without answering this question" or missing, then insert "<u>man or woman</u>"] <u>is supposed to</u>. For example, by calling you a fag, tranny, gay, dyke, or butch.

Do you think they knew that you or someone else <u>wanted them to stop</u>? If it happened more than once or by more than one person, do you think any of them ever knew?
> Yes 1
> No 2
> [If SH2b=2 (No) then skip to SH2d]

SH2c. You indicated that, after [Timeframe] someone from work made you embarrassed, angry, or upset by repeatedly <u>suggesting that you do not act like a</u> [If TB7=Man, then insert "<u>man</u>". If TB7=Woman, then insert "<u>woman</u>". If TB7 = ("Continue without answering this question" or missing, then insert "<u>man or woman</u>"] <u>is supposed to</u>. For example, by calling you a fag, tranny, gay, dyke, or butch.

Did they <u>continue</u> this unwanted behavior even <u>after</u> they knew that you or someone else wanted them to stop?
> Yes 1
> No 2
> [If SH2c=1 (Yes) then skip to SH3b, AND PerceivedHostileWorkEnvironment = TRUE]

SH2d. Do you think that this was ever severe enough that <u>most</u> [If TB7=Man, then insert "men". If TB7=Woman, then insert "women". If TB7 = ("Continue without answering this question" or missing, then insert "people of your gender"] in the military would have been offended if someone had said these things to them? If you're not sure, choose the best answer.
> Yes 1
> No 2
> [If SH2d=1 (Yes) then PerceivedHostileWorkEnvironment = TRUE]

[Ask if SH3=1 (Yes) else skip to SH4b]
SH3b. You indicated that, [Timeframe], someone from work made you uncomfortable, angry, or upset by repeatedly <u>making sexual gestures or sexual body movements</u>.

Do you think they knew that you or someone else <u>wanted them to stop</u>? If it happened more than once or by more than one person, do you think any of them ever knew?

    Yes 1

    No 2

[If SH3b=2 (No) then skip to SH3d]

SH3c. You indicated that, [Timeframe], someone from work made you uncomfortable, angry, or upset by repeatedly <u>making sexual gestures or sexual body movements</u>.

Did they <u>continue</u> this unwanted behavior even <u>after</u> they knew that you or someone else wanted them to stop?

    Yes 1

    No 2

[If SH3c=1 (Yes) then skip to SH4b, AND PerceivedHostileWorkEnvironment = TRUE]

SH3d. Do you think that this was ever severe enough that <u>most</u> [If TB7=Man, then insert "<u>men</u>". If TB7=Woman, then insert "<u>women</u>". If TB7 = ("Continue without answering this question" or missing, then insert "<u>people of your gender</u>"] in the military would have been <u>offended</u> by these gestures? If you're not sure, choose the best answer.

    Yes 1

    No 2

[If SH3d=1 (Yes) then PerceivedHostileWorkEnvironment = TRUE]

[Ask if SH4=1 (Yes) else skip to SH5b]

SH4b. You indicated that, [Timeframe], someone from work made you embarrassed, angry, or upset by <u>displaying, showing, or sending sexually explicit materials</u> like pictures or videos.

Do you think they knew that you or someone else <u>wanted them to stop</u>? If it happened more than once or by more than one person, do you think any of them ever knew?
> Yes 1
> No 2
> [If SH4b=2 (No) then skip to SH4d]

SH4c. You indicated that, [Timeframe], someone from work made you embarrassed, angry, or upset by <u>displaying, showing, or sending sexually explicit materials</u> like pictures or videos.

Did they <u>continue</u> this unwanted behavior even <u>after</u> they knew that you or someone else wanted them to stop?
> Yes 1
> No 2
> [If SH4c=1 (Yes) then skip to SH5b, AND PerceivedHostileWorkEnvironment = TRUE]

SH4d. Do you think that this was ever severe enough that <u>most</u> [If TB7=Man, then insert "<u>men</u>". If TB7=Woman, then insert "<u>women</u>". If TB7 = ("Continue without answering this question" or missing, then insert "<u>people of your gender</u>"] in the military would have been <u>offended</u> by seeing these sexually explicit materials? If you're not sure, choose the best answer.
> Yes 1
> No 2
> [If SH4d=1 (Yes) then PerceivedHostileWorkEnvironment = TRUE]

[Ask if SH5=1 (Yes) else skip to SH6b]
SH5b. You indicated that, [Timeframe], someone from work made you uncomfortable, angry, or upset by repeatedly <u>telling you about their sexual activities</u>.

Do you think they knew that you or someone else <u>wanted them to stop</u>? If it happened more than once or by more than one person, do you think any of them ever knew?
> Yes 1
> No 2
> [If SH5b=2 (No) then skip to SH5d]

SH5c. You indicated that, after [Timeframe], someone from work made you uncomfortable, angry, or upset by repeatedly <u>telling you about their sexual activities</u>.

Did they <u>continue</u> this unwanted behavior even <u>after</u> they knew that you or someone else wanted them to stop?
> Yes 1
> No 2
> [If SH5c=1 (Yes) then skip to SH6b, AND PerceivedHostileWorkEnvironment = TRUE]

SH5d. Do you think that this was ever severe enough that <u>most</u> [If TB7=Man, then insert "<u>men</u>". If TB7=Woman, then insert "<u>women</u>". If TB7 = ("Continue without answering this question" or missing, then insert "<u>people of your gender</u>"] in the military would have been <u>offended</u> by hearing about these sexual activities? If you're not sure, choose the best answer.
> Yes 1
> No 2
> [If SH5d=1 (Yes) then PerceivedHostileWorkEnvironment = TRUE]

[Ask if SH6=1 (Yes) else skip to SH7b]
SH6b. You indicated that, [Timeframe], someone from work made you embarrassed, angry, or upset by <u>asking you questions about your sex life or sexual interests.</u>

Do you think they knew that you or someone else <u>wanted them to stop</u>? If it happened more than once or by more than one person, do you think any of them ever knew?

     Yes 1
     No 2
     [If SH6b=2 (No) then skip to SH6d]

SH6c. You indicated that, [Timeframe], someone from work made you embarrassed, angry, or upset by <u>asking you questions about your sex life or sexual interests.</u>

Did they <u>continue</u> this unwanted behavior even <u>after</u> they knew that you or someone else wanted them to stop?

     Yes 1
     No 2
     [If SH6c=1 (Yes) then skip to SH7b, AND PerceivedHostileWorkEnvironment = TRUE]

SH6d. Do you think that this was ever severe enough that <u>most</u> [If TB7=Man, then insert "men". If TB7=Woman, then insert "women". If TB7 = ("Continue without answering this question" or missing, then insert "people of your gender"] in the military would have been offended if they had been asked these questions? If you're not sure, choose the best answer.

     Yes 1
     No 2
     [If SH6d=1 (Yes) then PerceivedHostileWorkEnvironment = TRUE]

[Ask if SH7=1 (Yes) else skip to SH8b]
SH7b. You indicated that, [Timeframe], someone from work made you uncomfortable, angry, or upset by making repeated <u>sexual comments about your appearance or body.</u>

Do you think they knew that you or someone else <u>wanted them to stop</u>? If it happened more than once or by more than one person, do you think any of them ever knew?
> Yes 1
> No 2
> [If SH7b=2 (No) then skip to SH7d]

SH7c. You indicated that, after [Timeframe], someone from work made you uncomfortable, angry, or upset by making repeated <u>sexual comments about your appearance or body.</u>

Did they <u>continue</u> this unwanted behavior even <u>after</u> they knew that you or someone else wanted them to stop?
> Yes 1
> No 2
> [If SH7c=1 (Yes) then skip to SH8b, AND PerceivedHostileWorkEnvironment = TRUE]

SH7d. Do you think that this was ever severe enough that <u>most</u> [If TB7=Man, then insert "men". If TB7=Woman, then insert "women". If TB7 = ("Continue without answering this question" or missing, then insert "people of your gender"] in the military would have been offended</u> if these remarks had been directed to them? If you're not sure, choose the best answer.
> Yes 1
> No 2
> [If SH7d=1 (Yes) then PerceivedHostileWorkEnvironment = TRUE]

[Ask if SH8a=1 (Yes) else skip to SH9b]

SH8d. You indicated that, [Timeframe], someone from work made you embarrassed, angry, or upset by <u>taking or sharing sexually suggestive pictures or videos of you</u> when you did not want them to.

Do you think that this was ever severe enough that <u>most</u> [If TB7=Man, then insert "**men**". If TB7=Woman, then insert "**women**". If TB7 = ("Continue without answering this question" or missing, then insert "**people of your gender**"] **in the military would have been offended** if it had happened to them? If you're not sure, please choose the best answer.

     Yes 1
     No 2
     [If SH8d=1 (Yes) then PerceivedHostileWorkEnvironment = TRUE]

[Ask if SH9a=1 (Yes) else skip to SH11b]

SH9b. You indicated that, [Timeframe], someone from work made you uncomfortable, angry, or upset by making repeated <u>attempts to establish an unwanted romantic or sexual relationship with you</u>.

Do you think they knew that you or someone else <u>wanted them to stop</u>? If it happened more than once or by more than one person, do you think any of them ever knew?
>Yes 1
>No 2
>[If SH9b=2 (No) then skip to SH9d]

SH9c. You indicated that, [Timeframe], someone from work made you uncomfortable, angry, or upset by making repeated <u>attempts to establish an unwanted romantic or sexual relationship with you</u>.

Did they <u>continue</u> this unwanted behavior even <u>after</u> they knew that you or someone else wanted them to stop?
>Yes 1
>No 2
>[If SH9c=1 (Yes) then skip to SH11b, AND PerceivedHostileWorkEnvironment=TRUE]

SH9d. Do you think that this was ever severe enough that <u>most</u> [If TB7=Man, then insert "<u>men</u>". If TB7=Woman, then insert "<u>women</u>". If TB7 = ("Continue without answering this question" or missing, then insert "<u>people of your gender</u>"] in the military would have been <u>offended</u> by these unwanted attempts? If you're not sure, choose the best answer.
>Yes 1
>No 2
>[If SH9d=1 (Yes) then PerceivedHostileWorkEnvironment = TRUE]

[Ask if SH11=1 (Yes) else skip to SH12a]
SH11b. You indicated that, [Timeframe], someone from work made you uncomfortable, angry, or upset by <u>touching you unnecessarily.</u>

Do you think they knew that you or someone else <u>wanted them to stop</u>? If it happened more than once or by more than one person, do you think any of them ever knew?
>Yes 1
>No 2
>[If SH11b=2 (No) then skip to SH11d]

SH11c. You indicated that, [Timeframe], someone from work made you uncomfortable, angry, or upset by <u>touching you unnecessarily.</u>

Did they <u>continue</u> this unwanted behavior even <u>after</u> they knew that you or someone else wanted them to stop?
>Yes 1
>No 2
>[If SH11c=1 (Yes) then skip to SH12a, AND PerceivedHostileWorkEnvironment = TRUE]

SH11d. Do you think that this was ever severe enough that <u>most</u> [If TB7=Man, then insert "<u>men</u>". If TB7=Woman, then insert "<u>women</u>". If TB7 = ("Continue without answering this question" or missing, then insert "<u>people of your gender</u>"] in the military would have been <u>offended</u> by this unnecessary touching? If you're not sure, choose the best answer.
>Yes 1
>No 2
>[If SH11d=1 (Yes) then PerceivedHostileWorkEnvironment = TRUE]

138

[Ask if SH12=1 (Yes) else skip to SH13a]
You indicated that, [Timeframe], someone from work made you feel as if you would get some workplace benefit in exchange for doing something sexual.

What led you to believe that you would get a <u>workplace benefit</u> if you agreed to do something sexual? *Select "Yes" or "No" for each item*

SH12a. They told you that they would give you a reward or benefit for doing something sexual.	Yes 1	No 2
SH12b. They hinted that you would get a reward or benefit for doing something sexual. For example, they reminded you about your evaluation/fitness report about the same time that they expressed sexual interest.	Yes 1	No 2
SH12c. Someone else told you they got benefits from this person by doing sexual things	Yes 1	No 2
SH12d. You heard rumors from other people that this person treated others better in exchange for doing sexual things.	Yes 1	No 2
SH12e. Based on what you knew about their personality, you thought you could get a benefit.	Yes 1	No 2

[If SH12a=1 (Yes) then PerceivedSexualQuidProQuo = TRUE]
[If SH12b=1 (Yes) then PerceivedSexualQuidProQuo = TRUE]
[If SH12c=1 (Yes) then PerceivedSexualQuidProQuo = TRUE]

[Ask if SH13=1 (Yes) else skip to SH14a]
You indicated that, [Timeframe], someone from work made you feel as if you would get punished or treated unfairly in the workplace if you did <u>not</u> do something sexual.

What led you to believe that you would get <u>punished or treated unfairly in the workplace</u> if you did <u>not</u> do something sexual? *Select "Yes" or "No" for each item*

Sh13a. They told you that you would be punished or treated unfairly if you did not do something sexual.	Yes 1	No 2
SH13b They hinted that you would be punished or treated unfairly if you did not do something sexual. For example, they reminded you about your evaluation/fitness report near the same time that they expressed sexual interest.	Yes 1	No 2
SH13c. Someone else told you they were punished or treated unfairly by this person for not doing something sexual.	Yes 1	No 2
SH13d. You heard rumors from other people that this person treated others badly unless they were willing to do sexual things.	Yes 1	No 2
SH13e. Based on what you knew about their personality, you thought you might get punished or treated unfairly.	Yes 1	No 2

[If SH13a=1 (Yes) then PerceivedSexualQuidProQuo = TRUE]
[If SH13b=1 (Yes) then PerceivedSexualQuidProQuo = TRUE]
[If SH13c=1 (Yes) then PerceivedSexualQuidProQuo = TRUE]

[Ask if SH14=1 (Yes) else skip to SH15a]

SH14a. You indicated that, after [Timeframe], someone from work said that [If TB7=Man, then insert "men". If TB7=Woman, then insert "women". If TB7 = ("Continue without answering this question" or missing, then insert "people of your gender"] are not as good as [If TB7=Man, then insert "women". If TB7=Woman, then insert "men". If TB7 = ("Continue without answering this question" or missing, then insert "the other gender"] at your particular job, or that they should be prevented from having your job.

Do you think their beliefs about [If TB7=Man, then insert "**men**". If TB7=Woman, then insert "**women**". If TB7 = ("Continue without answering this question" or missing, then insert "**people of your gender**"] ever **harmed or limited** your career? For example, did they hurt your evaluation/fitness report, affect your chances of promotion or your next assignment?

     Yes 1
     No 2
     [If SH14a=1 (Yes) then PerceivedGenderDiscrimination = TRUE]

141

[Ask if SH15=1 (Yes) else skip to next section]
SH15a. You indicated that, [Timeframe], someone from work <u>mistreated, ignored, excluded, or insulted you</u> because [If TB7=Man, then insert "<u>**you are a man**</u>". If TB7=Woman, then insert "<u>**you are a woman**</u>". If TB7 = ("Continue without answering this question" or missing, then insert "<u>**of your gender**</u>"].

Do you think this treatment ever <u>harmed or limited</u> your career? For example, did it hurt your evaluation/fitness report, affect your chances of promotion or your next assignment?

Yes 1
No 2
[If SH15a=1 (Yes) then PerceivedGenderDiscrimination = TRUE]

[Ask if SH16=1 (Yes) else skip to next section]
SH16a. You indicated that, [Timeframe], someone from work <u>mistreated, ignored, excluded, or insulted you</u> because of your sexual orientation.

Do you think this treatment ever <u>harmed or limited</u> your career? For example, did it hurt your evaluation/fitness report, affect your chances of promotion or your next assignment?

      Yes 1
      No 2
      [If SH16a=1 (Yes) then PerceivedSexualOrientationDiscrimination = TRUE]

[If PerceivedSexualQuidProQuo = TRUE, OR PerceivedHostileWorkEnvironment = TRUE, OR PerceivedGenderDiscrimination = TRUE then PerceivedEqualOpportunityViolation = TRUE]

IF A STUDENT MARKED "No" FOR ALL SH1– SH15, GO TO QUESTION SHFU1a BELOW. ↓	IF RESPONSES ABOVE ARE CODED AS CONSISTENT WITH MILITARY EQUAL OPPORTUNITY (MEO) VIOLATION (EITHER SEXUAL HARASSMENT OR GENDER DISCRIMINATION), CONTINUE ↓
SHFU1a. Are you aware of any of these things happening to <u>other</u> students [Timeframe]**?** *Select all that apply.* ☐ No. ☐ Yes, I saw this happen. ☐ Yes, a student told me this happened to them. ☐ Yes, an [If Enlisted non-prior service student, then "MTL,"] instructor or other leader informed me of this happening. ☐ Yes, I heard about this happening from someone else. [IF "NO," SKIP TO QUESTION SHC1. ELSE SKIP TO SHR1.]	**Think about the situation(s) you selected in this section as happening to you** [Timeframe]**. Now pick the behavior that you consider to be the most serious or that had the greatest effect on you. For the next questions, please think of that worst behavior.** **SHFU2. How many people did this to you?** *Mark one.* ☐ One person ☐ More than one person **SHFU6. Were they . . . ?** *Mark one.* ☐ Male(s) ☐ Female(s) ☐ Both male(s) and female(s) **SHFU3. Were they a/an . . . ?** *Select all that apply.* ☐ Non-prior service student ☐ Prior service student ☐ [If enlisted]Retrainee ☐ [If enlisted]MTL ☐ Instructor ☐ Someone else in my chain of command ☐ Other U.S. military personnel not listed above ☐ Military personnel from another country ☐ Civilian ☐ Don't know/other **SHFU3_officer.** [If officer AND (SFHU3 = "Instructor"), then ask:] **Was the instructor(s) a First Assignment Instructor Pilot (FAIP)?** o No o Yes [Ask only if TB6a = Yes] **SHFU4. At which installation were you assigned when this situation occurred?** If it happened on more than one installation, check all that apply. *[Display only installations selected in TB5 and TB6b]* **SHFU5. Did you tell any other students about any of these situations that happened to you?** ☐ Yes, I told another student. ☐ No, I did not tell another student.

	SHFU1b. The previous questions asked whether any of these situations happened to you personally. **Are you aware of any of these things happening to other students** [Timeframe]? *Select all that apply.*
	[Note: Questions SHFU1a and SHFU1b are identical.]
	☐ No.
	☐ Yes, I saw this happen.
	☐ Yes, a student told me this happened to them.
	☐ Yes, an [If Enlisted non-prior service student, then "MTL,"] instructor or other leader informed me of this happening.
	☐ Yes, I heard about this happening from someone else.
	GO TO NEXT PAGE (QUESTION SHR1).

For the situations in this section that happened to you personally, or that you were aware of happening to another student . . .

SHR1. Did you report any of the behaviors in this section to any of the sources below? *Please select all that apply or indicate that you did not report any incidents.*

- ☐ I told [If enlisted, then display "a student in an Airman Leader position (for example, a bay chief, teal rope, or red rope)" If officer, then display "a student in a leadership position, such as a Senior Ranking Officer"].
- ☐ [If enlisted non-prior service student, then display: "I told an MTL."]
- ☐ I told an instructor.
- ☐ I told someone else in my chain of command.
- ☐ I told an officer or NCO outside of my chain of command.
- ☐ I told someone in Air Force law enforcement: Office of Special Investigations (OSI) or Security Forces (SF).
- ☐ I told the Inspector General (IG).
- ☐ I told the Equal Opportunity (EO) Office.
- ☐ I wrote it down on paper and put it in a critique box/drop box.
- ☐ [If technical training student, then "I used the 2 AF hotline to report it."]
- ☐ I told a chaplain or chaplain assistant.
- ☐ I told the SARC (sexual assault response coordinator).
- ☐ I told an Air Force therapist or counselor.
- ☐ I told an Air Force doctor, nurse, or other medical professional.
- ☐ I told a staff member of the Airman and Family Readiness Center.
- ☐ Other
- ☐ **I did not report any incidents.**

IF THEY SELECTED "I DID NOT REPORT ANY INCIDENTS," GO TO QUESTION SHR2 BELOW. ↓	IF THEY SELECTED THAT THEY REPORTED TO ANY SOURCE, GO TO QUESTION SHR4 BELOW. ↓

SHR2. Please select the items below that describe why you did not report any incidents. *Select all that apply. More options will be shown on the next page.*

- ☐ I knew someone had already reported it.
- ☐ I thought someone else would report it.
- ☐ I only heard about it, so I wasn't sure if it was true.
- ☐ I didn't think there was anything wrong with it.
- ☐ I don't believe people should tell on one another.
- ☐ I didn't think anything would be done if I reported it.
- ☐ I didn't want anyone else to know it happened.
- ☐ I didn't think it was serious enough to report.
- ☐ I didn't think I would be believed.
- ☐ I was afraid reporting might cause trouble for my flight or class.
- ☐ I thought that reporting might delay my graduation or moving to my first duty assignment.

If you reported one incident, please answer the next questions about that one report. If you reported more than one incident, please think of the incident that you consider the most serious.

SHR4. How seriously do you feel your report was taken?
- ○ Very seriously
- ○ Somewhat seriously
- ○ Not very seriously
- ○ Not at all seriously
- ○ I don't know

146

Note: More options will be shown on the next page.
********** PAGE BREAK **********

Please select the items below that describe why you did not report any incidents. *Select all that apply.*

- ☐
- ☐ I handled it myself.
- ☐ I decided to put up with it.
- ☐ I didn't want the person who did it to get in trouble for it.
- ☐ I knew of others who were treated poorly for reporting.
- ☐ I was afraid the person who did it or their friends would try to get even with me for reporting.
- ☐ I didn't think my report would be kept confidential.
- ☐ I wanted to report it anonymously but didn't know a safe way to do that.
- ☐ I was afraid of getting into trouble for something I shouldn't have been doing.
- ☐ I was afraid students would punish me or mock me for reporting.
- ☐ I was afraid instructors would punish me or mock me for reporting.
- ☐ [If enlisted non-prior service student, then]I was afraid MTLs would punish me or mock me for reporting.
- ☐ Other

GO TO THE NEXT PAGE (QUESTION SHC1).

SHR5. What happened with the behavior after you reported it?
- ○ The behavior didn't happen again.
- ○ The behavior continued or got worse.
- ○ I don't know: The behavior was happening to someone else.

SHR6. What happened to you after the report? *Select all that apply.*
- ☐ I got support to help me deal with what happened.
- ☐ The person I reported it to praised me for reporting.
- ☐ I got in trouble for my own misbehavior or infraction.
- ☐ The person who did it or their friends tried to get even with me for reporting.
- ☐ Students tried to get even with me for reporting.
- ☐ Instructors tried to get even with me for reporting.
- ☐ [If enlisted non-prior service student, then]MTLs tried to get even with me for reporting.
- ☐ None of the above happened to me.

SHR7. If you could do it over, would you still decide to report the incident?
- ○ Yes.
- ○ No.

GO TO THE NEXT PAGE (QUESTION SHC1).

147

Climate for Sexual Harassment: Average Items to Form Scale

Air Force policy states: "Unwelcome sexual advances, requests for sexual favors, and other verbal or physical conduct of a sexual nature constitute sexual harassment when (1) submission to such conduct is made either explicitly or implicitly a term or condition of an individual's employment, (2) submission to or rejection of such conduct by an individual is used as the basis for employment decisions affecting such individual, or (3) such conduct has the purpose or effect of unreasonably interfering with an individual's work performance or creating an intimidating, hostile, or offensive working environment."

The following questions ask you about the extent to which these <u>sexual harassment</u> policies are enforced at [technical/flying] training. **For questions about** [technical/flying] **training leaders, we are referring to those Air Force NCOs and officers with training leadership responsibilities (for example, squadron commanders, directors of operations, flight commanders, flight chiefs, superintendents, and first sergeants).** Please respond based on what you believe about your leadership, even if you do not have direct knowledge about their attitudes or actions on this specific type of behavior.

	Strongly Disagree	Disagree	Neither Disagree nor Agree	Agree	Strongly Agree
SHC1. Air Force training leadership makes honest efforts to stop sexual harassment.	○	○	○	○	○
SHC2. Air Force training leadership encourages the reporting of sexual harassment.	○	○	○	○	○
SHC3. Air Force training leadership takes actions to prevent sexual harassment.	○	○	○	○	○
SHC4. Air Force training leadership would correct or discipline someone who engages in sexual harassment.	○	○	○	○	○

Section VI: Sexual Assault

Students will not see banner titles.

As requested by AETC, this section has minimally adapted the DoD-approved assessment instrument for Sexual Assault. Because it is standardized for all DoD uses, changes should not be made to the items unless the change is absolutely critical.

Please read the following special instructions before continuing the survey.

Questions in this next section ask about unwanted experiences of an abusive, humiliating, or sexual nature. These types of unwanted experiences vary in severity. Some of them could be viewed as an assault. Others could be viewed as hazing or some other type of unwanted experience.

They can happen to both women and men.

Some of the language may seem graphic, but using the names of specific body parts is the best way to determine whether or not people have had these types of experiences.

SA0. Before we proceed, please help ensure that the computer displays the appropriate set of questions for you by indicating one of the following:
- ○ **I am anatomically male.**
- ○ **I am anatomically female.**
- ○ **Continue without answering this question. I understand that I will see questions that refer to both male and female anatomy.**

When answering the questions in this section, please include experiences <u>no matter who did it to you or where it happened</u>. It could be done to you by a male or female, service member or civilian, someone you knew or a stranger.

Please include experiences <u>even if you or others had been drinking alcohol, using drugs, or were intoxicated</u>.

The following questions will ask you about events that happened [Timeframe].

Remember, all the information you share will be kept confidential.

SA1. [Timeframe]**, did you have any <u>unwanted</u> experiences in which someone put his penis <u>into your</u>** [If SA0 = female or unwilling to indicate sex, display: **"vagina,"**] **anus or mouth?**	○ No ○ Yes [If SA1=1 (Yes) ask "OB1a", else continue]
SA2. [Timeframe]**, did you have any <u>unwanted</u> experiences in which someone put any object or any body part <u>other than a penis</u> into your** [If SA0 = female or unwilling to indicate sex, display: **"vagina,"**] **anus or**	○ No ○ Yes [If SA2=1 (Yes) and *sexualAssault_12m* ≠ "True", ask "PF2a", else continue]

149

mouth? The body part could include a finger, tongue or testicles.	
SA3. [Timeframe], **did anyone <u>make you put</u> any part of your body or any object into someone's mouth, vagina, or anus when you did not want to?** A part of the body could include your [If SA0 = male or unwilling to indicate sex, display: "penis, testicles,"] tongue or fingers.	o No o Yes [If SA3=1 (Yes) and *sexualAssault_12m* ≠ "True", ask "PF3a", else continue] [Programming note: If *sexualAssault_12m* = "TRUE" on the basis of follow ups to SA1-SA3 then *penetrativeSA_12m* = "TRUE" else *penetrativeSA_12m* = "FALSE"]
SA4. [Timeframe], **did you have any <u>unwanted</u> experiences in which someone <u>intentionally touched</u> private areas of your body (either directly or through clothing)?** Private areas include buttocks, inner thigh, breasts, groin, anus, vagina, penis or testicles.	o No o Yes [If SA4=1 (Yes) and *sexualAssault_12m* ≠ "True", ask "PF4a", else continue]
S5. Please select "Yes" for this item to help us confirm that students are reading these items. [Screening item]	o No o Yes
SA5. [Timeframe], **did you have any <u>unwanted</u> experiences in which someone <u>made you touch</u> private areas of their body or someone else's body (either directly or through clothing)?** This could involve the person putting their private areas on you. Private areas include buttocks, inner thigh, breasts, groin, anus, vagina, penis or testicles.	o No o Yes [If SA5=1 (Yes) and *sexualAssault_12m* ≠ "True", ask "PF5a", else continue] [Programming note: If *SexualAssault_12m* = "TRUE" on the basis of follow ups to SA4-SA5 then *contactSA_12m* = "TRUE" else *contactSA_12m* = "FALSE"]
SA6. [TIMELINE], **did you have any <u>unwanted</u> experiences in which someone <u>attempted to</u> put a penis, an object, or any body part into your** [If SA0 = female or unwilling to indicate sex, display: "**vagina,**"] **anus or mouth, <u>but no penetration actually occurred</u>?**	o No o Yes [If SA6=2 (No) skip to SAE1]
[Ask only if SA6 = yes]**SA6a. As part of this attempt, did the person touch you anywhere on your body?** This includes grabbing your arm, hair or clothes, or pushing their body against yours.	o No o Yes [If *sexualAssault_12m* ≠ "True", ask "PF6a", else continue] [Programming note: If *sexualAssault_12m* = "TRUE" on the basis of follow ups to SA6 then *attemptedSA_12m* = "TRUE" else *attemptedSA_12m* = "FALSE"]

SAE1. [TIMELINE], did anyone show you private areas of their body or make you show them private areas of your body when you didn't want to? Private areas include buttocks, inner thigh, breasts, groin, anus, vagina, penis, or testicles.	o No o Yes

[Purpose Follow Up Module START]
[Purpose Follow up module: "X" in the question number refers to appropriate SA screener number (2-6)]

PFXa. Was this unwanted experience (or any experiences like this if you had more than one) abusive or humiliating, or intended to be abusive or humiliating? If you aren't sure, choose the best answer.

      Yes 1
      No 2
      [If PFXa=1 (Yes) skip to OBX item]

PFXb. Do you believe the person did it for a sexual reason? For example, they did it because they were sexually aroused or to get sexually aroused. If you aren't sure, choose the best answer.

      Yes 1
      No 2
      [If PFXb=1 (Yes) continue to OBX item]
      [If PFXb=2 (No) skip to next SA_screener question (SA3 –SA6)]

[Purpose Follow Up Module END]

[Offender Behavior Module START]
[Offender Behavior Module: "X" in the question number refers to appropriate screener number (1-6)]
[Programming Note: Please keep the instructions on the screen for all items OBXa-OBXk. Please present each item alone on the screen]

The following statements are about things that might have happened to you when you had this experience. In these statements, "they" means the person or people who did this to you.

Please indicate which of the following happened.

OBXa. They continued even when you told them or showed them that you were unwilling.
    Yes 1
    No 2
    [If OBXa=1 (Yes) *sexualAssault_12m*= "TRUE"]

OBXb. They used physical force to make you comply. For example, they grabbed your arm or used their body weight to hold you down.
    Yes 1
    No 2
    [If OBXb=1 (Yes) *sexualAssault_12m*= "TRUE"]

OBXc. They physically injured you.
    Yes 1
    No 2
    [If OBXc=1 (Yes) *sexualAssault_12m*= "TRUE"]

OBXd. They threatened to physically hurt you (or someone else).
    Yes 1
    No 2
    [If OBXd=1 (Yes) *sexualAssault_12m*= "TRUE"]

    [IF OBXd=1 (Yes) then ask]
OBXd_1. Did they threaten you (or someone else) with a weapon?
    Yes 1
    No 2

    [IF OBXd=1 (Yes) then ask]
OBXd_2. Did they threaten to seriously injure, kill, or kidnap you (or someone else)?
    Yes 1
    No 2

OBXe. They threatened you (or someone else) in some other way. For example, by using their position of authority, by spreading lies about you, or by getting you in trouble with authorities.
    Yes 1
    No 2
    [If OBXe=1 (Yes) *sexualAssault_12m*= "TRUE"]

OBXf. They did it when you were passed out, asleep, or unconscious.
>   Yes 1
>   No 2
>   [If OBXf=1 (Yes) *sexualAssault_12m*= "TRUE"]

OBXg. They did it when you were so drunk, high, or drugged that you could not understand what was happening or could not show them that you were unwilling.
>   Yes 1
>   No 2
>   [If OBXg=1 (Yes) *sexualAssault_12m*= "TRUE"]

OBXh. They tricked you into thinking that they were someone else or that they were allowed to do it for a professional purpose (like a person pretending to be a doctor).
>   Yes 1
>   No 2
>   If OBXh=1 (Yes) *sexualAssault_12m*= "TRUE"]
>   [If *sexualAssault_12m* = TRUE, then skip to next screening item SA2-SA6, Else continue.]

OBXi. They made you so afraid that you froze and could not tell them or show them that you were unwilling.
>   Yes 1
>   No 2
>   [If OBXi=1 (Yes) *sexualAssault_12m*= "TRUE"]

OBXj. They did it after you had consumed so much alcohol that the next day you could not remember what happened.
>   Yes 1
>   No 2
>   [If OBXj=1 (Yes) *sexualAssault_12m*= "TRUE"]

OBXk. It happened without your consent.
>   Yes 1
>   No 2
>   [If OBXk=1 (Yes) *sexualAssault_12m*= "TRUE"]

SAFU1a. The previous questions asked whether any of these situations happened to you personally. **Are you aware of any of these things happening to <u>other</u> students** [Timeframe]**?** *Select all that apply.*

☐ No.
☐ Yes, I saw this happen.
☐ Yes, a student told me this happened to them.
☐ Yes, an [If enlisted non-prior service student, then "MTL,"] instructor or other leader informed me of this happening.
☐ Yes, I heard about this happening from someone else.

[IF "NO," SKIP TO QUESTION SAC1. ELSE SKIP TO SAR1.]

SAFU9. On the previous page, you indicated that at least one of these situations happened to you personally. [Timeframe]**, how many different times did you have an unwanted experience involving touching or attempted touching of private areas of the body?** [INSERT DROP-DOWN BOX with 1, 2, 3, 4, 5, 6, 7, 8, 9, 10, 11+.]

SAFU10. Were any of the unwanted experiences framed as something being done as a part of entry into your career field?
☐ Yes, all of them
☐ Yes, some of them
☐ No
☐ Not sure

[Ask only if TB6a = Yes] **SAFU4. At which installation were you assigned when this situation occurred?** If it happened on more than one installation, check all that apply. *[Display only installations selected in TB5 and TB6b]*

SAFU5. Did you tell any other students about any of these situations that happened to you?
☐ Yes, I told another student.
☐ No, I did not tell another student.

If this happened to you <u>one</u> time, please answer the next questions about that one incident. If this happened to you <u>more than one</u> time [Timeframe]**, please think of the most serious event or the one that had the greatest effect on you.** [PROGRAMMING NOTE: Repeat this instruction on all screens for items SAFU2 to SAFU1b.]

SAFU2. How many people did this to you (during this one event)?
☐ One person
☐ More than one person
☐ Don't know

SAFU6. Were they . . . ?
☐ Male(s)
☐ Female(s)
☐ Both male(s) and female(s)
☐ Don't know

SAFU3. Were they . . . ? *Select all that apply.*

☐ Non-prior service student
☐ Prior service student
☐ [if enlisted] Retrainee
☐ [if enlisted] MTL
☐ Instructor
☐ Someone else in my chain of command
☐ Other U.S. military personnel not listed above
☐ Military personnel from another country
☐ Civilian
☐ Don't know/other

SAFU3_officer. [If officer AND (SAFU3 = "Instructor"), then ask:] Was the instructor(s) a First Assignment Instructor Pilot (FAIP)?

☐ No
☐ Yes

SAFU11. Where did it occur?

☐ In the dorms (including bays, latrine, closets, day room, flight offices)
☐ In another room or building on base (including classroom, chow hall, chapel)
☐ In an outdoor training area (e.g., tent, campsite)
☐ At another outdoor location (such as behind a building)
☐ In a car, truck, van, or other vehicle
☐ Off base
☐ Other

SAFU12. Did you receive any of the following services for ANY unwanted experience that occurred [Timeframe]**?**
Select all that apply.

☐ Help from the SARC (sexual assault response coordinator)
☐ Victim advocacy services (for example, someone to accompany you to appointments and explain what to expect)
☐ Counseling services
☐ Support from a chaplain
☐ Medical services
☐ Legal services
☐ Help making arrangements so you didn't have to come in contact with anyone who did it to you

SAFU1b. The previous questions asked whether any of these situations happened to you personally. **Are you aware of any of these things happening to other students** [Timeframe]?
Select all that apply.
[Note: Questions SAFU1a and SAFU1b are identical.]

☐ No.
☐ Yes, I saw this happen.
☐ Yes, a student told me this happened to them.
☐ Yes, an [If enlisted non-prior service student, then "MTL,"] instructor or other leader informed me of this happening.
☐ Yes, I heard about this happening from someone else.

GO TO NEXT PAGE (QUESTION SAR1).

For the situations in this section that happened to you personally, or that you were aware of happening to another student . . .

SAR1. Did you report any of the unwanted sexual experiences in this section to any of the sources below? *Please select all that apply, or indicate that you did not report any incidents.*

☐ I told [If enlisted, then display "a student in an Airman Leader position (for example, a bay chief, teal rope, or red rope)"; if officer, then display "a student in a leadership position, such as a Senior Ranking Officer"].
☐ [If enlisted non-prior service student, then display: "I told an MTL."]
☐ I told an instructor.
☐ I told someone else in my chain of command.
☐ I told an officer or NCO outside of my chain of command.
☐ I told someone in Air Force law enforcement: Office of Special Investigations (OSI) or Security Forces (SF).
☐ I told the Inspector General (IG).
☐ I told the Equal Opportunity (EO) Office.
☐ I wrote it down on paper and put it in a critique box/drop box.
☐ [If technical training student, then "I used the 2 AF hotline to report it."]
☐ I told a chaplain or chaplain assistant.
☐ I told the SARC (sexual assault response coordinator).
☐ I told an Air Force therapist or counselor.
☐ I told an Air Force doctor, nurse, or other medical professional.
☐ I told a staff member of the Airman and Family Readiness Center.
☐ Other
☐ **I did not report any incidents.**

IF THEY SELECTED "I DID NOT REPORT ANY INCIDENTS," GO TO QUESTION SAR2 BELOW. ↓	IF THEY SELECTED THAT THEY REPORTED TO ANY SOURCE, GO TO QUESTION SAR4 BELOW. ↓

SAR2. Please select the items below that describe why you did not report any incidents. *Select all that apply. NOTE: More options will be shown on the next page.*

☐ I knew someone had already reported it.
☐ I thought someone else would report it.
☐ I only heard about it, so I wasn't sure if it was true.
☐ I didn't think there was anything wrong with it.
☐ I don't believe people should tell on one another.
☐ I didn't think anything would be done if I reported it.
☐ I didn't want anyone else to know it happened.
☐ I didn't think it was serious enough to report.
☐ I didn't think I would be believed.

If you reported one incident, please answer the next questions about that one report. If you reported more than one incident, please think of the incident that you consider the most serious.

SAR4. How seriously do you feel your report was taken?
- ○ Very seriously
- ○ Somewhat seriously
- ○ Not very seriously
- ○ Not at all seriously
- ○ I don't know

□ I was afraid reporting might cause trouble for my flight or class.

□ I thought that reporting might delay my graduation or moving to my first duty assignment.

Note: More options will be shown on the next page.

********** PAGE BREAK **********

Please select the items below that describe why you did not report any incidents. *Select all that apply.*

□ I handled it myself.

□ I decided to put up with it.

□ I didn't want the person who did it to get in trouble for it.

□ I knew of others who were treated poorly for reporting.

□ I was afraid the person who did it or their friends would try to get even with me for reporting.

□ I didn't think my report would be kept confidential.

□ I wanted to report it anonymously but didn't know a safe way to do that.

□ I was afraid of getting into trouble for something I shouldn't have been doing.

□ I was afraid students would punish me or mock me for reporting.

□ I was afraid instructors would punish me or mock me for reporting.

□ [If enlisted non-prior service student, then]I was afraid MTLs would punish me or mock me for reporting.

□ Other

GO TO THE NEXT PAGE (QUESTION SAC1).

SAR5. What happened with the behavior after you reported it?

o The behavior didn't happen again.

o The behavior continued or got worse.

o I don't know: The behavior was happening to someone else.

SAR6. What happened to you after the report? *Select all that apply.*

□ I got support to help me deal with what happened.

□ The person I reported it to praised me for reporting.

□ I got in trouble for my own misbehavior or infraction.

□ The person who did it or their friends tried to get even with me for reporting.

□ Students tried to get even with me for reporting.

□ Instructors tried to get even with me for reporting.

□ [If enlisted non-prior service student, then]MTLs tried to get even with me for reporting.

□ None of the above happened to me.

SAR7. If you could do it over, would you still decide to report the incident?

o Yes

o No

GO TO THE NEXT PAGE (QUESTION SAC1).

Climate for Sexual Assault: Average Items to Form Scale

The Uniform Code of Military Justice (UCMJ) criminalizes various forms of unwanted sexual activity, including rape, sexual assault, and unwanted sexual contact. For the next sections, we use the term *sexual assault* to refer to all of these forms of unwanted sexual contact characterized by force, threats, intimidation, or abuse of authority, or when the victim does not or cannot consent to that sexual contact.

The following questions ask you about the extent to which military laws and policies on <u>sexual assault</u> are enforced at [technical/flying] training. **For questions about [technical/flying] training leaders, we are referring to those Air Force NCOs and officers with training leadership responsibilities (for example, squadron commanders, directors of operations, flight commanders, flight chiefs, superintendents, and first sergeants).** Please respond based on what you believe about your leadership, even if you do not have direct knowledge about their attitudes or actions on this specific type of behavior.

	Strongly Disagree	Disagree	Neither Disagree nor Agree	Agree	Strongly Agree
SAC1. Air Force training leadership makes honest efforts to stop sexual assault.	○	○	○	○	○
SAC2. Air Force training leadership encourages the reporting of sexual assault.	○	○	○	○	○
SAC3. Air Force training leadership takes actions to prevent sexual assault.	○	○	○	○	○
SAC4. Air Force training leadership would discipline someone who engages in sexual assault.	○	○	○	○	○

Section VII: Hazing

Below is a list of behaviors others may have done to you or had you do to someone else while you were in [technical/flying] training as part of joining your career field.

When responding to these items, only consider behaviors that *were clearly NOT related to training objectives, were outside of your official training, and were done as part of joining or initiating you into your career field*.

Please do not consider anything that happened to other students. Think only about whether these things happened to you during [technical/flying] training.

[Show instruction alone on screen with forward button. Then for subsequent screen include the instructions again with the questions beneath them.]

As part of joining your career field . . .	No	Yes
H1. Did anyone <u>tie up, tape, or restrain you</u> outside of your official training activities?	○	○
H2. Did anyone <u>kidnap, transport, or drop you off in an unfamiliar location</u> outside of your official training activities?	○	○
H3. Did anyone <u>deprive you of food, sleep, or cleanliness</u> outside of your official training activities?	○	○
H4. Did anyone <u>persuade or force you to eat or drink disgusting things</u> outside of your official training activities?	○	○
H5. Did anyone <u>verbally harass or ridicule you</u> outside of your official training activities?	○	○
H6. Did anyone <u>persuade or force you to hit, kick, or physically assault someone else</u> outside of your official training activities?	○	○
H7. Did anyone <u>persuade or force you to act in a demeaning or embarrassing way</u> outside of your official training activities?	○	○
H8. Did anyone <u>hit, kick, or physically assault you</u> outside of official combative training activities?	○	○
H9. Did anyone <u>force you to do physical exercises</u> outside of your official training activities?	○	○

As part of joining your career field . . .		
H10. Did anyone <u>throw or dunk you into water</u> outside of your official training activities?	o	o
H11. Did anyone <u>hose you down with water</u> outside of your official training activities?	o	o
S6. Please select "Yes" for this item to help us confirm that students are reading these items. [Screening item]	o	o
H12. Did anyone <u>persuade or force you to alter your body (for example, get a tattoo, brand, or piercing)</u>?	o	o
H13. Did anyone <u>persuade or force you to consume alcohol</u>?	o	o
H14. Did anyone <u>persuade or force you to smoke cigarettes, cigars, or use tobacco</u>?	o	o
H15. Did anyone <u>persuade or force you to use illegal drugs or prescription drugs not prescribed to you</u>?	o	o
H16. Did anyone <u>persuade or force you to act as a personal servant</u>?	o	o
H17. Did anyone <u>persuade or force you to wear embarrassing clothing that is not part of the uniform</u>?	o	o
H18. Did anyone <u>persuade or force you to participate in a mean prank on others</u>?	o	o
H19. Did anyone <u>persuade or force you to destroy property</u>?	o	o
H20. Did anyone <u>persuade or force you to verbally harass or ridicule someone else</u>?	o	o
H21. Did anyone <u>press or punch an object into your skin (for example, wings, badges, or medals)</u>?	o	o
H22. Did anyone <u>simulate putting any object or part of their body into or on your private areas</u>? By private areas, we mean vagina or penis, anus, breast, inner thigh, and buttocks.	o	o
H23. Did anyone <u>persuade or force you to simulate putting any object or part of your body into or on someone else's private areas</u>? By private areas, we mean vagina or penis, anus, breast, inner thigh, and buttocks.	o	o

Note that scoring of this domain should include whether any items in Section V were marked as occurring as part of career initiation.

HFU1a. The previous questions asked whether any of these situations happened to you personally. **Are you aware of any of these things happening to <u>other</u> students** [Timeframe]**?** *Select all that apply.*
- ☐ No.
- ☐ Yes, I saw this happen.
- ☐ Yes, a student told me this happened to them.
- ☐ Yes, an [If enlisted non-prior service student, then "MTL,"] instructor or other leader informed me of this happening.
- ☐ Yes, I heard about this happening from someone else.

HFU7a. Are you aware of any of these things happening to <u>other</u> students in your career field <u>when they receive their occupational badge or beret upon graduation</u>? *Select all that apply.*
- ☐ No.
- ☐ Yes, I saw this happen.
- ☐ Yes, a student told me this happened to them.
- ☐ Yes, an [If enlisted non-prior service student, then "MTL,"] instructor or other leader informed me of this happening.
- ☐ Yes, I heard about this happening from someone else.

[IF QUESTIONS HFU1a AND HFU7a ARE "NO," SKIP TO QUESTION HC1. ELSE SKIP TO HR1.]

HFU2. On the previous page, you indicated that at least one of these situations happened to you personally. How many people did these things to you?
- ☐ One person
- ☐ More than one person
- ☐ Don't know

HFU3. Were they a(n) . . . ? *Select all that apply.*
- ☐ Non-prior service student
- ☐ Prior service student
- ☐ [If enlisted]Retrainee
- ☐ [If enlisted]MTL
- ☐ Instructor
- ☐ Someone else in my chain of command
- ☐ Other U.S. military personnel not listed above
- ☐ Military personnel from another country
- ☐ Civilian
- ☐ Don't know / other

HFU3_officer. [If officer AND (HFU3= "Instructor"), then ask:] **Was the instructor(s) a First Assignment Instructor Pilot (FAIP)?**
- ○ No
- ○ Yes

HFU8. Please select the items below that describe your participation in any of this activity. *Select all that apply.*
- ☐ I willingly participated.
- ☐ Because others were participating, I felt social pressure to participate.
- ☐ I was verbally persuaded to participate.
- ☐ I was physically forced to participate.

[Ask only if TB6a = Yes] **HFU4. At which installation were you assigned when this situation occurred?** If it happened on more than one installation, check all that apply. *[Display only installations selected in TB5 and TB6b]*

HFU5. Did you tell any other students about any of these situations that happened to you?
- ☐ Yes, I told another student.
- ☐ No, I did not tell another student.

HFU1b. The previous questions asked whether any of these situations happened to you personally. **Are you aware of any of these things happening to other students [Timeframe]?** *Select all that apply.*

[Note: Questions HFU1a and HFU1b are identical.]

- ☐ No.
- ☐ Yes, I saw this happen.
- ☐ Yes, a student told me this happened to them.
- ☐ Yes, an [If enlisted non-prior service student, then "MTL,"] instructor or other leader informed me of this happening.
- ☐ Yes, I heard about this happening from someone else.

HFU7b. Are you aware of any of these things happening to other students in your career field when they receive their occupational badge or beret upon graduation? *Select all that apply.*

[Note: Questions HFU7a and HFU7b are identical.]

- ☐ No.
- ☐ Yes, I saw this happen.
- ☐ Yes, a student told me this happened to them.
- ☐ Yes, an [If enlisted non-prior service student, then "MTL,"] instructor or other leader informed me of this happening.
- ☐ Yes, I heard about this happening from someone else.

GO TO NEXT PAGE (QUESTION HR1).

For the situations in this section that happened to you personally, or that you were aware of happening to another student . . .

HR1. Did you report any of the behaviors in this section to any of the sources below? *Please select all that apply, or indicate that you did not report any incidents.*

- ☐ I told [If enlisted, then display "a student in an Airman Leader position (for example, a bay chief, teal rope, or red rope)"; if officer, then display "a student in a leadership position, such as a Senior Ranking Officer"].
- ☐ [If enlisted non-prior service student, then display: "I told an MTL."]
- ☐ I told an instructor.
- ☐ I told someone else in my chain of command.
- ☐ I told an officer or NCO outside of my chain of command.
- ☐ I told someone in Air Force law enforcement: Office of Special Investigations (OSI) or Security Forces (SF).
- ☐ I told the Inspector General (IG).
- ☐ I told the Equal Opportunity (EO) Office.
- ☐ I wrote it down on paper and put it in a critique box/drop box.
- ☐ [If technical training student, then "I used the 2 AF hotline to report it."]
- ☐ I told a chaplain or chaplain assistant.
- ☐ I told the SARC (sexual assault response coordinator).
- ☐ I told an Air Force therapist or counselor.
- ☐ I told an Air Force doctor, nurse, or other medical professional.
- ☐ I told a staff member of the Airman and Family Readiness Center.
- ☐ Other
- ☐ **I did not report any incidents.**

IF THEY SELECTED "I DID NOT REPORT ANY INCIDENTS," GO TO QUESTION HR2 BELOW. ↓	IF THEY SELECTED THAT THEY REPORTED TO ANY SOURCE, GO TO QUESTION HR4 BELOW. ↓
HR2. Please select the items below that describe why you did not report any incidents. *Select all that apply. Note: More options will be shown on the next page.* ☐ I knew someone had already reported it. ☐ I thought someone else would report it. ☐ I only heard about it, so I wasn't sure if it was true. ☐ I didn't think there was anything wrong with it. ☐ I don't believe people should tell on one another. ☐ I didn't think anything would be done if I reported it. ☐ I didn't want anyone else to know it happened. ☐ I didn't think it was serious enough to report. ☐ I didn't think I would be believed.	If you reported one incident, please answer the next questions about that one report. If you reported more than one incident, please think of the incident that you consider the most serious. **HR4. How seriously do you feel your report was taken?** ○ Very seriously ○ Somewhat seriously ○ Not very seriously ○ Not at all seriously ○ I don't know

- ☐ I was afraid reporting might cause trouble for my flight or class.
- ☐ I thought that reporting might delay my graduation or moving to my first duty assignment.

Note: More options will be shown on the next page.

********** PAGE BREAK **********

Please select the items below that describe why you did not report any incidents. *Select all that apply.*
- ☐ I handled it myself.
- ☐ I decided to put up with it.
- ☐ I didn't want the person who did it to get in trouble for it.
- ☐ I knew of others who were treated poorly for reporting.
- ☐ I was afraid the person who did it or their friends would try to get even with me for reporting.
- ☐ I didn't think my report would be kept confidential.
- ☐ I wanted to report it anonymously but didn't know a safe way to do that.
- ☐ I was afraid of getting into trouble for something I shouldn't have been doing.
- ☐ I was afraid students would punish me or mock me for reporting.
- ☐ I was afraid instructors would punish me or mock me for reporting.
- ☐ [If enlisted non-prior service student, then]I was afraid MTLs would punish me or mock me for reporting.
- ☐ Other

GO TO THE NEXT PAGE (QUESTION HC1).

HR5. What happened with the behavior after you reported it?
- ○ The behavior didn't happen again.
- ○ The behavior continued or got worse.
- ○ I don't know: The behavior was happening to someone else.

HR6. What happened to you after the report?
Select all that apply.
- ☐ I got support to help me deal with what happened.
- ☐ The person I reported it to praised me for reporting.
- ☐ I got in trouble for my own misbehavior or infraction.
- ☐ The person who did it or their friends tried to get even with me for reporting.
- ☐ Students tried to get even with me for reporting.
- ☐ Instructors tried to get even with me for reporting.
- ☐ [If enlisted non-prior service student, then]MTLs tried to get even with me for reporting.
- ☐ None of the above happened to me.

HR7. If you could do it over, would you still decide to report the incident?
- ○ Yes
- ○ No

GO TO THE NEXT PAGE (QUESTION HC1).

Climate for Hazing: Average Items to Form Scale

Hazing violates military policy and should not be a part of the Air Force training environment. Hazing can happen to someone when they first join the Air Force, when they join a new career field, when they move to a new base or unit, or when they are promoted. Hazing may involve threats, physical injuries, or emotional harm. Examples of hazing are being punched or kicked, being verbally harassed, or being forced to consume alcohol, drugs, or any other substance. Although some people willingly participate in their own hazing, it is still against the rules. Hazing does not have an official military or government purpose. Difficult military training that is done for an official purpose is not hazing.

The following questions ask you about the extent to which Air Force and AETC policies on hazing are enforced at [technical/flying] training. For questions about [technical/flying] training leaders, we are referring to those Air Force NCOs and officers with training leadership responsibilities (for example, squadron commanders, directors of operations, flight commanders, flight chiefs, superintendents, and first sergeants). Please respond based on what you believe about your leadership, even if you do not have direct knowledge about their attitudes or actions on this specific type of behavior.

	Strongly Disagree	Disagree	Neither Disagree nor Agree	Agree	Strongly Agree
HC1. Air Force training leadership makes honest efforts to stop hazing.	○	○	○	○	○
HC2. Air Force training leadership encourages the reporting of hazing.	○	○	○	○	○
HC3. Air Force training leadership takes actions to prevent hazing.	○	○	○	○	○
HC4. Air Force training leadership would discipline someone who engages in hazing.	○	○	○	○	○

Section VIII: Feedback and Support Systems

The questions in this section now ask you about [technical/flying] training feedback and support systems.

FSS1. Below is a list of people you may or may not see every day. How easy would it be for you to arrange to speak personally with the following people if you wanted to talk to them about problems at [technical/flying] training like the ones mentioned in this survey?

	Very Easy	Easy	Neither Easy nor Difficult	Difficult	Very Difficult	Doesn't Apply: We Don't Currently Have One
a. [If enlisted, then:]Student Airman Leader, such as red or teal rope [If Officer, then:]A student in a leadership position, such as a Senior Ranking Officer	o	o	o	o	o	o
b. Your instructor supervisor	o	o	o	o	o	o
c. [If enlisted non-prior service student, then:]Your flight chief	o	o	o	o	o	o
d. Your flight commander	o	o	o	o	o	o
e. Your squadron superintendent	o	o	o	o	o	o
f. Your first sergeant	o	o	o	o	o	o
g. Your director of operations or training resource branch chief	o	o	o	o	o	o
h. Your squadron commander	o	o	o	o	o	o
i. [If enlisted non-prior service student, then: "One of your MTLs"]	o	o	o	o	o	
j. One of your instructors						
k. A chaplain	o	o	o	o	o	
l. A SARC (sexual assault response coordinator)	o	o	o	o	o	
m. A military doctor or nurse	o	o	o	o	o	
n. A military therapist, counselor or mental health professional	o	o	o	o	o	
o. Military law enforcement: Office of Special Investigations (OSI) or Security Forces (SF)	o	o	o	o	o	
p. The Inspector General (IG)	o	o	o	o	o	

167

q.	Someone at the Equal Opportunity (EO) Office	○	○	○	○	○	
r.	A staff member of the Airman and Family Readiness Center	○	○	○	○	○	

FSS2. Which of the following people would you be able to recognize by sight if they walked past you?
Select all that apply. [Programing note: Omit any leader from this list that the student indicated in FSS1 that they do not currently have.]

- ☐ My flight commander
- ☐ My squadron superintendent
- ☐ My first sergeant
- ☐ My director of operations (DO) or training resource branch chief
- ☐ My squadron commander
- ☐ My chaplain
- ☐ The SARC (sexual assault response coordinator)
- ☐ My instructor supervisor
- ☐ [if enlisted and non–prior service, then:] **My flight chief**

	Strongly Disagree	Disagree	Neither Disagree nor Agree	Agree	Strongly Agree
FSS3. If instructors knew a student was being abused or mistreated, they would:					
a. Make honest efforts to stop it.	○	○	○	○	○
b. Probably report it.	○	○	○	○	○
c. Probably try to cover it up.	○	○	○	○	○
d. Expect the student to handle it.	○	○	○	○	○
[If enlisted non-prior service student, then:] **FSS4. If MTLs knew a student was being abused or mistreated, they would:**					
a. Make honest efforts to stop it.	○	○	○	○	○
b. Probably report it.	○	○	○	○	○
c. Probably try to cover it up.	○	○	○	○	○
d. Expect the student to handle it.	○	○	○	○	○

Technical Training/Flying Training Feedback and Support Systems

FSS7. Please indicate the extent to which you agree or disagree with the following statements.

	Strongly Disagree	Disagree	Neither Disagree nor Agree	Agree	Strongly Agree
a. I have a fellow student I can count on to look out for my well-being.	○	○	○	○	○
b. [If technical training student]I would be willing to use the 2 AF hotline to report a problem during technical training or to ask for help with it.	○	○	○	○	○
c. [If enlisted and technical training, then: "MTLs, "]Instructors or others in the chain of command discourage students from using the 2 AF hotline to report misconduct.	○	○	○	○	○
d. I would be willing to use a critique box/drop box to report a problem or to ask for help.	○	○	○	○	○
e. I would be able to put a comment in a critique box/drop box without anyone noticing.	○	○	○	○	○
f. Instructors [If enlisted non-prior service student, then "MTLs, "] or others in the chain of command discourage students from using critique boxes/drop boxes to report misconduct.	○	○	○	○	○
g. Instructors, [If enlisted non-prior service student, then "MTLs, "] or others in the chain of command discourage students from participating in this survey.	○	○	○	○	○
h. If I experienced abuse or mistreatment from an [If enlisted non-prior service student, then "MTL or"] instructor, there is at least one person in the chain of command I feel I could turn to for help (for example, a team chief, instructor supervisor, or first sergeant).	○	○	○	○	○
i. If I experienced abuse or mistreatment from an [If enlisted non-prior service student, then "MTL or "] instructor, there is at least one person in the Air Force outside of the chain of command I feel I could turn to for help (for example, a chaplain, SARC, or a doctor).	○	○	○	○	○

FSS8. Please indicate the extent to which you agree or disagree with the following statement:
"Overall, my commitment to the Air Force has strengthened through [technical/flying] **training.**

- o   Strongly disagree
- o   Disagree
- o   Neither disagree nor agree
- o   Agree
- o   Strongly agree

Section IX: Closing Questions

CQ1. How open and honest did you feel you could be when answering these survey questions?

- o Not at all open or honest
- o Somewhat open and honest
- o Completely open and honest

[If survey software permits access through both military and non-military devices, ask:]

CQ2. Did you take this survey on ….

- o A <u>personal</u> computer, tablet, or smartphone?
- o A <u>military</u> computer, tablet, or smartphone?

CQ3. [Display only if military computer in CQ2, or if access is possible only through a military computer, but CAC is not universally required] **Did you need to use your CAC card to access the survey?**

- o Yes
- o No

Submit survey

[Place an ending time stamp here.]

THANK YOU FOR PARTICIPATING IN THIS SURVEY

We want to emphasize to you that this survey is not an official channel for reporting abuse or misconduct.

If you have experienced any of the situations you were asked about as part of this survey and need help or would like to make an official report, there are several options for you to do so:

- ✓ You can talk to someone in your chain of command ([If enlisted non-prior service student, then: MTL, Chief MTL,] instructor, instructor supervisor, first sergeant, squadron commander).

- ✓ You can contact Air Force law enforcement (Office of Special Investigations or Security Forces).

- ✓ You can submit a complaint or report in one of the critique boxes/drop boxes in the training area.

- ✓ You can talk to your chaplain.

- ✓ You can contact the DoD Safe Helpline toll-free number for all locations across DoD at 877-995-5247 (24-hour confidential hotline) if you were sexually assaulted or know someone in the Air Force who was sexually assaulted.

The chaplain and SARC can provide CONFIDENTIAL help following a sexual assault if you have not made an official report and do not want them to tell anyone else what happened.

Appendix D. Responsible Comparisons of Survey Results

One of the challenges of analyzing and reporting survey data from such a diverse population spread across so many locations and pipelines is that groups that AETC might wish to compare or disaggregate could be quite small. Additionally, it could be challenging to understand whether differences in responses reflect true differences between populations. In this appendix, we provide guidance to assist with the presentation of survey results, particularly where the number of respondents may be low.

When reporting survey data, results could be reported separately for enlisted and officers, for men and women, for different bases, or for different pipelines. These comparisons of group responses will be impacted by the number of respondents. Two factors are at work here, so we conducted analyses to determine the minimum sample sizes that are adequate for (1) delivering stable estimates of misconduct and (2) protecting the confidentiality of all students in that group. Often there is a tension between the end user (who may prefer to learn about survey rates at fine levels of analyses; e.g., rates among women in each career field while training at each installation), statistical power considerations (a relatively large sample is required to be confident about each estimated rate of misconduct), and confidentiality considerations (groups must be large enough that the data cannot be used to identify any given person in the group based on their answers).

Ultimately, AETC leaders will want to understand whether an observed rate of misconduct is different from one time point to the next (e.g., in 2016 relative to 2017) or in one group relative to another group (e.g., men relative to women, Lackland AFB relative to Keesler AFB). To make these kinds of comparisons, it is necessary to have a large enough sample of students who complete the survey to be confident that a difference between groups would be observable.

As an example, imagine that members of community A have a slightly higher annual rate of death than members of community B. If researchers compared only 100 people from each community, they may not have enough deaths in a given year to be able to "see" that the annual death rate was higher in community A. Instead, they would need to compare 1,000 or even 10,000 people from each community before they could "see" the difference in annual rate of death.

In statistics, the analyses used to determine how many people must be observed before differences in the rate of such events as misconduct are apparent are called *power analyses* (Cohen, 1988). These techniques allow researchers to determine how many people must be in each group if they want to be able to say definitively that the groups either have the same rate of an event (e.g., death or misconduct) or have a different rate of the event.

To provide recommendations for the reporting of survey results, we conducted a series of analyses to help us understand how many Air Force students must be in each group in order to make a comparison between groups. Figure D.1 illustrates these analyses, with hypothetical rates of abuse and misconduct presented across the horizontal x-axis and the minimum detectible difference between groups on the y-axis. Imagine a hypothetical situation in which 20 percent of a group of students experienced sexual harassment, which is represented in Figure D.1 by the fourth grouping of bars. Within the grouping, darker bars reference a smaller group of students (e.g., 50 students), and the lighter bars represent larger groups of students (e.g., 1,000 students). For example, if the survey analysts are comparing groups of 50 students each, and the rate of sexual harassment is 20 percent for one group of students, then the second group would need to have a rate of sexual harassment that was higher than the first group by at least 25.8 percent in order for the analysts to claim that a second group was more likely to report sexual harassment than the first. Specifically, the second group would have to report sexual harassment at a rate of 45.8 percent or higher before the survey results would reliably detect that there was a significant difference between the two groups. Now imagine that the two groups of students to be compared had 1,000 students in each group, and the rate of sexual harassment in the first group was 20 percent (the lightest bar in the fourth group of bars in Figure D.1). In this case, a statistically significant difference could be detected if the rate in the second group was only 5.2 percent higher (e.g., sexual harassment rate of 25.2 percent).

Figure D.1. Minimum Detectable Difference Between Groups Given a Known Rate of Abuse

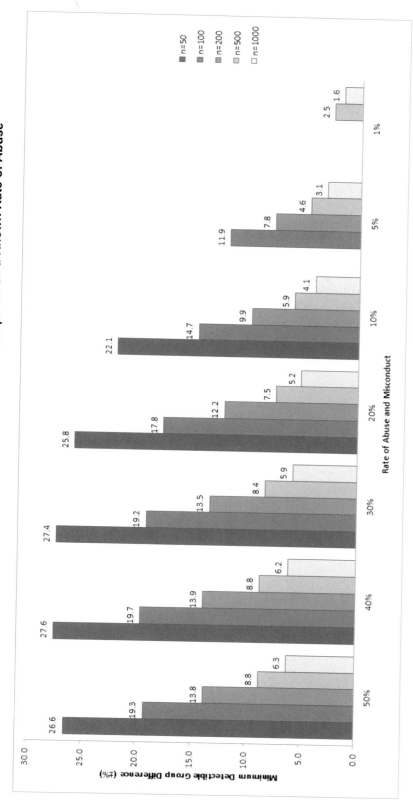

NOTE: When an expected bar is missing, it indicates that the sample size is insufficient to detect a group difference of any size.

175

Figure D.2 illustrates an alternative way to consider the power associated with a given sample size. This figure provides estimates of the *margin of error* around an estimated rate within a group. For example, if a survey estimated that a group of students had a rate of bullying of 10 percent, and the margin of error was 2 percent, that would mean that the researchers are reasonably confident that the true rate of bullying is somewhere between 8 percent and 12 percent. In Figure D.2, the x-axis shows rates of abuse from 50 percent to 1 percent. Taking a rate of abuse of 40 percent as an example, the first bar in the grouping is for a sample size of 50 students and corresponds to a margin of error of 13.6 percent. This means that a researcher can be reasonably confident that the true rate of abuse is within plus or minus 13.6 percent of the observed survey rate (40 percent) with a group size of 50; sometimes written as 40% ±13.6%. The size of the margin of error decreases as the sample sizes increases. For example, for a survey of 1,000 students, if the observed rate of bullying was 40 percent, the margin of error would drop to only 3 percent (40% ±3%).

These figures are provided to allow analysts to determine necessary minimum sample sizes as a function of the expected rate of misconduct or abuse in the environment. Alternatively, analysts may wish to calculate precise power analyses using exact group sizes and misconduct rates. In either case, power to detect differences between groups must be considered in order to ensure that random fluctuation around a prevalence estimate (due to measurement error) is not inadvertently interpreted as an indicator of a true trend in misconduct prevalence in the environment. Given the understandable human tendency to interpret any difference between groups as meaningful, analysts should be careful not to include group comparisons in reports or briefings without providing explicit guidance about whether differences are meaningful.

Figure D.2. Margins of Error Given a Known Rate of Abuse for Varying Sample Sizes

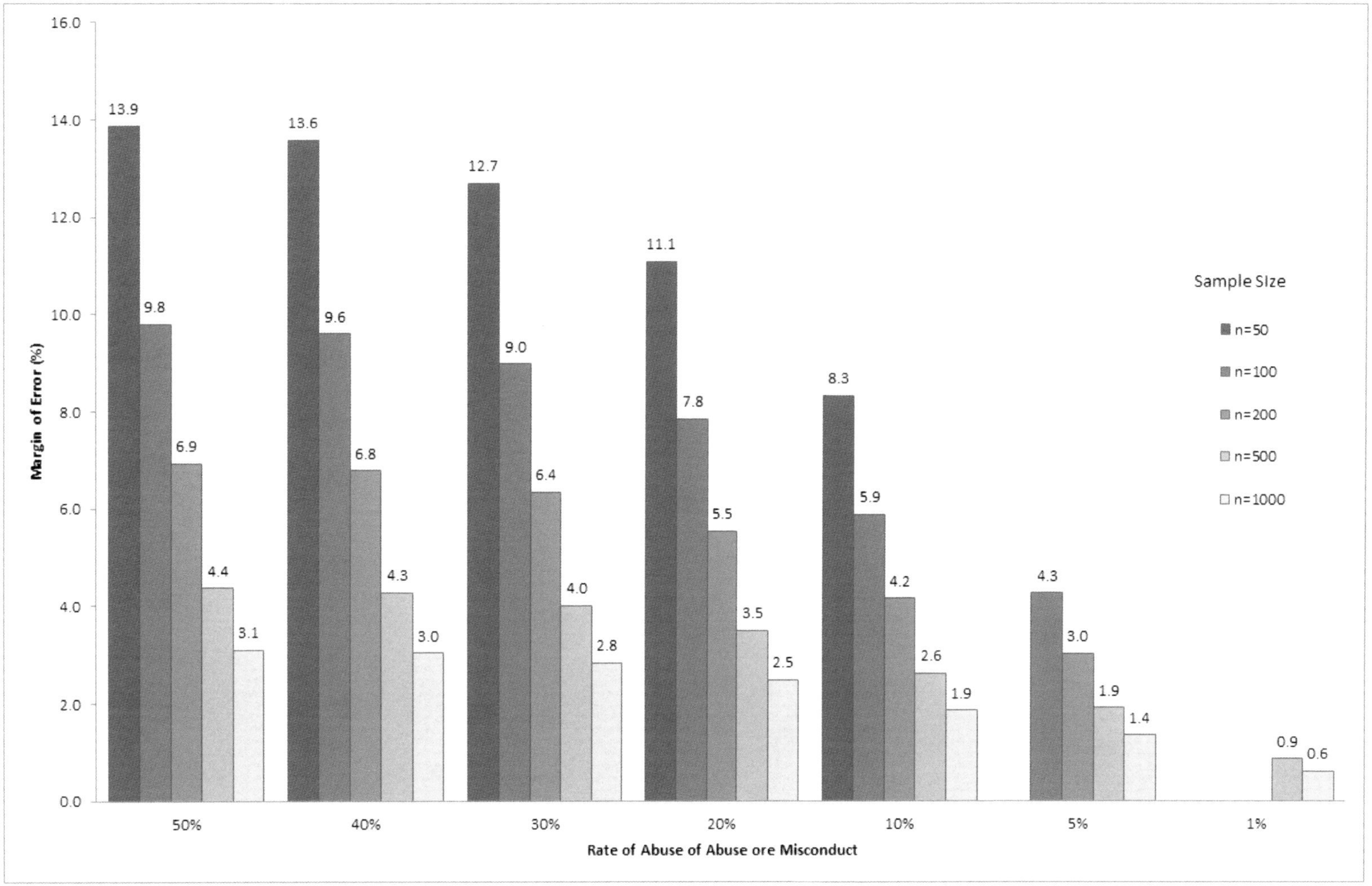

NOTE: When an expected bar is missing, it indicates that the sample size is insufficient to estimate the given rate of abuse.

177

References

AETC—*See* Air Education and Training Command.

Air Education and Training Command Instruction 36-2205, "Volume 4: Formal Flying Training Administration and Management—T1A, T6A, and T38C," September 5, 2014. As of June 22, 2016:
http://static.e-publishing.af.mil/production/1/aetc/publication/aetci36-2205v4/aetci36-2205v4.pdf

Air Education and Training Command Instruction 36-2216, "Administration of Military Standards and Discipline Training," December 6, 2010, Incorporating Change 1, December 2011.

Air Education and Training Command Instruction 36-2640, "Technical and Basic Military Training Evaluations," July 15, 2014.

Air Education and Training Command Instruction 36-2909, "Recruiting, Education, and Training Standards of Conduct," December 2, 2013.

Air Education and Training Command Instruction 36-2909, "Recruiting, Education, and Training Standards of Conduct," Second Air Force Supplement, February 3, 2015.

Air Education and Training Command, "Fact Sheet: Air Education and Training Command," October 6, 2014. As of March 10, 2016:
http://www.af.mil/AboutUs/FactSheets/Display/tabid/224/Article/104471/air-education-and-training-command.aspx

———, "Flying Training Pipelines," slides provided to authors, October 2, 2015a.

———, "Tech Training Pipelines," slides provided to authors, October 2, 2015b.

Air Force Instruction 36-2101, "Classifying Military Personnel (Officer and Enlisted)," U.S. Air Force, 2013. As of April 4, 2016:
http://static.e-publishing.af.mil/production/1/saf_mr/publication/afi36-2101/afi36-2101.pdf

Air Force Instruction 36-2909, "Professional and Unprofessional Relationships," U.S. Air Force, 1999. As of April 4, 2016:
http://jpp.whs.mil/Public/docs/03_Topic-Areas/02-Article_120/20150116/49_AFI_36_2909_Relationships.pdf

Air Force Instruction 36-2201, *Air Force Training Program*, U.S. Air Force, September 15, 2010, Incorporating Through Change 3, 7 August 2013.

Air Force Instruction 38-101, "Air Force Organization," U.S. Air Force, 2017. As of December 14, 2018:
https://static.e-publishing.af.mil/production/1/af_a1/publication/afi38-101/afi38-101.pdf

Air Force Magazine, "Community Assessment Survey Embraces Total Force," April 10, 2013. As of February 29, 2016:
http://www.airforcemag.com/DRArchive/Pages/2013/April%202013/April%2010%202013/Community-Assessment-Survey-Embraces-Total-Force.aspx

Air Force Policy Directive 10-35, *Battlefield Airmen*, U.S. Air Force, March 23, 2009.

Allan, Elizabeth J., and Mary Madden, *Hazing in View: College Students at Risk,* Orono, Me.: University of Maine, 2008. As of April 28, 2016:
http://umaine.edu/hazingresearch/files/2012/10/hazing_in_view_web.pdf

Allen, Peter J., and Lynne D. Roberts, "The Ethics of Outsourcing Online Survey Research," in Rocci Luppicini, ed., *Ethical Impact of Technological Advancements and Applications in Society,* Hershey, Pa: Information Science Reference, 2012, pp. 160–175.

American Psychological Association, "How Technology Changes Everything (and Nothing) in Psychology: 2008 Annual Report of the APA Policy and Planning Board," *American Psychologist,* Vol. 64, No. 5, 2009, pp. 454–463.

Ausink, John A., Richard S. Marken, Laura Miller, Thomas Manacapilli, William W. Taylor, and Michael R. Thirtle, *Assessing the Impact of Future Operations on Trainer Aircraft Requirements.* Santa Monica, Calif.: RAND Corporation, MG-348-AF, 2005.

Christian, Michael S., Jill C. Bradley, J. Craig Wallace, and Michael J. Burke, "Workplace Safety: A Meta-Analysis of the Roles of Person and Situation Factors," *Journal of Applied Psychology*, Vol. 94, No. 5, 2009, pp. 1103–1127.

Cohen, Jacob. *Statistical Power Analysis for The Behavioral Sciences,* 2nd eds., Hillsdale, N.J.: Lawrence Earlbaum Associates, 1988.

Culbertson, Amy, and Waymond Rodgers, "Improving Managerial Effectiveness in the Workplace: The Case of Sexual Harassment of Navy Women," *Journal of Applied Social Psychology*, Vol. 27, No. 22, 1997, pp. 1953–1971.

Davis, Lisa, Amanda Grifka, Kristin Williams, and Margaret Coffey, eds., *2016 Workplace and Gender Relations Survey of Active Duty Members*, Alexandria, Va.: Office of People Analytics, OPA Report No. 2016-050, May 2017.

Defense Equal Opportunity Management Institute, *Information You Need to Know Before You Request a DEOCS Assessment,* April 2015a. As of February 23, 2016:
https://www.deocs.net/DocDownloads/FrequentlyAskedQuestionsApr2015.pdf

———, *Sample of Locally Developed Questions List,* October 2015b. As of February 23, 2016:
https://www.deocs.net/DocDownloads/DEOCSLDQS_2015Oct.pdf

———, *DEOMI Organizational Climate Survey (DEOCS)*, January 2016. As of February 23, 2016:
https://www.deocs.net/DocDownloads/SampleDEOCSSurvey12Jan2016.pdf

Defense Manpower Data Center, *2012 Workplace and Gender Relations Survey of Active Duty Members: Nonresponse Bias Analysis Report*, Alexandria, Va., Report No. 2013-059, January 2014.

DEOMI—*See* Defense Equal Opportunity Management Institute.

Deputy Secretary of Defense, "Hazing and Bullying Prevention and Response in the Armed Forces," memorandum, December 23, 2015.

Doane, A. N., M . L. Kelley, E. S. Chiang, and M. A. Padilla, "Development of the Cyberbullying Experiences Survey," *Emerging Adulthood,* Vol. 1, No. 3, 2013, pp. 207–218.

DoD—*See* U.S. Department of Defense.

DoD Directive—*See* Department of Defense Directive.

DoD Instruction—*See* Department of Defense Instruction.

Department of Defense Directive 1350.2, "Department of Defense Military Equal Opportunity (MEO) Program," U.S. Department of Defense, August 18, 1995, incorporating Change 1, May 7, 1997, certified current as of November 21, 2003.

Department of Defense Instruction 1020.03, "Harassment Prevention and Response in the Armed Forces," U.S. Department of Defense, February 8, 2018.

Doss Aviation, "Welcome to DOSS Aviation and USAF Initial Flight Training" webpage, undated. As of October 29, 2018:
http://www.dossaviation.com/usaf-ift

Einarsen, Stale, "Harassment and Bullying at Work: A Review of the Scandinavian Approach," *Aggression and Violent Behavior,* Vol. 5, No. 4, 2000, pp. 379–401.

Einarsen, Stale, and Anders Skogstad, "Bullying at Work: Epidemiological Findings in Public and Private Organizations," *European Journal of Work and Organizational Psychology*, Vol. 5, No. 2, 1996, pp. 185–201.

Evans, Joel R., and Anil Mathur, "The Value of Online Surveys," *Internet Research,* Vol. 15, No. 2, 2005, pp. 195–219.

Fitzgerald, Louise F., Vicki J. Magley, Fritz Drasgow, and Craig R. Waldo, "Measuring Sexual Harassment in the Military: The Sexual Experiences Questionnaire (SEQ—DoD)," *Military Psychology*, Vol. 11, No. 3, 1999, pp. 243–263.

Goffman, Erving, *Asylums: Essays on the Social Situation of Mental Patients and Other Inmates,* New York: Anchor Books, 1961.

Harrington, Lisa M., Kathleen Reedy, John Ausink, Bart E. Bennett, Barbara A. Bicksler, Darrell Jones, and Daniel Ibarra, *Air Force Non-Rated Technical Training: Opportunities for Improving Pipeline Processes*, Santa Monica, Calif.: RAND Corporation, RR-2116-AF, 2017. As of September 21, 2018: https://www.rand.org/pubs/research_reports/RR2116.html

Herbert, Tracy Bennett, and Christine Dunkel-Schetter, "Negative Social Reactions to Victims: An Overview of Responses and Their Determinants," in Leo Montada, Sigrun-Heide Filipp, and Melvin J. Learner, eds., *Life Crises and Experiences of Loss in Adulthood*, Hillsdale, N.J.: Lawrence-Erlbaum Associates, April 1992, pp. 497–518.

Hoover, Nadine C., and Norman J. Pollard. *Initiation Rites in American High Schools: A National Survey: Final Report*, Alfred, N.Y.: Alfred University, 2000.

Hulin, Charles L., Louise F. Fitzgerald, and Fritz Drasgow, "Organizational Influences on Sexual Harassment," in M.S. Stockdale, ed., *Sexual Harassment in the Workplace: Perspectives, Frontiers, and Response Strategies*, London: Sage Publications, 1996, pp. 127–150.

Jaycox, Lisa H., Terry L. Schell, Coreen Farris, Amy Street, Dean Kilpatrick, Andrew R. Morral, and Terri Tanielian, Questionnaire Development, In A. R. Morral, K. L. Gore and T. L. Schell (Eds.), *Sexual Assault and Sexual Harassment in the U.S. Military: Volume 1. Design of the 2014 RAND Military Workplace Study,* Santa Monica, Calif.: RAND Corporation, RR-870/1-OSD, 2014, pp. 37–55. As of October 5, 2018: https://www.rand.org/pubs/research_reports/RR870z1.html

Jaycox, Lisa H., Terry L. Schell, Andrew R. Morral, Amy Street, Coreen Farris, Dean Kilpatrick, and Terri Tanielian, "Sexual Assault Findings: Active Component," in A. R. Morral, K. L. Gore and T. L. Schell, eds., *Sexual Assault and Sexual Harassment in the U.S. Military: Volume 2. Estimates for Department of Defense Service Members from the 2014 RAND Military Workplace Study*, Santa Monica, Calif.: RAND Corporation, RR-870/2-OSD, 2015, pp. 9–30. As of October 6, 2018: https://www.rand.org/pubs/research_reports/RR870z2-1.html

Joint Base San Antonio, "479th Flying Training Group," webpage, undated. As of March 10, 2016: http://www.jbsa.mil/MissionPartners/12thFlyingTrainingWing/479thFlyingTrainingGroup.aspx

Kalton, G., *Introduction to Survey Sampling*, Newbury Park, Calif.: Sage Publications, 1983.

Keller, Kirsten M., Miriam Matthews, Kimberly Curry Hall, William Marcellino, Jacqueline A. Mauro, and Nelson Lim, *Hazing in the U.S. Armed Forces: Recommendations for Hazing Prevention Policy and Practice*, Santa Monica, Calif.: RAND Corporation, RR-941-OSD, 2015. As of November 29, 2018: https://www.rand.org/pubs/research_reports/RR941.html

Keller, Kirsten M., Laura L. Miller, Sean Robson, Coreen Farris, Brian D. Stucky, Marian Oshiro, and Sarah O. Meadows, *An Integrated Survey System for Addressing Abuse and Misconduct Toward Air Force Trainees During Basic Military Training*, Santa Monica, Calif.: RAND Corporation, RR-964-AF, 2015. As of September 22, 2018: https://www.rand.org/pubs/research_reports/RR964.html

Lytell, Maria C., Sean Robson, David Schulker, Tracy C. McCausland, Miriam Matthews, Louis T. Mariano, Albert A. Robbert, *Training Success for U.S. Air Force Special Operations and Combat Support Specialties*, Santa Monica, Calif.: RAND Corporation, RR-2002-AF, 2018. As of September 22, 2018: https://www.rand.org/pubs/research_reports/RR2002.html

Manacapilli, Thomas, Carl F. Matthies, Louis W. Miller, Paul Howe, P.J. Perez, Chaitra M. Hardison, H. G. Massey, Jerald Greenberg, Christopher Beighley, and Carra S. Sims, *Reducing Attrition in Selected Air Force Training Pipelines*, Santa Monica, Calif.: RAND Corporation, TR-955-AF, 2012. As of September 21, 2018: https://www.rand.org/pubs/technical_reports/TR955.html

Miller, Laura L., and Eyal Aharoni, *Understanding Low Survey Response Rates Among Young U.S. Military Personnel*, Santa Monica, Calif.: RAND Corporation, RR-881-AF, 2015. As of September 22, 2018: https://www.rand.org/pubs/research_reports/RR881.html

Molnar, David, and Stuart Schechter, "Self-Hosting vs. Cloud Hosting: Accounting for the Security Impact of Hosting in the Cloud," presented at the Proceedings of the Ninth Workshop on the Economics of Information Security, Arlington, Va., June 7–8, 2010. As of November 11, 2015: http://www.econinfosec.org/archive/weis2010/papers/session5/weis2010_schechter.pdf

Nielsen, M. B., S. B. Matthiesen, and S. Einarsen, "The Impact of Methodological Moderators on Prevalence Rates of Workplace Bullying: A Meta-analysis," *Journal of Occupational and Organizational Psychology*, Vol. 83, No. 4, 2010, pp. 955–979.

Nosek, Brian A., Mahzarin R. Banaji, and Anthony G. Greenwald, "E-Research: Ethics, Security, Design, and Control in Psychological Research on the Internet," *Journal of Social Issues*, Vol. 58, No. 1, 2002, pp. 161–176.

Olweus, D., "School Bullying: Development and Some Important Challenges," *Annual Review of Clinical Psychology,* Vol. 9, 2013, pp. 751–780.

Ostroff, C., A. J. Kinicki, and M. M. Tamkins, "Organizational Culture and Climate," *Handbook of Psychology*, Vol. 12: *Industrial and Organizational Psychology*, Hoboken, N.J.: Wiley, 2003, pp. 565–593.

Probst, T. M., T. L. Brubaker, and A. Barsotti, "Organizational Injury Rate Underreporting: The Moderating Effect of Organizational Safety Climate," *Journal of Applied Psychology*, Vol. 93, No. 5, 2008, pp. 1147–1154.

Raphael, K. G., Cloitre, M., and Dohrenwend, B. P., "Problems of Recall and Misclassification with Checklist Methods of Measuring Stressful Life Events. *Health Psychology*, Vol. 10, No. 1, 1991, pp. 62–74.

Reid, Mike, "We're Listening—The 2013 Community Assessment Survey," *Colorado Springs Military Newspaper Group*, March 28, 2013. As of February 29, 2016: http://csmng.com/2013/03/28/were-listening-the-2013-community-assessment-survey/

Rock, L. M., R. N. Lipari, P. J. Cook, and A. D. Hale, *2010 Workplace and Gender Relations Survey of Active Duty Members: Overview Report on Sexual Assault*, Arlington, Va.: Defense Manpower Data Center, March 2011.

Sexton, N. R., H. M. Miller, and A. M. Dietsch, "Appropriate Uses and Considerations for Online Surveying in Human Dimensions Research," *Human Dimensions of Wildlife*, Vol. 16, 2011, pp. 154–163.

Sheppard Air Force Base, "Euro-NATO Joint Jet Pilot Training Program (ENJJPT)," Wichita Falls, Tex., 2012. As of February 29, 2016: http://www.sheppard.af.mil/Library/FactSheets/Display/tabid/3418/Article/367537/euro-nato-joint-jet-pilot-training-program-enjjpt.aspx

Stonemetz, Hillary, "Prior Service Program Open but Strictly Limited," Air Force Recruiting Service Public Affairs, April 25, 2014. As of April 25, 2016: http://www.af.mil/News/ArticleDisplay/tabid/223/Article/484041/prior-service-program-open-but-strictly-limited.aspx

Strang, Joshua, "Hecker Assumes Command of 19th Air Force," Air Education and Training Command, June 24, 2015. As of February 29, 2016: http://www.aetc.af.mil/News/ArticleDisplay/tabid/5115/Article/601567/hecker-assumes-command-of-19th-air-force.aspx

Stark, S., O. S. Chernyshenko, A. R. Lancaster, F. Drasgow, and L. F. Fitzgerald, "Toward Standardized Measurement of Sexual Harassment: Shortening the SEQ-DoD Using Item Response Theory," *Military Psychology*, Vol. 14, 2002, pp. 49–72.

Thomas, William A., "Minimizing the Loss of Student Pilots from Voluntary Attrition," December 1, 2009. As of April 6, 2016: http://www.airpower.maxwell.af.mil/airchronicles/apj/apj09/win09/thomas.html

Ullman, S. E., M. M. Foynes, and S. S. S. Tang, "Benefits and Barriers to Disclosing Sexual Trauma: A Contextual Approach," *Journal of Trauma and Dissociation*, Vol. 11, No. 2, April 2010, pp. 127–133.

U.S. Air Force, "Officer AFSC Classifications," November 20, 2012. As of April 1, 2016: http://www.af.mil/AboutUs/FactSheets/Display/tabid/224/Article/104484/officer-afsc-classifications.aspx

———, *Air Force Enlisted Classification Directory (AFECD),* April 30, 2015a.

———, "Enlisted AFSC Classifications," August 17, 2015b. As of April 1, 2016:
http://www.af.mil/AboutUs/FactSheets/Display/tabid/224/Article/104609/enlisted-afsc-classifications.aspx

U.S. Air Force Personnel Center, "Climate Survey Is Opportunity to Share Opinions with AF Leaders," March 30, 2015. As of February 29, 2016:
http://www.af.mil/News/ArticleDisplay/tabid/223/Article/581943/climate-survey-is-opportunity-to-share-opinions-with-af-leaders.aspx

U.S. Code, Title 10, Subtitle A, Part II, Chapter 80, Section 1561, Complaints of Sexual Harassment: Investigation by Commanding Officers, 2006.

U.S. Department of Defense, "Command Climate Assessments," Washington, D.C., memorandum from the Undersecretary of Defense for Personnel and Readiness to Secretaries of the Military Departments, Chairman of the Joint Chiefs of Staff, Chiefs of the Military Services, Chief of the National Guard Bureau, and General Counsel of the Department of Defense, July 25, 2013. As of October 4, 2018:
https://www.deomi.org/DownloadableFiles/humanRelations/documents/SecWrightMemo.pdf

U.S. General Accounting Office, *DoD Service Academies: More Changes Needed to Eliminate Hazing,* report to Congressional requestors, GAO/NSIAD-93-36, Washington, D.C., 1992.

Waldron, Jennifer J., and Christopher L. Kowalski, "Crossing the Line: Rites of Passage, Team Aspects, and Ambiguity of Hazing," *Research Quarterly for Exercise and Sport,* Vol. 80, 2009, pp. 291–302.

Williams, J. H., L. F. Fitzgerald, and F. Drasgow, "The Effects of Organizational Practices on Sexual Harassment and Individual Outcomes in the Military," *Military Psychology,* Vol. 2, No. 3, 1999, pp. 303–328.

Willness, C. R., P. Steel, and K. Lee, "A Meta-Analysis of the Antecedents and Consequences of Workplace Sexual Harassment," *Personnel Psychology,* Vol. 60, 2007, pp. 127–162.

Ybarra, M. L., D. Boyd, J. D. Korchmaros, and J. K. Oppenheim, "Defining and Measuring Cyberbullying Within the Larger Context of Bullying Victimization, *Journal of Adolescent Health,* Vol. 51, No.1, 2012, pp. 53–58.